New England

TIME-LIFE Library of America

New England

**Connecticut Maine
Massachusetts New Hampshire
Rhode Island Vermont**

By Joe McCarthy
and the Editors of
TIME-LIFE BOOKS

Time Incorporated, New York

The Author: Joe McCarthy, a native of Cambridge, Massachusetts, had written a number of articles and a book about New England and its people before undertaking this assignment for the TIME-LIFE Library of America. During World War II he was a correspondent, and later, managing editor of *Yank,* the U.S. Army's weekly newspaper. In 1948 he began his career as a freelance writer; since then his by-line has appeared in most of the nation's major magazines. Among the books he has written are *The Remarkable Kennedys* and the LIFE World Library's *Ireland.* He was co-author of the LIFE Science Library's *The Engineer.*

The Consulting Editor: Oscar Handlin, Charles Warren Professor of American History at Harvard University and director of the university's Charles Warren Center for Studies in American History, is one of America's foremost social historians. His work on U.S. immigrants, *The Uprooted,* won the Pulitzer Prize in 1952.

New England Consultant: Edward Chase Kirkland, Frank Munsey Professor of American History, Emeritus, Bowdoin College, is the author of *Men, Cities and Transportation.*

The Cover: The white church, the snug-looking houses and weathered barns, the rolling hills and autumn foliage give East Corinth, Vermont, a 19th Century look.

TIME-LIFE BOOKS

Editor
Maitland A. Edey
Executive Editor
Jerry Korn
Text Director   **Art Director**
Martin Mann   Sheldon Cotler
Chief of Research
Beatrice T. Dobie
Picture Editor
Robert G. Mason
Assistant Text Directors:
Harold C. Field, Ogden Tanner
Assistant Art Director:
Arnold C. Holeywell
Assistant Chief of Research:
Martha Turner

Publisher
Rhett Austell
General Manager: Joseph C. Hazen Jr.
Circulation Director: Joan D. Manley
Marketing Director: Carter Smith
Business Manager: John D. McSweeney
Publishing Board: Nicholas Benton,
Louis Bronzo, James Wendell Forbes

TIME-LIFE Library of America

Series Editor: Oliver E. Allen
Editorial Staff for *New England:*
Assistant Editor: James A. Maxwell
Picture Editor: Grace M. Brynolson
Designer: John Newcomb
Assistant Designer: Jean Lindsay
Staff Writers: Peter Chaitin, John von Hartz,
Jonathan Kastner, Victor Waldrop, Peter Yerkes
Chief Researcher: Clara E. Nicolai
Text Research: Terry Drucker, Paula Arno,
Vista Grayson
Picture Research: Ellen Youngblood, Victoria
Thompson, Myra Mangan
Art Assistant: Mervyn Clay

Editorial Production
Color Director: Robert L. Young
Assistant: James J. Cox
Copy Staff: Marian Gordon Goldman,
Patricia Miller, Florence Keith
Picture Department: Dolores A. Littles,
Barbara Sullivan
Traffic: Douglas B. Graham
Studio: Patricia Byrne, Jean Held

The text chapters of this book were written by Joe McCarthy, the picture essays by the editorial staff. Valuable aid was provided by these individuals and departments of Time Inc.: LIFE staff photographers Alfred Eisenstaedt and Dmitri Kessel; the Chief of the LIFE Picture Library, Doris O'Neil; the Chief of the Bureau of Editorial Reference, Peter Draz; the Chief of the TIME-LIFE News Service, Richard M. Clurman; Correspondents Ruth Mehrtens and Sue Wymelenberg (Boston), C. Elliott Stocker (Providence) and Frank Sleeper (Portland).

Contents

Introduction

I never knew how much I loved New England—indeed, that I loved it at all—until I broke away, got married and went to live in New York. At that period, the late 1920s, New England was still in the doldrums that followed its Indian Summer, when William Dean Howells, once a pilgrim to the region's spectacular Flowering, had begun the literary flight away. To people in their twenties at that time, New York spelled freedom.

Almost right away, however, on visits back home I heard myself remarking, "You know, I can't seem to think what I was rebelling against." While I was still New England's child, it was as if I had not been able to see around me for the blind, collective drive to get out. Now Boston suddenly looked perfectly delightful. I don't believe all my contemporaries who escaped to New York experienced the same *metanoia*—change of attitude—toward their beginnings that I did, but I do remember meeting, at a New York party, one New Englander who had made news in his day by the violence of his own exodus. I said something about our both being Boston rebels; after a minute he said wryly, "You mean Boston unregenerates." That was not exactly it—a sort of regeneration did take place. With my feet planted somewhere else, outside, I could all at once turn and see New England for the marvel that it is.

After a while I began to reap the benefits of having had a New England girlhood.

I was helped by the fact that the outside, for me, had been New York; for as John Jay Chapman—a New Yorker who loved Boston—wrote, "The present in New York is so powerful that the past is lost." New England, on the other hand, has more of an earlier past in a better state of preservation than any other part of the country. Ipswich, Massachusetts, alone has 40 houses built before 1725. If you are free to enjoy the past, there is any amount of it in New England to enjoy. As I received back, bit by bit, like a gift, the very thing I had renounced, I could see that it was not only the past that was being liberated to me, but part of myself was liberated too; for the future is only a dream or a hope, and the present is something you are in the process of living; but the past is a fact. It really happened. It is your inheritance, if you are able to claim it.

Once you cease to be a part of the past, it becomes your treasured knowledge. A traveler with an untrained ear would have trouble deciding solely from the landscape and the attitudes and accents of the natives whether he was in Vermont, southern New Hampshire, western Massachusetts or the northern Housatonic Valley of Connecticut. But a born New England ear can derive infinite amusement playing the game of distinguishing New England origins by speech: telling the laconic, deliberate flatness developed over the centuries on Mount Desert Island in Maine from the higher-keyed, more truculent flatness of Rhode Island's old South County; or distinguishing Robert Kennedy's blend of Cape Cod and South Boston from the hot-potato-in-the-mouth tones employed in Beverly Farms and Hamilton.

Mr. McCarthy points out in the present volume how "New England was settled by one kind of people: Puritans from much the same English background with the same basic religious beliefs, the same simple tastes and the same high principles." The fascination lies in the exceptions. The high jinks practiced in the 1620s at Merrymount, 30 miles from Plymouth, where Thomas Morton and his crew danced around Maypoles whose symbolism would have been perfectly obvious to an Elizabethan mind, included a gun- and rumrunning establishment on the premises. The Plymouth brethren were scandalized.

Likewise the Puritans of the Massachusetts Bay Colony considered Anne Hutchinson as anything but a co-religionist. When I was at school we used to sing about how the settlers were seeking "freedom to worship God"; but it didn't mean freedom for anybody with the slightest difference in religious persuasion from their own. Possessed (like their enemies the papists) of "the one and only truth," they would have thought it hypocrisy to be tolerant.

The rule that such exceptions prove is that it took all kinds to make traditional New England. The impression the tourist today gains—of its being all one region—is more the result of a long-ago, often forced, integration of diverse elements than of original uniformity. Like old England's melting pot of Briton, Saxon, Dane, Norman and everybody since, New England is a blend, but the blending got done and out of the way some time ago.

Today New England, the doldrums far behind, moves in the forefront of national and international progress, propelled by the same force that always has supplied New England's motive power: brains. The original impulse that founded Harvard in 1636 has once more, out of Harvard, M.I.T. and the other universities, brought forth in the space age the electronic virtuosity that, with an accompanying economic upsurge, sets New England like some persistent phoenix at the country's intellectual apex. Mr. McCarthy quotes the French geographer Jean Gottmann as saying in a 1961 study of the northeastern seaboard of the United States, which includes most of New England, that it gave him the feeling of looking at "the dawn of a new stage in human civilization."

Social changes that have followed the economic are no less striking. In the light of a bright common future, differences of race, creed, color and the right school no longer seem so desperately important as they used. The old farming life of New England persists as an undercurrent to the trend to commute —to the jet-engine factories, to the electronics laboratories, to new types of mills—but the villages where the chores do get attended to after work now help draw a tourist trade that brings in millions every year. Not only in the eyes of the world, but in its own eyes, New England is on what my generation used to call the up and up; it has got shed of the past. The new Prudential Center risen from the dreariest part of the Back Bay, the ramps over and around the North Station, look as unlike Victorian Boston as the landscape of Mars.

Fine, but it all has its sad side. The older, simpler way of life—the little white steamers that used to ply among the Maine islands with an orchestra playing out on deck; the long-gone trains that carried passengers between banks covered in summer with a profusion of Dorothy Perkins roses; the dear departed dowdy fashions sold at "The Boston Store"; the Yankee fishermen who didn't think it worth learning to swim, not with them boots; the up-and-down Yankee housewives who saved string and egg crates as being perfectly good, for gracious' sakes; the Yankee storekeeper who wouldn't stock Turkey red cotton because it was in too great demand; to say nothing of the concomitant, nowadays unfashionable virtues like thrift, intransigence, taciturnity and minding your own business—who remembers it now? Who remembers that salmon and peas were required eating on the Fourth of July, and how they came to be?

New England's past has too much character to be lightly abandoned, but not the least of the opportunities afforded by its new manifestation is for a different relationship to a past it used merely to be neck-deep in. Its triumphant struggle up out of the past demonstrates that rebellion against the existing environment need not always be acted out by running away. Rebellion can be made real, at a profounder level, by working on the environment itself; creating in effect a new environment. When such a vantage point in the present is gained—outside and apart from the past—it is possible to turn and look back with new objectivity at what is, after all, inherited property. The same dynamic holds for macrocosm as for microcosm: the most the past can feel for the future is longing, but the future is capable of making itself whole when it claims the past. In such a *metanoia* the Yankee virtues might be reclaimable as a thrift and intransigence of the spirit; a more all-inclusive own business to mind.

The poet David McCord, an example of those born elsewhere who, once exposed to New England's charms, fall flat and stick with it through thick and thin, expressed the feeling of everyone who loves the region when he said, in an address at the opening of Old Sturbridge Village in 1960, "New England is the authorized version of America: her land and people chapter and verse for more than three hundred years." New England does have the curious trick of righting itself, and once more leading the country. Lost, the trick renews itself on a new level. In the Latin of James Jeffrey Roche, a Boston Irish poet and journalist, "*Dies erit praegelida/Sinistra quum Bostonia.*" Which, being translated, is to say, "It will be a cold day when Boston gets left." As Mr. Braownin', the Rhode Island farmer who drove for my Aunt Susan on the side, used to remark between expostulations to his horse, "When ye say Boston, means New England. And when ye say *that*, might's well say the world. *Git* up thar, what ye 'baout?"

—NANCY HALE
Novelist and short-story writer

Lobster boats, anchored in a cove off Maine's Deer Isle, typify New England for most Americans. From the days of the first settlements, the sea—a source of food and the passageway to world commerce—played a major role in shaping the history of the region.

1

The United Region

A stranger driving through New England for the first time and seeing the rocky coast, the mountains, the hills and lakes, the neat little towns with old narrow streets is likely to have the momentary feeling that he has been transported, car and all, to the British Isles, probably Scotland. The impression will be fleeting, however. Although the six states in the northeastern corner of the nation are markedly different from the other parts of the United States, the all-pervasive Yankee atmosphere clearly stamps the area as New England, U.S.A.

The awareness of the unity of New England is a lasting one. Road signs assure the traveler that he is successively going through Connecticut, Rhode Island, Massachusetts, Vermont, New Hampshire and Maine, but he has the sensation of passing through not a half-dozen states, but one. A distinctive character flavors almost the entire region and makes state borders seem irrelevant. The dignified village green in Litchfield, Connecticut, for example, is virtually duplicated in Wiscasset, Maine, some 280 miles away, and in a hundred towns in between. The oneness is real as well as apparent. During the Depression of the 1930s, a governor of Connecticut seriously proposed that, for reasons of economy, New England become one state. The concept was not adopted, of course, but few natives found the idea ridiculous.

Both the similarities among the six New England States and their difference, as a sectional group, from the rest of America are rooted in their singular common history and their even more singular

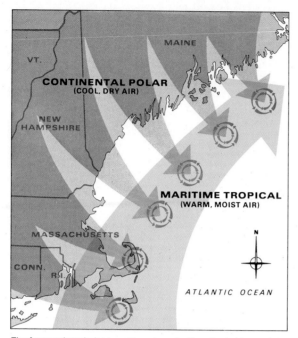

The frequently turbulent weather along the New England coast is caused by cyclonic systems that are constantly being formed by the mixture of warm southern air masses with cool northern masses. Such storms are called "northeasters" because the spinning winds in a cyclone appear from land to be proceeding from the northeast.

geography, with its seclusion, its stern and stony terrain, and its hard climate. Unlike other colonies on the Atlantic Seaboard and the territories in the South and West, all of New England was settled by one kind of people: Puritans from much the same English background with the same basic religious beliefs, the same simple tastes and the same high principles. Isolated on the south and east by salt water, on the north by forest wilderness and along the New York border on the west by mountain ranges, New England remained an almost completely homogeneous Yankee stronghold until well into the 19th Century, when the first big waves of immigrants came from Europe and Canada.

By that time the hard core of New England character, toughened by the harsh environment, was already formed. As historian James Truslow Adams put it, "the gristle of conscience, work, thrift, shrewdness, duty, became bone." Another ingredient in the bone of New England, stubborn independence, made it the place where the first shots of the Revolution were fired.

The physical attractions that lure vacationers today to New England—the magnificent mountains, luxuriant forests and majestic seacoast, the quaint old houses, stone walls and covered bridges, and the wealth of historic sites—are also reminders of the Yankee's struggle in those early years of isolation. The steep and rocky hillsides, with most of their topsoil scraped away by ice-age glaciers, were unfit for large-scale farming. The New Englander could barely raise enough for his family's needs. The stone walls, which now seem so picturesque to tourists, are monuments to the work required to clear the small fields of rocks by hand. The long and bitter winters also discourage agriculture. Early Yankee farmhouses were attached under one roof to the woodshed and the barn so that the farmer could get the kitchen stove started in the morning and feed his livestock without going outdoors into the freezing cold and snow.

The New England climate played as big a role as did the frustrating soil in shaping the strong Yankee character. Mark Twain, a resident of Hartford, Connecticut, for many years, claimed that he had counted 136 different varieties of weather within one 24-hour period in the spring. Describing a New England winter, the writer Jean Stafford wondered whether the Pilgrims modestly gave too much credit to God for seeing them through the cold; their own determined endurance was one of the marvels of history. In old rural New England every small boy was an expert at thawing out the pump with a kettle or two of boiling water. Even now in places with a town water supply, pipes five feet under the ground often freeze solid. But the Yankee, consulting his almanac, reassures himself that there will never be another year like 1816, usually referred to as "Eighteen Hundred and Froze to Death," when there was frost in every month and snow in July and August—along with a drought —and even the maple sap was skimpy. State-of-Mainers, as Maine people call themselves to emphasize their pride in the statehood they finally won from Massachusetts in 1820, say that they have two seasons, winter and July, or "nine months of winter and three months of damn poor sleddin'."

The winter weather encouraged the early townspeople to build their homes close together, for mutual aid and comfort, around the village common and near their white church. The community living fostered the New England town meeting, the forum where every qualified citizen has a voice in local government. From these democratic sessions came the satisfying taste of self-government that stirred up the first protests against British rule.

The long winters also gave the early Yankee time to meditate over the Bible and *Pilgrim's Progress*, thus nurturing his characteristic religious fervor. And the cold months allowed him plenty of hours to make things that his meager income from the soil would not permit him to buy—shoes, harness, tools, furniture. These home-learned skills prepared him for the job opportunities that came with the arrival of industry.

By the beginning of the 18th Century many Yankees had recognized that New England's resources —excellent lumber, fine natural harbors and swift streams for generating power—would, if properly exploited, pay better returns for labor than farming in that difficult region ever could. These astute men abandoned the plow to devote their efforts to shipping, industry and business. The ingenuity, thrifty shrewdness and resourcefulness that they had developed in their struggle with the soil and climate made them well suited to follow these new pursuits.

The Yankee's survival in his isolated war against the elements has also given him his special tight-lipped and proud aloofness; he feels slightly superior to people who have not been toughened by such a rigorous exposure. Henry Cabot Lodge, the Massachusetts Senator who died in 1924, reflected this attitude when he said: "New England has a harsh climate, a barren soil, a rough and stormy coast, and yet we love it, even with a love passing that of dwellers in more favored regions."

New England's coastline was a major factor in shaping and unifying the character of the area. Starting at an arm of Passamaquoddy Bay at present-day Calais, in northern Maine, and following a jagged course for some 6,000 miles to what is now Stamford, Connecticut, on Long Island Sound, the coast offered innumerable natural harbors, large and small. Good ports encouraged trade and the growth of industry. The coastal waters, abundant with life, provided a ready supply of food.

All of inland New England is wrinkled by mountains that rise high in the north and taper down into sloping foothills extending across Massachusetts and Connecticut southward toward Long Island Sound. The range of the White Mountains starts in Maine and runs into northern New Hampshire, where their spectacular peaks form the Presidential Range, topped by Mount Washington, at 6,288 feet the highest point in the Northeast. The weather on Mount Washington is so fierce that timber growth stops at about 4,800 feet, compared with 10,000 to 11,000 feet in the Rockies. On one wild April day in 1934, the wind at the bleak summit was clocked at 231 miles per hour, the fastest ever recorded anywhere. The top of the mountain, thronged by tourists during summer months but closed to visitors from fall until late spring, can be reached by car on a road that climbs 4,700 feet in eight miles. On the opposite side of

the mountain there is an 1869 cogwheel railroad with small and elderly steam engines that burn a ton of coal and use 1,000 gallons of water on each trip to and from the summit. The engineers and the firemen emerge so blackened by soot after each trip that they look like miners.

The magnificent White Mountains region of New Hampshire, New England's Switzerland, has 86 well-defined peaks in an area of some 1,200 square miles, eight of the pinnacles more than a mile high and 48 others from 3,000 to 5,000 feet. The mountains, running north and south, are divided into four principal formations by deep notches (as the Yankees call their valley gaps or passes). Excellent highways run through three of the notches, Pinkham, Crawford and Franconia, with dazzling views of the mountain heights that loom up on both sides of the roads. Within a few miles of the resort village of North Conway, in the valley southeast of the lofty Presidential Range, is some of the greatest scenery in America.

The peaks of the White Mountains seem to have more impressive grandeur than higher mountains in other parts of the United States because they rise more steeply from the valleys at their feet. Mount Washington, for example, towers a steep 4,000 feet above its base at Pinkham Notch, which is itself more than 2,000 feet above sea level. The famous face of the Old Man of the Mountains, overlooking Franconia Notch, about 35 miles west of Mount Washington, juts its stone profile out of a sheer cliff that springs upward in an almost straight line above the heads of the tourists peering at it from the floor of the valley 1,500 feet below.

Until a few years ago there was no good scenic road across the mountains from east to west to supplement the old, heavily traveled routes through the notches. However, such a road, the Kancamagus Highway, now exists, although it is still unmentioned in most tourist guidebooks. It extends westward from Conway, New Hampshire, for 34 miles to Lincoln, south of Franconia Notch, without a single filling station or refreshment stand anywhere along its entire length to mar the quiet beauty of its forests and heights. Most of the White Mountain region now is a national forest preserve, blessedly kept unspoiled, but it has very little of its original primeval timber. In 1867 the state of New Hampshire sold the greater part of this priceless heritage for the small sum of $26,000 to private lumbering companies that raped the woodlands. The United States government had to pay more than six million dollars in 1911 to get the same

A mountain's vegetation

A variety of plant life ranging from tall hardwood forests to tiny alpine flowers is supported on the wind-swept slopes and summit of New Hampshire's 6,288-foot-high Mount Washington. These drawings show examples of the different kinds of plant life found at various altitudes above sea level. All figures are approximate.

On the lower slopes, at elevations of about 2,000 to 2,600 feet above sea level, is the hardwood forest of sugar maples and red oaks *(bottom drawing)* common to all New England, mixed with other hardwoods like beech and yellow birch. As one ascends to the mixed-forest area *(second from bottom)*—about 2,600 to 3,500 feet up—the hardwoods become fewer while the sturdier birch and ash, and the cold-resistant conifers, like the hemlock and balsam fir, flourish. In the coniferous forest *(second from top)*, ranging from about 3,500 to 4,800 feet, the conifers predominate but change in form as one continues to climb, for the increasing cold, stony soil and hurricane-speed winds stunt the trees' growth until even the sturdiest, like the black spruce shown here, become distorted dwarfs. Near the 4,800-foot line, the upper limits of tree life, only a few small species survive, growing in a dense, ground-hugging mat often just a few inches high.

Above the tree line in the Alpine zone (above 4,800 feet) grow true mountaintop flowers *(top)*. Here Lapland rosebay, resembling a small, red-purple azalea, and brown, bristly deer's-hair nestle among the bleak gray boulders and carpet occasional level expanses called alpine gardens.

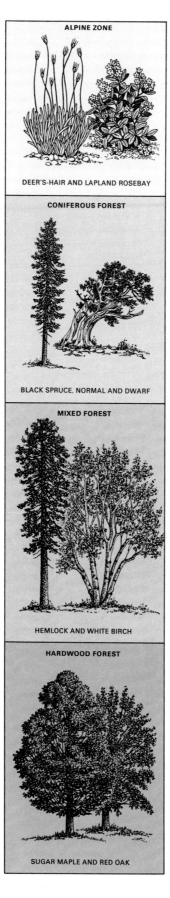

ALPINE ZONE

DEER'S-HAIR AND LAPLAND ROSEBAY

CONIFEROUS FOREST

BLACK SPRUCE, NORMAL AND DWARF

MIXED FOREST

HEMLOCK AND WHITE BIRCH

HARDWOOD FOREST

SUGAR MAPLE AND RED OAK

property back and establish it as a national forest.

New Hampshire's sparse farmland begins to appear on the foothills of the White Mountains as they extend southward around Lake Winnipesaukee and Lake Sunapee and on to the state's biggest city, Manchester. This is the country where Robert Frost tried for 10 bitter years to be a farmer before turning to teaching and writing. Without constant and heavy fertilizing, 95 per cent of New Hampshire's sandy, stony soil is unfit for growing anything except trees.

The same rocky formation rolls on farther south and finally drops sharply into salt water at the tidal estuary of the Thames above New London. Here in eastern Connecticut the geological pattern discouraged farming just as it did in the north. As a consequence, Norwich was a manufacturing town larger than New Haven and Hartford in colonial days. Watches, clocks, warming pans and combs were among the products made in Norwich. New London, like nearby Mystic, developed as a whaling and shipbuilding port.

West of the White Mountains and their foothills, between New Hampshire and Vermont, the winding Connecticut River, New England's longest stream, flows serenely southward for 407 miles. Rising in three small lakes in the north woods of New Hampshire near the Quebec border, the river passes down through Springfield in Massachusetts and Hartford in Connecticut and empties into Long Island Sound at Saybrook. Unlike the hilly country that confines the river narrowly on both sides for much of its course, the Connecticut Valley itself has fertile meadowlands that grow onions and celery and, in the southern parts, the tobacco leaf that is used as the outer wrapper for cigars.

Although Springfield has strong colonial roots, it and the other Connecticut River cities in western Massachusetts, such as Chicopee and Holyoke, have a brisk non-New England look, probably because they have done most of their growing as manufacturing centers since the Civil War. Farther down in the valley is Hartford, Connecticut's capital and the state's largest and most attractive city. It began as a river town, but because the Connecticut River is navigable that far north, Hartford gradually developed as a deepwater port for oceangoing shipping engaged in the West Indies trade. The city became an insurance center as a result of this seaborne shipping; for a percentage of the profits, underwriters would agree to share with a ship's owner the risk of a voyage. The city lost its importance as a port in the early 19th Century, but it is still the insurance capital of the U.S.

Despite Hartford's age, most of the mementos of its past days are now found only in museums. Except for some sacred relics, such as the handsome Old State House designed by Charles Bulfinch in 1796, the Victorian mansion once inhabited by Mark Twain, and Noah Webster's birthplace, an ancient salt-box house, much of the old Hartford has been erased by an extensive rebuilding program. The early riverfront settlement in the core of the city has been replaced by the impressive $40 million Constitution Plaza. This sparkling modern complex of office buildings, its focal point a skyscraper shaped much like a ship—the converging curved sides form a "prow" and "stern" at the two ends of the structure—includes a variety of retail shops, a radio-television studio and a hotel with a swimming pool, all on a landscaped, raised mall with a parking garage underneath. West of the Connecticut Valley, New Haven, the home of Eli Whitney and Yale University, has undergone similar rejuvenation.

Western New England between the Connecticut River Valley and the New York border is dominated by the Green Mountains of Vermont, the Berkshire Hills of Massachusetts and the Litchfield Hills of Connecticut, but it is all basically Green Mountain country. The lush picture-postcard greenery of the hills around Lenox and Stockbridge in Massachusetts and Goshen and Cornwall in Connecticut is simply a little more of Vermont under another name. The same uniformity extends to other parts of the region. The twisting shoreline of Rhode Island—250 miles long, although the state itself is only 48 miles long and 37 miles wide—looks very much like parts of the Maine coast.

The spiritual solidarity of the six states is heightened by the traditional reverence all show for Boston, a much more important city from the Yankee view than Washington or New York. Wrote a New England minister, the Reverend F. B. Zinckle, in 1868: "Boston . . . is often called the 'hub of the world' since it has been the source and fountain of the ideas that have reared and made America."

Along with their possession of a common cultural capital, the New England States often cooperate closely in politics, functioning almost as a political unit. The six governors frequently meet to discuss, on a regional basis, problems that would be considered purely state matters elsewhere in the nation.

Although partisans of Pennsylvania and Virginia might disagree with the argument, it has often been said that New England is different from the rest of the states because it reached maturity when other sections of the nation were still in their adolescence. New England, wrote Bernard De Voto, "is the first

American section to be finished, to achieve stability in the conditions of its life. It is the first old civilization, the first permanent civilization in America."

The stranger from Iowa, climbing the steep, cobblestone streets of Boston's stately Beacon Hill or snapping pictures of the elegant homes of sailing-ship owners in Portsmouth, New Hampshire, does see a civilization that may seem to him more European than American because it is two centuries older than his own back home.

Somewhat to his surprise, the visitor finds that many of the more aged communities in New England are small-scaled. Travelers from the wide-open spaces of the West, turning off high-speed turnpikes into the old, winding back roads of southern and central New England, are intrigued to find themselves in miniature rural scenes that suggest Currier and Ives prints or Grandma Moses Christmas cards. Small farms with small stone-walled patches of field are scattered between numerous small villages, many of them with small mills or factories beside small streams. Some of the seaside towns—like Marblehead and Rockport in Massachusetts, with their picturesque little houses crowded closely together along narrow streets that lead to diminutive docks on minute, boat-filled harbors or coves—seem like Lilliputian settlements.

When growth and change do come to some of the old settlements, the effect is often incongruous. For example, the old downtown section of Boston, where some of the sidewalks are so narrow that shoppers have to step into the gutter to pass one another, has always had the sedate look of a small, cultured city of long ago, such as Edinburgh in the 18th Century Georgian period. Now the new 52-story Prudential Tower, massive and gleaming, soars above the low slate roofs and chimney tops of the Back Bay area, not many blocks away. In that antiquated setting the structure seems much more enormous than a higher building would in New York or Chicago. Older Proper Bostonians still frown in disbelief at the rushing commuter traffic that sweeps through the North End on an elevated expressway near Paul Revere's 17th Century Elizabethan-style house with its diamond-shaped casement windowpanes. Outside the city the cars circle around the suburban complex of modern electronics plants on Route 128, streaming in a bumper-to-bumper flow beneath an overpass that now carries the historic road traveled by Revere on his famous ride. An even more startling intrusion jars the old, small and once-quiet college town of Amherst, Massachusetts: five huge, new 22-story dormitories on the crowded and expanding University of Massachusetts campus tower

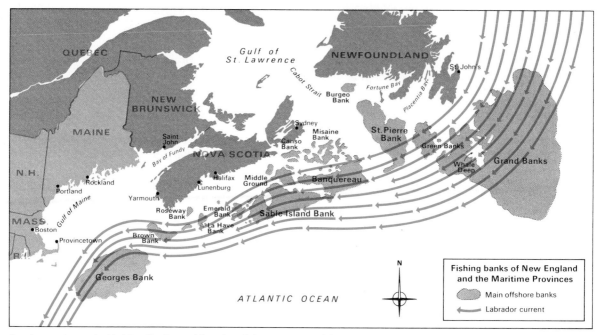

Running south past the Maritime Provinces of Canada and the coast of Maine, the icy Labrador Current travels over a number of "banks," underwater shelves where the water is relatively shallow. In these warmer waters flourish the minute organisms known as plankton, a staple in the diet of many fish—a fact that explains the richness of the northwest Atlantic fisheries. Yankee fishermen learned long ago that these banks off Canada and New England teemed with cod, mackerel, flounder and shellfish. The banks' fame is international: ever since the days of the Vikings, fishermen have crossed the Atlantic Ocean from Europe to try their luck here.

above the surrounding greenery of the Connecticut River Valley. In this setting the buildings look like a quintet of skyscrapers.

However, because settlers did not reach the woods and mountains of upper Maine and northern New Hampshire until late in the 19th Century, this large area of New England has none of the Old World smallness of the seacoast cities and towns and the more southerly rural villages. Much of this north country, around Moosehead Lake, the Rangeley Lakes and Mount Katahdin in Maine, and above Dixville Notch in New Hampshire, is still uninhabited wilderness. A motorist can drive for more than 30 miles on lumber-company roads in some parts of the region without seeing another person or a house and without meeting another car.

Still farther north in Maine, beyond the mountains and lakes, along the St. John River on the Canadian border, lies still another country no more like the rest of New England in appearance, soil quality and civilization than Arkansas is like Maryland. It is a private world of its own, almost as large as Massachusetts, with a population that speaks Canadian French. This is the fine, fertile potato-growing land of Aroostook County, one of the richest farming areas in the United States. Many of the families along the St. John River are descendants of the French Acadians, who were banished from Nova Scotia around the middle of the 18th Century. Almost everyone in the county is a speculator who gambles heavily on potatoes. It is said that in the vintage year of 1925, when the crop was plentiful and the prices good, 3,500 potato growers in one area paid off the mortgages on their farms.

Maine, to most people, is lobsters and seacoast resorts—Kennebunkport and the Casco Bay towns, Boothbay Harbor, Rockland, Castine and beautiful Mount Desert Island with its Cadillac Mountain, the highest shorefront peak on the North Atlantic Seaboard. But as long and impressive as the coastal area is—2,500 miles of shore twisting in and out along the 250 crow-flight miles between Kittery and Calais—it is a comparatively small part of Maine, a state nearly as big as all of the other five New England States combined. A student from New York at a college in Biddeford, south of Portland, was surprised to learn recently that he had a shorter drive to his home on Long Island than a classmate had to *his* home at Fort Kent in Aroostook County.

It is this large, noncoastal region that provides the state with its biggest industry—wood products. Pine-scented Maine has been chiefly a logging state since its colonial times. There were sawmills in Berwick and York before 1640, and most of the Maine coastal and river cities, such as Portland, Brunswick, Bath, Waterville, Augusta and Bangor, grew as lumber-shipping ports. About 1849, when Bangor shipped more than five million feet of construction boards to Gold Rush-booming California, the town had a flourishing "Barbary Coast" district of its own on Washington, Hancock and Exchange Streets, a wide-open lumberjacks' pleasure resort known as the "Devil's Half-Acre."

"There stands the city of Bangor, fifty miles up the Penobscot, at the head of navigation for vessels of the larger class," the author Henry D. Thoreau wrote at the time, "the principal lumber depot on this continent . . . still hewing at the forest of which it is built, already overflowing with the luxuries and refinements of Europe, and sending its vessels to Spain, to England, and to the West Indies for its groceries."

Since those deliriously prosperous days, Maine's virgin forests have been seriously depleted, and the state's hold on the lumber market is no longer as firm as it once was. More than 80 per cent of the state is still in timberlands, however, and wood products, especially pulp and paper, still comprise Maine's biggest business. Radio and television stations in both Maine and northern New Hampshire are kept busy broadcasting commercials for power-driven chain saws. With such a saw, it is possible for an experienced working team of two lumberjacks, getting from $8 to $8.50 per cord, to earn as much as $50 each for one day of cutting in the woods.

Lumber is also big business in New Hampshire, and today as always, tales of logging and log-driving exploits are popular there. Around Berlin, which has one of the nation's biggest paper mills, natives still talk of the huge amount of virgin timber that was cut when the site of the city was cleared in the late 1820s. On one winter day, they say, a team of four oxen hauled 40,000 feet of pine logs from the woods to the Androscoggin River.

The green trees on the lovely mountains that run through the middle of Vermont gave the state its name. The early French settlers called the area *verdmont* (green mountain); English settlers simply dropped the "d." In this instance, calling a state a mountain was only a mild hyperbole; Vermont has less level ground than almost any other state in the Union. Its people like to claim that if Vermont were stamped flat, it would be bigger than Texas.

Despite the terrain and generally poor soil, there was considerable farming at one time in Vermont, but the contour of the land was better suited to the scythe than to mechanized equipment even when it became available. Vermont was the last sanctuary

The term "down East," commonly denoting the Maine coast, comes from the days of sailing vessels. Because New England's prevailing winds are from the southwest, a ship like the schooner above could sail from other Atlantic Coast ports to the easterly parts of Maine by running with the wind behind it: downwind to the east.

of the old rural Yankee, self-reliant and independent, sticking to the old ways of providing for his needs. Late in the last century, long after such practices had been abandoned in the rest of New England, some Vermont farmers were still using oxen for work in the fields, growing flax for bed linen, carding wool from their sheep for homespun clothing, and making their own wooden maple-sap and milk buckets and farming tools. A number of years ago the author Dorothy Canfield Fisher heard a Vermonter transplanted to Kansas say of his native hills: "What ought to be done with the old state is to turn it into a national park of a new kind —keep it just as it is, with Vermonters managing just as they do—so the rest of the country could come in to see how their grandparents lived."

Today, of course, life in Vermont is not so far behind the times. There are now IBM and General Electric plants in Burlington, and the small town of Springfield is one of the nation's leading producers of machines for making automobile gears. But as a visitor can readily see, Vermont as a whole has been less changed by the industrial revolution than any state in the Northeast. It has more cattle, fewer cities and towns, fewer hired laborers—and therefore fewer foreign-born immigrants—and less manufacturing than any other part of New England. The

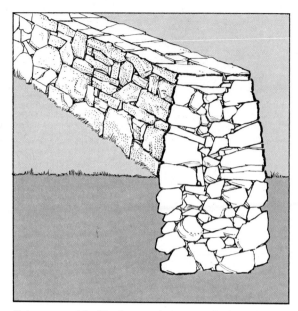

Picturesque and durable, the mortarless stone walls that still lace New England's fields were built with fine skill. As this cross section shows, they are set on a base that may go as deep as three and a half feet below the surface to prevent frost heaves from toppling them. For even greater stability, the base of a wall is often wider than its top. New England boasted 100,000 miles of stone walls in the days before modern farming methods discouraged their use.

state also has the smallest population of the region, only about 400,000 people. All of which, in today's crowded world, makes the charming and peacefully quiet Green Mountains increasingly attractive as a vacationland and as a year-round residence for affluent people seeking a sanctuary free from noise, congestion and heavy traffic. "Vermont is the only place within a day's drive from New York that's fit to live in," a Wall Street banker said recently.

The solitude in such a spacious countryside, now so appealing, was often trying to the Yankees who lived there alone in the days before the automobile, telephones or television. Along with the struggle against the soil and the climate, the northern New Englanders in past centuries fought loneliness. "It wasn't so bad on the men, because they had plenty of hard work to do," says one Vermonter, discussing the home life of his grandfather's time, "but it was very lonely for the woman." Rudyard Kipling, who lived in Vermont for four years in the 1890s, wrote of meeting a woman from a farmhouse on an opposite hilltop. "Be you the new lights 'crost the valley yonder?" she asked him. "Ye don't know what a comfort they've been to me this winter."

The Green Mountains are softer, lower and somewhat more fertile than the steeper peaks of New Hampshire. In Vermont's lean early years even the

summits were farmed or used as pastureland. Like the steadfast people who have lived on them, the mountains are solid underneath; granite and marble taken from the mountains are among the state's most important products, along with milk, lumber and paper pulp. Before the automobile, Vermont's mountains and its waterfront along Lake Champlain attracted only summer tourists. Now, because of fall foliage, a stunning spectacle of flaming red and gold, every motel vacancy in western New England is filled on early October weekends, and in the winter the snow brings an invasion of skiers to the slopes at such centers as Stowe, Bromley, Sugarbush, Pico and Killington.

When the Green Mountains descend into Massachusetts, they become the steep Hoosacs, where the Mohawk Trail provides motorists with a high climb over slanting walls of gorgeous forests. Then the hills roll on into the picturesque Berkshires, the beautiful, secluded area where Nathaniel Hawthorne once picnicked with Herman Melville, where Edith Wharton entertained Henry James, and where the music of the Tanglewood concerts now resounds in July and August.

The foothills are still steep around Litchfield, Connecticut, the beautifully preserved Georgian colonial village where the author of *Uncle Tom's Cabin*, Harriet Beecher Stowe, was born while her famous preacher father, Lyman Beecher, was serving as the town's minister. Litchfield is regarded by northern Yankees these days as New England's last outpost in Connecticut; the southern part of that state, in their opinion, has become a suburb of New York. There is a sound basis for this view; the commuting population from the shore of Connecticut's Long Island Sound has increased mightily in the last 20 years. From New Haven west to the state border at Greenwich, few pockets of true rural living still exist. The value of rural land in Connecticut today is much higher than anywhere else in New England because it is close to expanding urban and industrial areas.

Ever since Revolutionary times Connecticut has marched ahead of the rest of New England in the manufacturing of a wide variety of industrial products—brass items, firearms, machinery, silverware, hats, clocks, textiles, tools. Now the state's big employers, along with the insurance companies in Hartford, are the makers of jet aircraft engines, helicopters and nuclear-powered submarines. This third-smallest state in the nation is one of the most prosperous; in recent years it has ranked either first or second in per capita income.

The even smaller state of Rhode Island has been

How a leaf changes color

The spectacular autumn colors of New England's famous sugar-maple leaf are the result of the leaf's varying chemical composition. The leaf contains several color-producing chemicals. Which of these is dominant depends largely on temperature and the amount of moisture present. Under some conditions, the leaf goes through only one color change—from green to yellow, for example—before falling to the ground. Under other circumstances, it may pass through a full cycle—from green to vivid yellow to flaming red to somber brown. In spring and summer, the tree's growing period, the leaf is green because green-colored chlorophyll is the dominant chemical pigment. This substance, through a process known as photosynthesis, converts air, water and light energy into sugar to nourish the tree. In the fall the supply of chlorophyll comes to an end, and depending on weather and other factors, one of the other color-producing substances—carotenoids, anthocyanins or tannins—becomes dominant and the leaf goes through its beautiful transition.

During the spring and summer, the maple produces chlorophyll, and the leaves are green. During the day the chemical is partially depleted, but at night the tree creates more chlorophyll, restoring the balance.

As the chill of early fall arrives, the tree decreases its production of chlorophyll, and a similar chemical, carotenoid, which has been part of the leaf since it was a bud, becomes dominant and colors the leaf yellow.

As winter approaches and the maple tree is about to shed all of its leaves and rest until spring, the cold, dry weather destroys all of the leaf's pigments except tannin, which is the most durable of the chemicals. The tannin gives the leaf its brown color.

As fall continues, the carotenoids gradually lose their dominance in the leaf's chemistry. If there are warm days and cold nights, light converts sugar in the leaf into anthocyanin, which becomes the dominant chemical and turns the leaf red.

almost as heavily industrialized for decades. A professor recalls that when he was teaching at Brown University in 1925 he and his wife could never seem to find a place for a Sunday picnic. Any spot reachable by a trolley line from Providence was within sight and smell of a factory. Indeed, Rhode Island was the birthplace of the American factory. In 1790 an Englishman, Samuel Slater, built a cotton-yarn mill that was so mechanized it could be, and was, operated by child laborers; a second Slater mill still stands in Pawtucket as a museum exhibit.

Rhode Island was industrialized primarily by sailing-ship wealth, which also established a culture as solid and mellowed as Boston's. Rising above the factories in Providence is one of the most handsome state capitol buildings in the United States. It is built of white marble and has a huge dome exceeded in size only by the one on St. Peter's in Rome. Along the nearby streets—whose names, such as Benefit and Benevolent, reflect the tolerant beliefs of Roger Williams, the colony's founder—are fine churches, libraries, the world's most famous collection of Americana, excellent art galleries, and such houses as the one built by John Brown, merchant and shipbuilder, which John Quincy Adams in 1789 called "the most magnificent . . . private mansion that I have ever seen on this continent."

Providence stands about 28 miles from the sea, at the head of Narragansett Bay, a sheltered expanse of salt water that is filled with islands, pleasant coves and beaches and that takes up about a sixth of the little state's 1,214 square miles. At the opposite end of the bay, facing the ocean on Aquidneck Island, is Newport, which for several decades before the Revolution rivaled New York, Boston and Philadelphia in wealth and culture. Newport's affluence was built on the triangular trade with Africa and the West Indies involving rum, slaves and molasses.

To the British, Newport was important enough to justify sending a force of 9,000 soldiers in 1776 to seize it. Occupied for the next three years, it was left ransacked and commercially crippled. During the 1890s, it reached the peak of its renaissance as a gaudy summer playground for the wealthy. Astor, Vanderbilt and Belmont money superimposed on the previous century's conservatism a splashy gilt that gives today's visitor an exhibit of the contrasting tastes of those two ages of American prosperity. Not far from the huge and ornate palaces of the Vanderbilts are such exquisite examples of colonial architecture as the mid-18th Century Hunter House, with its beautifully paneled rooms, and Trinity Church, built in 1726, which displays New

England's first church bell, a wineglass-shaped pulpit and a baptismal font hammered from a single sheet of silver. Illustrative of Rhode Island's early religious freedom at a time when the rest of New England was not so tolerant, Newport has the oldest synagogue in America, built in 1763 on a diagonal line on its small lot so that it faces eastward toward Jerusalem.

The New England seacoast's sparkling variety of scenery—from the rocks of Maine to the sand dunes of Cape Cod and the beautiful offshore islands of Nantucket and Martha's Vineyard—has drawn vacationers from all over America for a longer period than any other area of the continent. As far back as 1654 a resident of Saco, Maine, received a license from the local court "to keep an ordinary [tavern] to entertain strangers for their money."

The most celebrated holiday mecca on the coast is Cape Cod, which extends for 65 miles into the Atlantic from the southeast corner of Massachusetts. On the map Cape Cod looks like an arm bent at the elbow to flex its muscles. The upper part of the arm, between the shoulder at the mainland and the elbow at Chatham and Orleans, has two distinctly different shores—the north and south sides, or as the natives call them, "the New England side and the New York side." The north shore is definitely Yankee; its water on Cape Cod Bay is colder, and its villages at Sandwich, Barnstable, Dennis and Brewster were the homes of sailing-ship captains, prim and old-fashioned, with the sedate saltiness of Joseph C. Lincoln's Cape Cod stories.

The southern, or New York, side of the upper arm of the cape has the warmer water of Nantucket Sound, more yacht clubs and country clubs, and the more recently built luxurious summer colonies of wealthy New Yorkers, Middle Westerners and Boston Irish. It was in Hyannis Port that Joseph P. Kennedy, then a prosperous young Bostonian with eight children, established his seaside compound in the late 1920s. Older Cape Codders and staid Bostonians who summer there frown upon these showy newcomers. A Yankee mother from Boston once refused to let her little son attend a child's party given by the Kennedys at Hyannis Port because she had heard that the Kennedys had a soda fountain in their house.

To the disapproval of the dignified north shore, the main road on the south shore of the cape, Route 28, between Hyannis and Harwich Port, has become a neon-lighted jumble of motels, curio shops and thick-shake drive-ins. But beyond Chatham, the charming and well-preserved town at the cape's bent elbow, and for the rest of the way northward along the lower forearm to the fist at Provincetown, Cape Cod is for the most part a blissfully unspoiled beachland—now a National Seashore—of huge, towering dunes and great stretches of white sand washed by the surf of the immense blue ocean.

Provincetown, the fishermen's settlement and artists' colony at the tip of the cape, was the first landing place of the Pilgrims. After a brief exploration of the unbroken sand dunes, they continued on to Plymouth, on the mainland shore of Cape Cod Bay between the cape and Boston. Even in the early days transients converted Provincetown into an unconventional place; in 1714 the nearby respectable village of Truro refused the task of policing this "bacchanalian" resort. Ever since 1916, when Eugene O'Neill, enjoying the informality of the Portuguese fishing community and its magnificent beaches, began to write and stage his early plays in Provincetown, it has been crowded in the summer with painters, sculptors and writers, and with the tourists who come to stare at them. After Labor Day Provincetown again reverts to its older role as a port for trawlers and seiners.

The people who first touched the bleak shore of New England at Provincetown on November 11, 1620, and "fell upon their knees & blessed ye God of heaven, who had brought them over ye vast & furious ocean," came here as settlers, rather than as fortune seekers, traders or missionaries. Despite recent changes, the permanence of the civilization they established still stands unshaken and sure. A few miles from the bridge at Concord where the Minutemen turned back the British Redcoats, the Massachusetts Institute of Technology's Lincoln Laboratory plays a leading role in the Western world's missile-guidance research. The steady expansion of urban areas diminishes town-meeting government. "There are two New Englands," a Vermonter says. "The places that still hold town meetings and those that don't, and the latter is getting bigger." But the new skyscrapers in Boston are somehow overshadowed by Faneuil Hall, the scene of protest meetings before the Revolution, and by the spire of the Old North Church, where the signal lanterns were hung to warn the people when and how the British were coming.

According to Cleveland Amory, a lady who was born on Beacon Hill and lived for most of her later years in another part of the country finally returned to Boston and was asked if she liked being home again. "Like it?" she said. "Why I never thought of it that way. Liking Boston is like saluting the flag."

Most Yankees tend to feel that way about all of New England.

A man-made wall of rounded granite boulders, mementos of the glaciers that deposited them while retreating northward from New England at the end of the last ice age, follows the dips and rises of the undulating terrain as it winds across a Vermont pasture.

A lovely land of great antiquity

The beautiful, softly rolling landscape of New England presents a calm, peaceful face, seemingly that of a region newborn and unwrinkled by age. In fact, New England is geologically very old, and its gentle façade is a result of its antiquity and of titanic forces that began shaping it in the dim past. When the Green Mountains of Vermont, for example, were thrust up from the earth 425 million years ago, they were among the highest in the world; it has taken erosive forces all the eons since to lower and soften them to their modern contours. Similarly, the rest of ancient New England has had its edges smoothed off, not only by the forces of wind and water, but by the abrasive action of successive waves of glaciers, the last of which shaped Cape Cod, the final section of the region to come into existence, toward its present conformation a scant 12,000 years ago.

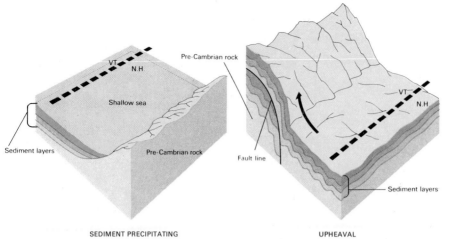

SEDIMENT PRECIPITATING   UPHEAVAL

The Green Mountains began to be formed 425 million years ago, when sediments settled in an inland sea *(far left)*. These sediments were then compressed *(left)* by subterranean pressures on both sides of a fault line, or plane of weakness, extending deep into the earth. Masses of material were thrust above and beyond the fault line—in effect, depositing half of New Hampshire atop Vermont to create the then-towering Green Mountains. They have been so eroded since then that even the rock sediments that once lay at the bottom of the inland sea have disappeared from the peaks, exposing there an even older layer of rock known as Pre-Cambrian.

Workmen clamber in a granite quarry near Barre, Vermont. The great subterranean pressures that created the state's mountains later metamorphosed much of the original rock into marble and granite; Vermont contains some of the nation's most extensive deposits.

The soft, weathered hills of the Green Mountains tenderly enfold the tiny village of Pawlet in southern Vermont. A prosperous 19th Century milling center, Pawlet is today a dairy community, dependent for its income on the scattered, sloping pastures that surround it.

The Green Mountains, lords of Vermont

The Green Mountains—so called because of the verdant growth that covers their flanks—"stretch extended straight," as the New England poet Robert Frost once wrote, running through Vermont from north to south in three more or less parallel ridges the full 159-mile length of the state. Among the oldest of the ranges of North America, they today deserve the title of "mountains" only by courtesy; so eroded have they been over the centuries since their birth that their tallest peak, Mount Mansfield, perhaps reaching a height of 12,000 feet when it first came into existence eons ago, today rises to a mere 4,393 feet.

Minuscule as the Green Mountains may be, few Vermonters denigrate them; their beauty and their gentle slopes attract thousands of vacationists and skiers to the state in summer and winter, and the innumerable pastures that dot the foothills of the mountains, watered by the sparkling streams cascading from the summits, support the dairy industry that is one of Vermont's major economic props.

The weathered peaks of New Hampshire

Brought into being roughly 75 million years later than the neighboring Green Mountains of Vermont, the White Mountains that rise in northern New Hampshire are well named. The granite of which they were formed, bared by hundreds of thousands of years of erosion, glints gray-white on their peaks and flanks, sharply contrasting with the evergreens that cling tenaciously to the thin deposits of soil remaining on parts of the mountain slopes. This contrast of colors, coupled with the White Mountains' erosion-sculpted contours, lends them great beauty, and like the Green Mountains, they draw great numbers of vacationists and skiers each year. Unlike the Green Mountains, however, they do not constitute a single range and are not the result of movement along a fault line. They consist, instead, of several separate clumps of peaks, all created by a completely different geologic process known as granitic intrusion, shown in the diagrams at right.

Tumbling down over satin-smooth ledges, the Swift River rushes toward the village of Conway, New Hampshire. Hastening streams like this one have over the millennia not only helped to carry away the soft materials that once overlay the White Mountains but gradually worn down the granite bedrock itself, reducing once-towering peaks to manageable mountains beloved by hikers.

Transported from their birthplace by a tremendous force, rocks and boulders lie strewn on a Mount Washington slope, deposited there by a glacier some 12,000 years ago. The glaciers, grinding their way southward and then retreating northward, added their mammoth weight and abrasive action to the erosive forces that lowered the White Mountains to their present heights.

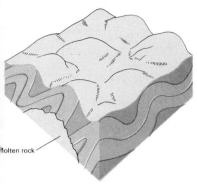 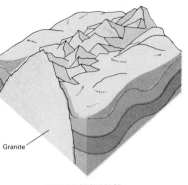

Molten rock

Granite

GRANITIC INTRUSION

EROSION OF SURFACE

The evolution of the White Mountains began 350 million years ago when molten rock was forced upward toward the wrinkled surface of the earth by subterranean pressures *(far left)*. Cooling and hardening, the molten rock became a granite underlay beneath softer surface materials. As the eons wore on, the soft surface material was largely removed by erosion, leaving exposed the hard granite that forms today's mountain peaks *(left)*.

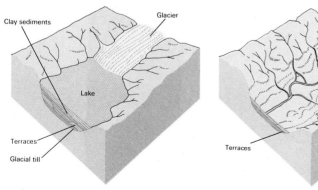

Clay sediments

Glacier

Lake

Terraces

Glacial till

RETREATING GLACIER

Terraces

PRESENT VALLEY

Bound toward its outlet in Long Island Sound, the Connecticut River detours around a New Hampshire point *(center)* in this northeastward-looking view taken from Vermont. The foothills of the White Mountains rise in the left background.

The glacier retreating northward from the Connecticut Valley has left deposits of sand and stone known as glacial till *(far left)*. Above this layer, the glacier's melting sides, dumping more glacial till, have formed wedge-shaped terraces. Far to the south, glacial till has dammed the valley, creating a glacial lake in which soft sediments slowly settled. When the dam broke and the lake vanished *(left)*, the valley was bequeathed a floor of fertile sediment through which the river could easily wander.

A valley's fertile, glacier-formed floor

Running past the mountains and rocky fields of New England is the valley of the long, lazy Connecticut River. From time immemorial—ever since the White Mountains to the east and the Green Mountains to the west were formed—there has been a valley here. About 12,000 years ago an enormous glacier began its retreat from the ice-clogged valley. It is to this glacier that the present valley owes its fertility and many of its present topographical features. Although other parts of New England were left rocky and barren by the retreat of the "rotting," or melting, glaciers at the end of the ice age, the glacier here produced a massive dam in the vicinity of what is now Middletown, Connecticut, and a lake that filled the valley for a distance of 157 miles to the north. On the rich, sediment-laden floor of this long-gone lake today flourish the dairy, tobacco and truck farms of the Connecticut Valley, and on the terraces left behind by the retreating glacier rest such New England towns as Hanover and Lebanon, New Hampshire.

The glacier-scarred, rock-strewn coast of Maine

For most of its length the coast of Maine is rocky and wave-battered. The evergreen forests stand a respectful distance from the waves that smash relentlessly against the granite facing of the shore. Measured in a straight line this dramatic coastline is 250 miles long, but into it glaciers and the tireless sea have carved countless bays and inlets to create a shoreline of 2,500 miles. The multitude of harbors helps make the Maine coast a sport- and commercial-fishing center, as well as a yachtsman's paradise. Off this irregular shore lie thousands of largely uninhabited sea- and glacier-shaped islets visited only by lobstermen and seagoing campers.

Worn smooth by the pounding of the ocean, a bastion of granite *(above)* guards the Maine coast. It has given way slowly—gouges left by glaciers thousands of years ago are still visible—but the waves incessantly reduce it, pushing the shoreline steadily inland.

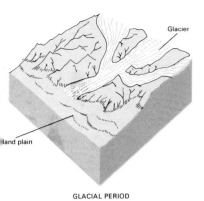

GLACIAL PERIOD   POST-GLACIAL PERIOD

Prior to the ice age, the area of Maine's present coast consisted of a series of angular hills rising from an inland plain *(far left)*. As the glaciers inched their way along, they smoothed hilltops and deepened river valleys. Because so much of the ocean's water froze at this time, the sea level fell. At the same time the weight of the ice caused the land to sink. Later, as the glacier melted, the oceans rose *(left)*, impinging on the lowered land, forming bays in what had once been river valleys and making islands out of the peaks of hills.

Unmindful of spray and noise, tourists witness the spectacle of Thunder Hole on Mount Desert Island, Maine. Surf rushing into a water-carved chasm compresses the air inside, which in turn blasts the water 40 feet into the air with a thunderous explosion.

A five-foot boulder carried from a point 20 miles away by a glacier rests atop Cadillac Mountain on Mount Desert Island. Even for a glacier, this was no small achievement; at 1,532 feet, Cadillac Mountain is the highest point on the North American coast.

27

The shifting sands of Cape Cod

Shaped like a beckoning arm, the 65-mile spit of sand that is Cape Cod juts out from the Massachusetts coast, luring thousands of vacationers to its beaches and resort towns each year. Along with the neighboring offshore islands of Martha's Vineyard and Nantucket, it was the final section of New England to come into existence. With its birth, the region in effect completed the geological story it had opened 425 million years ago. The geological process continues, however. The cape, like nearby sections of Maine and the rest of New England (and indeed of the world), is constantly being altered in size and shape by the forces of wind and water—so much so, in its case, that parts of its coastline can change beyond recognition in a matter of years.

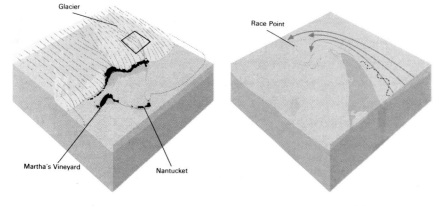

GLACIER'S FARTHEST ADVANCE   FORMATION OF UPPER CAPE

Its advance blocked by warm ocean currents, the last glacier to cover New England halted 12,000 years ago *(dotted line, far left)* and began to recede. It left in its wake great deposits of rocky materials *(black areas)* that became the islands of Martha's Vineyard and Nantucket and the southern base of Cape Cod. The boxed area, enlarged in the drawing at left, encompasses the tip of the present cape. It came into existence later as ocean currents whittled away at the Atlantic shoreline *(dashes)*, carrying huge quantities of sand northward to bring Cape Cod to its present conformation.

A fisherman sculls through a salt marsh near Prout's Neck, on the coast of southern Maine. Like the neighboring tip of Cape Cod, this low-lying section of the Maine coastline has been largely shaped by the constant ebb and flow of ocean waves and currents.

Swirling currents surround Race Point, northernmost extremity of Cape Cod, in this southward-looking aerial view. A century ago, the point was an offshore sand bar; the sand-bearing currents have since firmly attached it to the mainland.

28

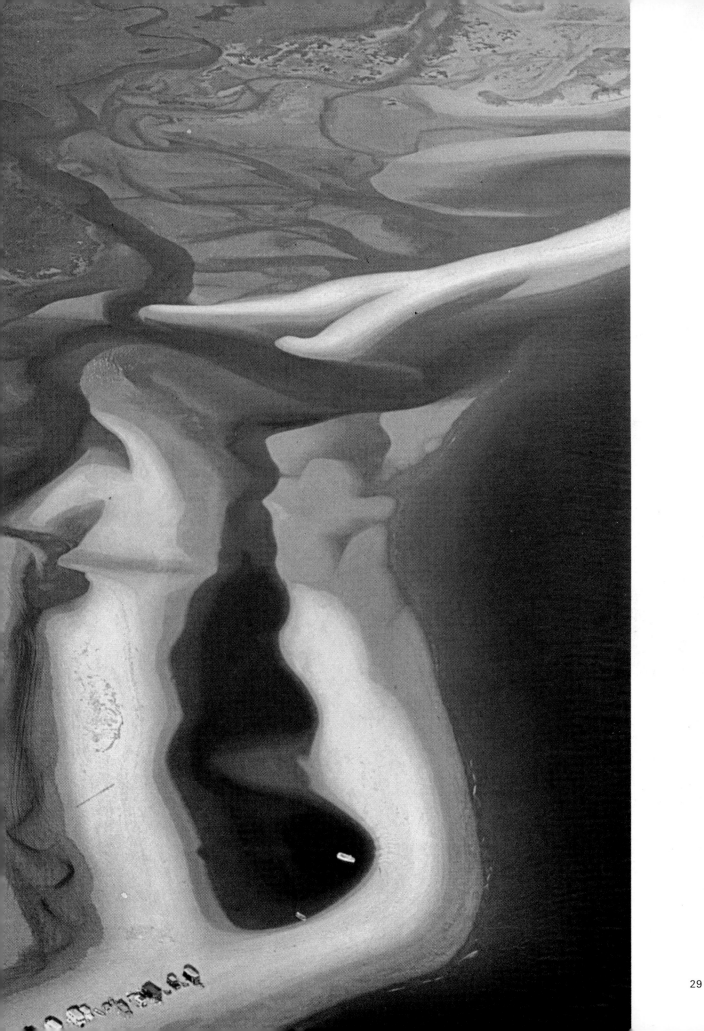

2

The Yankee Character

Of all the stock characters found in American regional humor—the Texas oil millionaire, the Appalachian mountaineer, the Hollywood producer, the New York provincial, to name but a few—the salty, taciturn New England Yankee is easily the best established. The many stories about the Yankee, as about the others, are sometimes true and sometimes apocryphal but they are revealing of his character. There is, for example, the reply of the Maine fisherman—or New Hampshire apple grower or Rhode Island clam digger—when he is asked if he has lived in his native village all his life. "Not yet," the Yankee replies.

A similarly explicit response is made to a motorist from New York when he stops his car at a Vermont country store and calls to a group of local men, "I want to go to Bennington." There is a long moment of silence and then one of the Yankees slowly removes his pipe from his mouth and says, "We've no objections."

Historian Samuel Eliot Morison, a summer resident of Northeast Harbor, in Maine, recounts the

dialogue he had with a villager one day at the post office.

"Saw your book on Columbus," the native said.

"How'd you like it?"

"Didn't read it. But my wife read it."

"How'd she like it?"

"Didn't say."

As with all regional humor, there is an element of caricature about the Yankee variety. However, good caricature is always based on solid truth. There are, of course, Yankees who are nonsalty, who are, in fact, as warm and outgoing as the purveyors of Southern hospitality are supposed to be, and there are talkative Yankees who may answer the question, "Is the train on time?" with a history of railroads. But astringent repartee and the simple expression of literal truth are very much a part of the Yankee character, a reflection of the hardheaded realism inherited from the original English Puritan settlers.

As an ethnic group in New England today, the Yankees—who may have received their name from the guttural Indian pronunciation of "English" or "*Anglais*" that came out "Yengees"—are, in many areas, greatly outnumbered by descendants of later immigrants, especially those from Ireland, Italy and French Canada. But for about 200 years after

Vermonter Calvin Coolidge is dour and taciturn as he faces the camera during a vacation from the White House. To most Americans, Coolidge seemed the personification of Yankee frugality and shrewdness during his Presidency, from 1923 to 1929.

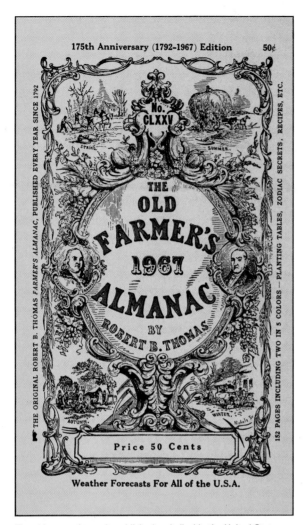

The oldest continuously published periodical in the United States, *The Old Farmer's Almanac* has prospered because it has offered New Englanders useful, down-to-earth information and afforded the rest of the world a nostalgic glimpse into a rugged past. Published in Dublin, New Hampshire, the *Almanac* is particularly well known for its often accurate long-range weather predictions, frequently stated with folksy humor ("Pshaw, rainy and raw"), and for its homespun aphorisms ("A man between two lawyers is a fish between two cats"; "Changing beds won't cure a fever"). The *Almanac* contains tables giving such information as the best times to plant and harvest, but also serves another function: designed as a source of entertainment for long winter evenings, it is an anthology of anecdotes, puzzles and scientific discoveries.

the arrival of the Puritans in 1620, New England was a Yankee domain. Consequently, the older traditions, customs and culture of the area—influences that have also affected the rest of the United States—are rooted in the Yankee character.

Realism, the searching out and acceptance of truth regardless of how bleak it may be, is the dominant feature of that character. Its development was conditioned largely by the stern, uncompromising Puritan religion that was based on rigid Calvinist theology. The Puritans believed that man was wholly sinful by nature; only through severe and unremitting discipline could he achieve good. Therefore hard work was considered a religious duty. But more was demanded of the good Puritan. He must engage in constant self-examination; he must search for truth, truth almost certain to be bitter, and steel himself to face it unwaveringly. Harriet Beecher Stowe, a perceptive observer of her native New England, wrote of her people in that colonial period: "Working on a hard soil, battling with a harsh, ungenial climate . . . they asked no indulgence, they got none, and they gave none. They shut out from their religious worship every poetic drapery, every physical accessory that they feared would interfere with the abstract contemplation of hard, naked truth, and set themselves grimly and determinately to study the severest problems of the unknowable and the insoluble. . . . They never expected to find the truth agreeable. . . . Their investigations were made with the courage of the man who hopes little, but determines to know the worst of his affairs. They wanted no smoke of incense to blind them, and no soft opiates of pictures and music to lull them; for what they were after was *truth*, and not happiness, and they valued *duty* far higher than enjoyment."

The outlook of Yankees has softened, of course, since those early days when churches were kept so cold in the winter that the minister wore black gloves with the tips of the index finger and thumb cut off so that he could turn the pages of the Bible. Religious convictions are no longer displayed so intensely as in the time when Lyman Beecher, Mrs. Stowe's Calvinist preacher father, was the parson in Litchfield, Connecticut. One Sunday a minister in a nearby town, who believed in the doctrine of predestination, was to exchange pulpits with Beecher, who, despite his denomination's teachings, believed in free will. As the two ministers met on horseback halfway between their churches, the other pastor said, "Doctor Beecher, is it not marvelous: since the beginning of time it was ordained that you and I should exchange pulpits today."

Beecher turned his horse around and galloped back toward Litchfield, shouting, "Then I won't do it!"

The early willingness, even eagerness, to face the truth and live with it, no matter how discouraging it seemed, developed other traits of the New England Puritan stock—a spartan hardiness and reserve, with a concomitant distaste for excessive emotional display and wasted words; shrewd thrift and resourcefulness; and, above all, sturdy individualism and the steadfast maintenance of moral convictions. The memories of every New England town are filled with the sounds of the aroused Yankee conscience making itself heard.

In Arlington, Vermont, as Dorothy Canfield Fisher has recalled, those sounds include the tolling of the church bell on the day John Brown, the antislavery raider, was hanged, and the angry voice of Patrick Thompson, a storekeeper, at a town meeting where the argument was advanced that the cost of needed repairs on bridges would make the building of a high school impossible. "What kind of a town would we rather have, fifty years from now?" Thompson shouted. "A place where nit-wit folks go back and forth over good bridges? Or a town which has always given its children a fair chance, and prepares them to hold their own in modern life? . . . I say, 'if we have to choose, *let the bridges fall down!*'" The town meeting decided to build the high school.

In the 1950s the late Senator Joseph McCarthy ran afoul of Yankee principles, and two of the encounters proved major factors in his subsequent downfall and disgrace. McCarthy's reputation as a Communist-hunter was at its peak early in the decade. The fact that the reputation was based almost entirely on bombast and wild, unsubstantiated accusations did little to diminish his destructive power; before one charge could be disproved, half a dozen new and more sensational ones would be made. In the atmosphere of hysterical fear he created, few influential men were willing to defend traditional American standards of fair play. Even the President of the United States and his Secretary of State bowed before McCarthy. But in New England there were men who did not bow.

McCarthy had one of his first experiences with the Yankee conscience in 1953 when he attempted to trample on academic freedom at Harvard by stirring up public sentiment against several faculty members. The university's administrators and faculty, instead of knuckling under as the Wisconsin Senator had come to expect, stoutly held to their principles and even counterattacked—a rare show of courage at the time. McCarthy decided to look for other victims.

He had a far more serious collision with Yankee integrity the following year during the so-called Army-McCarthy hearings, actually an investigation by the Senate Investigations Subcommittee of McCarthy's charges that Communists had infiltrated the Army's Signal Corps laboratories at Fort Monmouth, New Jersey. The Army's counsel was Joseph Welch, a dignified, elderly, Harvard-trained lawyer, whose spiritual home was New England even though he had been born in Iowa. He had lived and practiced law in Boston ever since leaving law school.

The hearings were televised, and the national audience was enormous. Few viewers will forget the moment when McCarthy attempted to discredit Welch by implying that one of Welch's young associates in Boston was a Communist sympathizer. Welch, McCarthy said, had tried to get the young man hired as "the assistant counsel for this committee" so that he would have the opportunity to be "looking over the secret and classified material."

When McCarthy had ended his long harangue, Welch turned and gazed at him with a mixture of sadness and contempt. "Until this moment, Senator," Welch said, "I think I never really gauged your cruelty and your recklessness. . . . Little did I dream you could be so reckless and so cruel as to do an injury to that lad. . . . Have you no sense of decency, sir? At long last have you left no sense of decency? If there is a God in heaven, it will do neither you nor your cause any good. . . ." McCarthy visibly withered under the blast.

It was a turning point in the Senator's public life. A month later another New Englander willing to swim against the tide, Senator Ralph Flanders of Vermont, set in motion a resolution calling for McCarthy's censure by the Senate. Despite furious opposition by McCarthy's supporters, a resolution to "condemn" was finally passed by a vote of 67 to 22. For all practical purposes, McCarthy's career was shattered.

The tradition of fighting for unpopular causes is a bright thread that runs throughout the historical fabric of New England. The classic example is that of the young John Quincy Adams, who was forced to resign from the U.S. Senate in 1808 because he had turned against his Federalist Party and his constituents in Massachusetts to support the Louisiana Purchase and the Embargo Act of Thomas Jefferson, the archenemy of Adams' own father. (And the elder John Adams—then in retirement at Quincy after being defeated for a second term

New England bridges

Wooden bridges are among New England's best-known landmarks. The simplest designs were the king post and queen post, useful when a single timber could span a narrow stream, but not safe where several timbers end to end were needed. An early advance over these was the Warren truss, basically a barn set up over water. The Burr truss, king posts with an arch for added support, permitted even longer spans. The most popular design was the Town lattice truss, strong and easily built with short timbers. The still stronger Long truss was briefly used by railroads. The Howe truss took over because it used iron supporting bars. Wood coverings prevented weather from damaging the joints holding the timbers together.

BURR TRUSS

KING POST

QUEEN POST

WARREN TRUSS

TOWN LATTICE TRUSS

as President by Jefferson—strongly backed his son's stand.) Another Senator from Massachusetts, Daniel Webster, sacrificed any last chance he might have had of becoming President, and antagonized his antislavery following in New England, by delivering his famous Seventh of March speech in 1850 in favor of Henry Clay's compromise effort to pacify the South. His fellow Yankee, the writer James Russell Lowell, called Webster "the most meanly and foolishly treacherous man I ever heard of." Webster's explanation was simple: "Necessity compels me to speak true rather than pleasing things."

Deserted by his friends in the North and receiving no support from the South when he tried to get the Whig Presidential nomination in 1852, Webster died a few months later, discouraged and disappointed. John Quincy Adams, however, shook off his youthful setback in the Senate to become a successful diplomat and a distinguished Secretary of State. In 1825 he became the sixth President of the United States; he served only one term and then went back to Quincy, Massachusetts, penniless and debt-ridden. However, two years later he returned to Washington as a Congressman and spent the next 17 years there as a member of the House of Representatives. It was the happiest period of his

eventful life. "My election as President of the United States was not half so gratifying to my inmost soul," Adams wrote in his diary when he won his seat in the House.

While President, Adams had often walked five miles in the early morning and, regardless of the weather, had taken long swims in the Potomac River—against the current of course. As a Congressman in his seventies, he would get up at 5 o'clock in the morning, light a fire with flint and steel—he despised the newfangled lucifer matches—sponge himself vigorously from head to foot with cold water and read the Bible for an hour before breakfast. He died at the age of 80 in the House of Representatives after suffering a stroke during a roll call. "This is the end of earth," he said as he was dying, "but I am composed."

Such a regimen of strictly ordered work, prayer, exercise and study was the general rule among the older Yankees. Novelist John P. Marquand, author of *The Late George Apley* and many other books dealing with New Englanders, has described how carefully his elderly great-aunt, Mary Russell Curzon, organized her daily routine in her Newburyport, Massachusetts, home during his childhood.

Miss Curzon each day rose early, ate a frugal breakfast, did her housework and then worked on

LONG TRUSS

HOWE TRUSS

embroidery until 10:30, when she went outdoors to look around the yard and garden, feed kitchen scraps to her pigs and wait for the arrival of the postman. From 11 to 12 she read her mail and wrote letters, and after her noon lunch she worked on a hooked rug until it was time for another walk outside and a trip to the woodshed to fill her wood basket with pine cones and white-pine kindling for the fireplace. She had a hired woman to help out with the housework and cooking. (The independent New England rural people refuse to work as servants, but they can be engaged, as social equals of the employer, to "help out.") One day when her helper was away and she was alone, Miss Curzon was splitting wood for kindling when her hatchet slipped and gashed her leg deeply above her knee. She went into her house, threaded a needle and stitched the wound herself.

At dusk Miss Curzon would help the hired woman light the lamps and candles and draw the shutters. After supper she recorded the events of the day in her diary, making notes of the callers, of the weather, of the breaking of a limb from a tree, of whether or not there was ice on the river. Then she felt that the duties of the day were done and she was free to play backgammon or dominoes and to read for pleasure. She read every evening, either the

Atlantic Monthly or *Littell's Living Age* magazine, Pepys's *Diary* or Gibbon, and "if she was in a lighter mood," a novel by Sir Walter Scott. At exactly 11 o'clock she checked the doors to make sure they were locked and then went upstairs to sleep on the bed on which she had been born and on which she died in her 87th year.

Scholarly study is a Yankee characteristic, stemming from the early Puritan emphasis on intellectual improvement for older people as well as for youths. Abigail Homans, a great-grandniece of John Quincy Adams', says that her uncle Brooks Adams thought that a suitable book for a young woman recovering from an operation was John Henry Cardinal Newman's *Apologia*, a profound religious autobiography. Boston's Julia Ward Howe, who wrote "The Battle Hymn of the Republic," and her friends had a favorite party game that required them to translate Mother Goose rhymes into Greek and German. The taste for erudition was not confined to the genteel Boston homes. Vermont's Calvin Coolidge, President of the United States from 1923 to 1929, had the appearance and the manner of a homely, rustic Yankee hick, but he read Dante's *Divine Comedy* in its original Italian.

While he was in the White House, Coolidge was even more closely identified with his native New England than Lyndon B. Johnson has been with Texas. Coolidge seemed to embody so strongly all of the traits and peculiarities associated with old-fashioned Yankee character—calm silence, thrift, quaintly plain tastes, cracker-barrel wit, shrewd common sense—that to most Americans of his time he was a reassuring symbol of the simplicity and virtues of a bygone age. They felt that as long as he was rocking comfortably in his rocking chair in the Executive Mansion everything was bound to be all right.

Coolidge's silence and frugality were legendary. While Governor of Massachusetts, he once drove 30 miles from Boston to an inland city with a friend. As they approached the seacoast on the return trip, the Governor spoke to his companion for the first and only time during the drive. "It is cooler here," he said. When New England's Yankee Division returned from France after World War I, the troops marched in a five-hour parade reviewed by the governors of the six states. The Governor of New Hampshire, standing beside Coolidge in the reviewing stand, reported later that in all of that time Coolidge spoke to him only once. "Governor," he said midway through the parade, "I think you will find that if you put one foot on the rail and lean in my position for a while, then change to the

A Nice Indian Pudding.

No. 1. 3 pints fcalded milk, 7 fpoons fine Indian meal, ftir well together while hot, let ftand till cooled; add 7 eggs, half pound raifins, 4 ounces butter, fpice and fugar, bake one and half hour.

No. 2. 3 pints fcalded milk to one pint meal falted; cool, add 2 eggs, 4 ounces butter, fugar or molaffes and fpice q. f. it will require two and half hours baking.

No. 3. Salt a pint meal, wet with one quart milk, fweeten and put into a ftrong cloth, brafs or bell metal veffel, ftone or earthern pot, fecure from wet and boil 12 hours.

A Sunderland Pudding.

Whip 6 eggs, half the whites, take half a nutmeg, one point cream and a little falt, 4 fpoons fine flour, oil or butter pans, cups, or bowls, bake in a quick oven one hour. Eat with fweet fauce.

A Whitpot.

Cut half a loaf of bread in flices, pour thereon 2 quarts milk, 6 eggs, rofe-water, nutmeg and half pound of fugar; put into a difh and cover with pafte, No. 2. bake flow 1 hour.

A Bread Pudding.

One pound foft bread or bifcuit foaked in one quart milk, run thro' a fieve or cullender, add 7 eggs, three quarters of a pound fugar, one quarter of a pound butter, nutmeg or cinnamon, one gill rofe-water, one pound ftoned raifins, half pint cream, bake three quarters of an hour, middling oven.

A Flour Pudding.

Seven eggs, one quarter of a pound of fugar, and a tea fpoon of falt, beat and put to one quart milk, 5 fpoons of flour, cinnamon and nutmeg to your tafte, bake half an hour, and ferve up with fweet fauce.

A boiled Flour Pudding.

One quart milk, 9 eggs, 7 fpoons flour, a little falt, put into a ftrong cloth and boiled three quarters of an hour.

This page from a late-18th Century New England cookbook carries the first printed recipe ("A Nice Indian Pudding") calling for the New World staple, corn ("Indian meal"). Before this time, most cookbooks used in this country were published in England and did not concern themselves with foods grown only in America. The recipes above were part of a collection called *American Cookery*, published in Hartford, Connecticut, in 1796 by Miss Amelia Simmons, who described herself as an "American Orphan." Using ingredients indigenous to her native land, she provided the first directions for making such dishes as mince pie and cranberry sauce.

other foot, it will rest you." (Although he was popularly known as "Silent Cal," when he did speak, his words were often worth repeating; in *The Home Book of Quotations* he has more entries than Franklin D. Roosevelt and twice as many as Warren G. Harding, Alfred E. Smith or Herbert Hoover.)

Coolidge's reputation for frugality was, perhaps, on a firmer foundation. The Coolidge home in Northampton, Massachusetts, was about 100 miles from Boston, the state capital, but he saw no need to move his family to Boston when he was serving as lieutenant governor. He rented a room for $1.50 a day in the Adams House, a Boston hotel. When he became Governor, he splurged and took the adjoining room as well, paying $2.50 for the suite. He still did not bring his family to Boston, however.

One day during an election campaign a Coolidge worker brought to the Adams House rooms a political ward leader from a nearby city. As was customary Coolidge took out a bottle of rye whiskey and poured drinks for the two men and himself. Later in the day the same worker returned for another strategy meeting with another ward leader. This time Coolidge poured only one drink and handed it to the newcomer.

"What about me?" the worker asked.

"You had yours this morning," Coolidge said.

Coolidge was at the Adams House with his wife on the June evening in 1920 when he received a telephone call from the G.O.P. convention in Chicago. Coolidge answered the telephone himself, listened, said a few words, hung up and then said to his wife, "Nominated for Vice President."

"You are not going to accept it, are you?" Mrs. Coolidge asked.

"I suppose I'll have to," he said. Three years later Warren G. Harding died, and Coolidge became President. He was elected to a full Presidential term in 1924.

During his uneventful years as President, Coolidge avoided putting on airs, paid all his personal bills himself, and poked into the White House kitchen's refrigerators now and then to check on possible extravagance. Once he complained because six hams were cooked for dinner for 60 guests. He is believed to have saved as much as $50,000 a year from his annual salary of $75,000. When his first paycheck was delivered, he looked it over, folded it neatly, tucked it into a vest pocket and said to the messenger, "Call often." His brief Vermont-country-store-type quips delighted the public. Asked by a visitor what he thought of a Rupert Hughes book debunking George Washington, Coolidge nodded toward a window and said, "I see his monument is still there." The famous remark attributed to him about the clergyman's sermon on sin ("He's against it") is alleged to be apocryphal, but it has a genuine Green Mountain Yankee ring to it.

So does the Gluyas Williams cartoon that appeared in a now-defunct humor magazine when Coolidge was departing from the White House. It shows him sitting grimly on his packed luggage with one rubber on the floor beside his feet while the frightened White House staff carries on a desperate search in the background. The caption unnecessarily explains, "Mr. Coolidge refuses point-blank to leave the White House until his other rubber is found." Anybody who knows the New England Yankee would know that the cartoon contains as much truth as caricature.

Tidy tightness has always been a Yankee trait. Despite the excitement of those hectic early days of the Revolution, Paul Revere remembered to submit an itemized bill to the Massachusetts Bay Colony's Provincial Congress for "riding for the Committee of Safety" in April and May 1775 and "my expenses for Self & horse during that time." The congress settled with him for £10 and four shillings, cutting him down from the £11, one shilling that he asked for.

Helen Howe in her memoirs of her New England girlhood, *The Gentle Americans*, tells how Frederick Pickering Cabot, a member of one of the wealthiest Yankee families, sold eggs from his farm from door to door on Beacon Hill even after he became a judge in a Boston court. Cabot was also president of the Boston Symphony Orchestra's board of trustees, and one Friday afternoon during a concert in Symphony Hall, he came out on the stage to make an announcement. A child in the audience cried, "That's our egg man!"

Frugality is not restricted to individuals in New England. The state government of New Hampshire somehow manages to make ends meet without a state income tax or sales tax. "We tax sin," a legislator in Concord explains, pointing out that much of the necessary revenue comes from lottery sweepstakes, levies on horse-racing bets and state-owned liquor stores. If the residents do not like their state government, they have little basis for complaining that they cannot be heard. New Hampshire, with a population of about 680,000, has a House of Representatives of 400 members, or an official voice for every 1,700 citizens, including children. "You could call us flagrantly democratic," a former governor of the state says. The large legislature is scarcely a financial extravagance, however; each senator and representative receives a mere $200

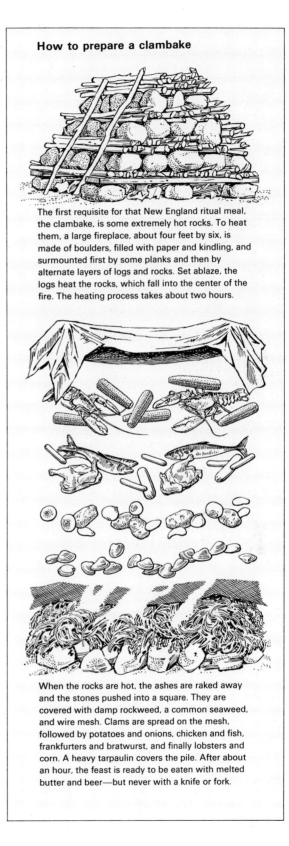

How to prepare a clambake

The first requisite for that New England ritual meal, the clambake, is some extremely hot rocks. To heat them, a large fireplace, about four feet by six, is made of boulders, filled with paper and kindling, and surmounted first by some planks and then by alternate layers of logs and rocks. Set ablaze, the logs heat the rocks, which fall into the center of the fire. The heating process takes about two hours.

When the rocks are hot, the ashes are raked away and the stones pushed into a square. They are covered with damp rockweed, a common seaweed, and wire mesh. Clams are spread on the mesh, followed by potatoes and onions, chicken and fish, frankfurters and bratwurst, and finally lobsters and corn. A heavy tarpaulin covers the pile. After about an hour, the feast is ready to be eaten with melted butter and beer—but never with a knife or fork.

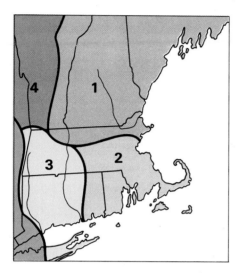
biennially. The spirited independence of New England inevitably breeds a degree of eccentricity, and therefore some rather odd goings on take place in the large New Hampshire legislature. A number of years ago, for example, the representatives voted on a proposed law to require all residents to obtain at least eight hours of sleep per night. The measure lost, presumably on the theory that, though carousing is a sin, infringing on freedom is a greater one.

Like old England, New England has always cherished its eccentrics as folk heroes. In Massachusetts, Yankees still speak fondly of the self-titled Lord Timothy Dexter of Newburyport, who made considerable money shipping warming pans to the tropical West Indies where they were used as molasses ladles. At one point in his life Lord Dexter turned to literature and wrote a book of personal philosophy and reminiscence titled *A Pickle for the Knowing Ones: or, Plain Truths in a Homespun Dress*. The text was unpunctuated, but there was a solid page of periods, commas, question marks, exclamation points, colons and semicolons in the back of the book. Readers were invited to "peper and solt it as they plese."

Edward Dickinson, father of the poet, Emily, is another favorite character in Yankee lore. Squire Dickinson, a stern Calvinist lawyer and a pillar of Amherst College, was a man who never smiled and seldom spoke. One evening he rushed to the church and rang the bell excitedly. The townspeople came running to him and found that he wished to call their attention to the beautiful sunset.

One of the most prized Yankee eccentrics was the poet Amy Lowell. Miss Lowell was the sister of Abbott Lawrence Lowell, President of Harvard University from 1909 to 1933, and one day he received a telephone call from the owner of a garage. A woman customer needed gasoline for her car, the man said, but she had no money, no license or identification. But she had said that President Lowell at Harvard was her brother and would vouch for her.

"Where is she now?" Lowell asked.

"Sitting on the curbstone, smoking a cigar," the garage owner said.

"That's my sister," Lowell said.

During Lowell's 24 years as president, Harvard went through one of the greatest periods of growth and expansion in its long history. But with all the momentous developments that took place at the university under his administration, he never once in all of that term of office allowed himself to be interviewed by a newspaper reporter. The same ingrained New England distaste for limelight, undue fuss or anything that might be misconstrued as ostentation made Charles Francis Adams III, great-great-grandson of John Adams, feel tortured when his appointment as Secretary of the Navy in 1929 forced him to pose for news photographers. Adams was asked to sit at his desk and pretend he was working by writing on a sheet of paper. After the picture-taking ordeal, a reporter looked at the paper and saw that Adams had scrawled "this is hell this is hell this is hell."

Making large sums of money, however, has not been considered ostentatious by New Englanders. Even in colonial times the Yankees were famous for shrewd business dealings. The helpful art of double-entry bookkeeping is thought to have been introduced into American business about 1740 by Obadiah Brown of the Brown trading and manufacturing dynasty in Rhode Island. Cleveland Amory, discussing the sources of present-day New England wealth in *The Proper Bostonians*, tells of a 19th Century Yankee merchant and banker who was "persuaded" to buy a mortgage on a Midwestern farm. The investor's great-great-grandson said to Amory, "Knowing him, no one was surprised when his 'farm' turned out to be six square miles in the center of Chicago!"

Amory's research also brought him to the diaries of William Appleton, a Boston Yankee who amassed a fortune after starting in business at 20 with an inheritance of $700 and "two hundred I drew in a Lottery." Appleton was described by his son-in-law as a man who never did an unkind thing and never said a kind word, a characterization that fits many tight-lipped Yankees. (So does the Boston wife's description of her husband as an expert organizer of United Fund charitable drives who does not know how to give a Christmas gift.) Appleton wrote of himself at the age of 75, a year before his death in 1862: "I must be busy. I don't know how to stop. . . . I can't help seeing openings for profit, neither can I help availing of them. I pray God to keep me from being avaricious, and proud of my success; but I cannot bear the shame of falling below my own powers and being left behind by those who are not my equals."

The successful Yankee's profound veneration for wealth led him, not unexpectedly, to political concepts that fortified his interests. After the American Revolution the economic aristocracy in Boston, Hartford and Providence embraced the Federalist political views of Alexander Hamilton, for the Federalists were dedicated to the idea of government by a wealthy and cultured gentry who would protect private property and capital. Politically they

Paul Revere regularly submitted bills for his services as courier and printer for the Massachusetts Provincial Congress, the colony's clandestine government. On this account covering April 21 to May 7, 1775, he requested compensation of five shillings per day for labor, but a thrifty congress cut the charge back to four. Revere claimed additional amounts for "expences for self & horse" and for "keeping two Colony Horses 10 Day." The item of three pounds covering "Printing 1000 impressions" was for engraving and printing a supply of the Revolutionary government's first paper money.

were close to British Toryism and opposed to Jeffersonian democracy, which they regarded as a dangerous and atheistic doctrine. Two of the New England high priests of Federalism, Fisher Ames and George Cabot, held that government by the common people was "tyranny" and "government of the worst." Infatuation with Federalism coincided with a decline of Calvinism in New England and a trend toward the new and milder Unitarianism, "the Boston religion," which, because it was less doctrinaire, was more acceptable to the newly rich merchant on Beacon Hill. And later, the Anglican (Episcopal) Church, which had been frowned upon in colonial and Revolutionary times, also gained wealthy new adherents.

Well before the Civil War the growing concentration of wealth had divided the society of homogeneous Yankee stock into two distinct groups—the influential, well-heeled upper crust, centered mostly around Boston, and the far more numerous, less privileged middle class. The distinction between them was often purely financial. Calvin Coolidge did not qualify for the top level of society because he was the son of a Vermont farmer and merchant of modest means. Yet his Yankee bloodline was as clearly blue as that of his aristocratic, wealthy Coolidge cousins in Boston, going back, as theirs did, to the same ancestor, John Coolidge, a Puritan who became a citizen of the Massachusetts Bay Colony in 1636. Eminent status could not be handed down from one generation to another. Families that lost their wealth also lost their standing and faded out of the aristocracy.

The Federalist families, especially the rich ones in Boston and along the North Shore of Massachusetts, became in a real sense a small Brahmin-like caste, remaining socially aloof from other Yankees and non-New Englanders. They married among themselves because, among other reasons, they did not know anyone else. Thus most of the Proper Bostonian families—the Cabots, Lowells, Adamses, Forbeses, Saltonstalls, Lawrences, Peabodys, Searses, Endicotts and others—were interrelated by blood as well as by position. Many of their sons bore several Brahmin names—Cabot Lowell, Lowell Cabot, Endicott Peabody. When the longtime Irish Mayor of Boston, James Michael Curley, heard that a man named Endicott Peabody Saltonstall had been appointed to a local office, the Mayor exclaimed, "What, all three of them?"

Family clannishness and ancestor worship, traditionally strong among all Yankees, are especially intense in lineage-conscious Proper Boston. The Boston *Transcript*, the traditional Brahmin newspaper until its death in 1941, each week devoted a full column to genealogical notes. A Chicago bank, making inquiries in Boston about a young Bostonian whom it was considering for employment, received so much information about his family tree that it sent back word that the bank's only interest was in hiring the applicant, not in breeding him. The respected former Senator Leverett Saltonstall, whose family has had nine unbroken generations of Harvard graduates, was once asked by John Gunther what he believed in most.

"Well, it might sound more impressive if I said something like 'democracy' or 'the country,' but let's not be pretentious," Saltonstall thoughtfully replied. "What I believe in most is Harvard and my family."

Although the Proper Bostonians represent only a small segment of Boston and an even smaller influence on the Yankee region as a whole, the widespread tales of their curious tribal customs and provincial snobbery have shaped and colored the outsider's impression of New England character. Shortly after he became President, John F. Kennedy remarked to a friend that even if he returned to Boston as the former occupant of the White House he would be barred from that Brahmin redoubt, the Somerset Club, because of his Irish Catholic descent. But then, firemen also had trouble getting into the Somerset Club, even for official business. When they went there in 1945 to put out a fire in the kitchen, they were stopped at the front door and told to use the service entrance.

The Proper Bostonian's condescending attitude toward the rest of the country—and the rest of the world—was summed up by the reaction of a Back Bay lady when she heard that her friend Robert Cutler, of the Old Colony Trust Company, had made quite a reputation in Washington as an aide to President Eisenhower. "Well, I suppose he has," she said. "But after all, it's not Boston—it's just *national.*"

The most severe critics of the Yankees are the articulate Boston Irish who remember the comparatively recent years of anti-Catholic discrimination when many help-wanted ads in Boston newspapers carried the line, "Protestants Only" or "No Irish Need Apply." "Their character?" commented an Irish attorney in a Boston law firm with the names of five Yankee senior partners on its office door. "It can be narrow, cranky, impossible, humorless, intolerant and then once in a while, when the chips are down, it opens up, self-consciously, and you get a quick look at the greatness that they try to keep hidden underneath. Let me tell you about a Yankee, a crusty old man if there ever was one, the head of our firm here."

When the Irish lawyer first went to work in the firm as a young man, just out of the Navy after World War II, the elderly senior partner seemed unaware of his presence. He was silent and unapproachable when they met in the elevator or in the hall, and after several months of his remote coolness the younger man gave up hope of ever getting a pleasant word from the older man.

The young lawyer had been working in the office for less than a year when his wife died while giving birth to a child. The next day he was sitting in his home in South Boston when the doorbell rang.

"I went to the door, and there he was, standing there alone, his hat in his hand. This man was old, in his late seventies, and he wasn't well. It was a stifling hot day in July, terribly hot, and it was a Sunday, and he had come by train, all by himself, all the way from Maine where he was at his summer home, a trip of about four hours in that awful heat—just to pay his respects and to ask me if there was anything he could do."

The lawyer paused and added, "And the next time I saw him again in the office, it was like it was before—he acted as if he hardly knew me. That's a Yankee."

A rock of stability, the 160-year-old Peacham Congregational Church rises from the landscape. It claims about a third of the town's citizens as members, and most local children attend its Sunday school. Nearby, a sign proclaims the town's date of settlement.

A quiet, unchanging way of life

Many New England villages, with their stately colonial homes, seem almost unchanged over the decades. Often this is merely the town's façade, behind which the forces of industrialization will have basically altered the community's way of life. There are, however, a few isolated places in New England that sound a true and delightful echo of a bygone era. One such place is Peacham, a Vermont hill town of about 500 souls. Here, in miniature, is another era—a community of self-reliant farmers, skilled artisans and small merchants who get together in an annual town meeting to levy taxes and provide for their common needs. Here Thomas Jefferson's dream of a nation of small landholders and craftsmen is still alive. What for most Americans is but a dim ancestral memory of quiet and peaceful country pleasures is for Peacham a continuing reality.

Photographs by Clemens Kalischer

A transplanted New Yorker, the Reverend Adolph Koch picks up his mail at the Peacham post office. Once a philosophy teacher at Columbia University, Dr. Koch, now retired, is one of the many Peachamites who came from afar in search of the quiet life.

In the Peacham library Mrs. Stuart O'Brien *(center)* and her daughter Cathy *(left)* chat with an older girl. The library, established in 1810, is supported largely by private contributions. It boasts a shelf of books by Peacham's permanent and summer residents.

Stops along the daily rounds

A Currier & Ives print come to life, the town of Peacham clings to its hillside in the northeastern part of Vermont. Here, in the center of the village, are most of the places frequently visited by Peachamites in pursuit of their business or pleasure. The post office, library and general store are all important establishments, not only for the services they perform but also because they provide convenient, though informal, meeting places where citizens can exchange pleasantries, talk about the harvest or perhaps discuss a forthcoming hunting trip with fellow townsmen before returning to the workaday routine.

A retired dairyman, Warren Farrington comes out of the general store. Though over 70, Farrington typifies the rugged characteristics often ascribed to Vermonters. In summer he works full time in a nearby state park; in winter he often labors in the woods *(page 46)*.

A general sharing of power and responsibility

Perhaps nowhere in the world does Jefferson's ideal of an informed and active citizenry receive greater expression than in such small New England towns as Peacham. The adult resident who does not take part in some community activity is an exception, and the majority attend the annual and special town meetings to make their views known and their votes felt. Many Peachamites do considerably more. They devote a large proportion of their time to town offices and serve as unpaid officials of community organizations, expecting no reward save the satisfaction of having done something for their community.

Fire Chief George Meech *(left)* and former chief George Tuzo examine a piece of department equipment. The chief is the only permanent member of his department, for when a blaze breaks out all able-bodied citizens—male and female—may respond to the alarm.

A community leader, Harold Somers poses with his wife in their parlor. Although he is a retired dairy farmer, Somers still cuts timber on his land and tends his fields. He has served many terms as a town official and is always called upon when knotty problems arise.

The town clerk, Mrs. Henry Bradley examines a document held by Maurice Chandler during a meeting with selectmen. Though in her mid-70s, Mrs. Bradley has also served as town treasurer since 1958 with the unanimous endorsement of successive town meetings.

Pillars of the faith, the four deacons of the Congregational Church —*(left to right)* Howard Stark, Harold Abbott, Warren Farrington and Francis Somers—confer with their minister, Jerry Buckley *(back to camera)*. The deacons are elected by church members.

Traditional methods and time-honored skills

Although Peacham contains automobiles and tractors aplenty, the old ways of doing things die hard in the Vermont hills. The horse still plays an important role in farming around the town, and the local handy man-craftsman continues to employ water-powered machinery. Competing with newer means is proving to be increasingly difficult, however, especially in dairy farming, long Peacham's primary economic bulwark. The typical family-sized farm with hand-operated equipment just cannot compete with the large, highly mechanized establishments. Each year a few more local dairymen retire and their sons leave town. Often they are replaced by cityfolk, attracted to Peacham by the very 19th Century atmosphere that causes the younger natives to leave.

This 19th Century mill *(above)* is operated by artisan Ben Thresher, whose machinery—including lathes, saws and drill presses—is all water-powered. The mill contains a cluttered blacksmith shop complete with a flaming forge, and although Thresher *(right)* does not shoe horses, he performs countless other tasks for Peachamites, from cabinetmaking to fashioning stanchions for cow barns.

Impervious to the cold, Warren Farrington *(left)* snakes out a log from a neighbor's farm with the help of his sturdy horse. Logging is a popular way for many people to supplement their incomes. The trees grow quickly in the Vermont hills and there is a ready market for maple logs.

Working together for the family's good

In the days when most Americans lived on small farms, each family formed an economic—as well as social—unit. In Peacham that time has not yet vanished. Among its farming families, like the Kemptons (*shown here*), each child learns that he must share the family's labor, thus contributing to its well-being. The parents, George and Patricia Kempton, are up each morning at 5 and immediately begin their daily rounds of chores: milking the cows, feeding them hay, cleaning out the barn, preparing meals. Later, after the five children have been packed off to school, the adults continue their work, but in the late afternoon the young pitch in to help with the tasks. For the Kemptons, at least, the result has been a warm and close-knit family life in which each member feels secure in his position and accepts his responsibilities to every other member.

The members of the Kempton family join together for an ample dinner that is being served by Mrs. Kempton. The teenager at right is a student at Peacham Academy—a local private school—who helped out on the Kempton farm during his winter vacation.

Reading their mail as they have lunch, the senior Kemptons enjoy a quiet moment before they resume work. George Kempton's position as a member of the school board and Mrs. Kempton's work with preschoolers have made them highly esteemed in the town.

Intent upon the work at hand, Pat Kempton carefully kneads dough for home-baked bread. Though her husband was Vermont-born and-raised, Mrs. Kempton grew up a city girl in New Jersey. She has had little trouble adjusting to life on a working farm, however.

Sheltered for the winter, the Kemptons' cows wait for Sammy Kempton to serve their dinner of hay. Feeding the cows is one of the children's responsibilities and each Kempton youngster is expected to work about an hour each day on farm or household chores.

Reaching for a traditional treat, a youngster at the town ski run waits for Ted Farrow, a retired farmer, to pour hot maple syrup into her snow-filled coffee can. Farrow serves the syrup through an open window of the ski-tow warming hut.

Ladies of the Christmas Club—one of several women's organizations—meet in a member's home for cards and conversation. This club, like some others, really exists to facilitate exchanges of visits, something Peachamites call "neighboring."

At a church potluck supper held in the library basement, postmaster Don Willcox (right above) and Mr. and Mrs. Orman Hooker, who are retired farmers, fill their plates from a variety of casseroles. The affair is held monthly and all attending contribute a dish.

Enjoying the company of good neighbors

Flinty and silent, that is the stereotype many people apply to Vermonters—but the citizens of Peacham seem cast from a different mold. Informal social and community service clubs abound and no class or religious barriers exist to bar any Peachamite from full participation. Partly this is because there are no firm class distinctions in Peacham—the town knows neither vast wealth nor abject poverty—and most residents share an Anglo-Saxon background. In short, Peacham is a homogeneous community secure enough in its own values to admit outsiders into its circle of activities with hospitality. This is reflected in the fact that many city dwellers find Peacham a perfect spot to have vacation homes. During the summer the cityfolk and Peachamites join together to exchange views on world and national problems, a town tradition called "Meetings of Minds."

A deep and abiding intimacy with nature

For Peachamites, nature is not a sometime thing to be enjoyed during annual vacations; it is an ever-present reality to be savored at length and at leisure. Each season brings its own delights. Spring means the rising of the maple sap; summer, picnics at mountain streams; autumn, walks in the woods ablaze with color. But perhaps it is winter that is best. Then the sound-muffling snow lies deep, and sometimes the silence of the streets is almost total, broken only by the tolling of the town church bell, announcing every half hour, both day and night.

With a hare in hand retired farmer Ben Berwick has reason to smile as he returns from hunting with his son, Ben Jr. Many Peacham boys learn to handle guns at an early age. The surrounding hills abound in game, particularly deer, which are a menace to crops.

Peacham boys build a snow fort, taking their design from New England's fieldstone walls. Their winter games, such as skating and sledding, are not unusual, but Peachamites have the advantage of being able to participate almost upon stepping out from their homes.

Though the sun has set and snow is falling, Peacham's enthusiastic young skiers hold tight to the rope tow for one last glide down the town's gentle ski run before darkness settles in. The tow is privately financed by a group of community-minded citizens.

3

Colonists
to Revolutionists

There was a threatened mutiny aboard the *Mayflower* in mid-November 1620 when she dropped anchor off what is now Provincetown on Cape Cod. The Pilgrims, or the "visible Saints" as they called themselves, had just announced that the colony would be established in this cold and forbidding region. The non-Pilgrims, or "Strangers," who comprised 61 of the 102 passengers, were infuriated. When the ship had left England, they had been told that they would be taken to "some place aboute Hudson's river for their habitation"—territory controlled by the Virginia Company, a privately owned concern, chartered by the King of England, which had jurisdiction over all land from slightly south of the present Wilmington, North Carolina, to just about what is now Rye, New York. Cape Cod was far north of the company's jurisdiction. The Strangers felt duped by the Saints, who had chartered the vessel.

Both the change of plan by the Pilgrims and the resultant anger of the Strangers were understandable; the two groups had come to the New World for

different reasons. The Saints were a radical Puritan sect that had severed all relations with the Anglican Church and had endured severe persecution in England. They had left their native land primarily to escape religious oppression. They probably feared further difficulties in territory that was under the aegis of the staunchly loyal Virginia Company.

The Strangers had come mainly in search of better economic opportunities than England afforded. The adults in the group were "goodmen" (ordinary settlers), hired hands and indentured servants, most of them at least nominal members of the Anglican Church. They therefore had nothing to fear from the Virginia Company, and the lands it controlled, according to all reports, were far more promising than this bleak coast of New England. Landing here was a bitter disappointment, especially after the high hopes that had sustained them during the extremely rough 66-day voyage.

The Saints handled the tense predicament with remarkable diplomatic skill. Among themselves they drew up a document that was to become famous as the Mayflower Compact. It stated, in part: "We whose names are underwritten, the loyall subjects of our dread soveraigne Lord, King James . . . doe by these presents solemnly & mutualy in ye presence of God, and one of another, covenant &

Paul Revere's engraving of the Boston Massacre of 1770 gives a biased view of the incident—the Bostonians had provoked the soldiers with insults and a barrage of snowballs—and it served as propaganda to heighten the colonists' resentment of the British.

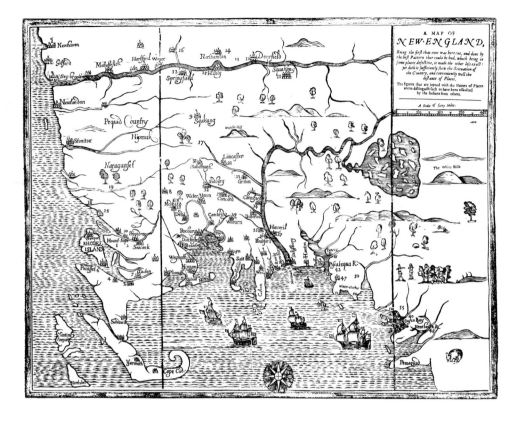

A MAP OF
NEW-ENGLAND,

Being the first that ever was here cut, and done by the best Pattern that could be had, which being in some places defective, it made the other less exact: yet doth it sufficiently shew the Scituation of the Country, and conveniently well the distance of Places.

The figures that are joyned with the Names of Places are to distinguish such as have been assaulted by the Indians from others.

A Scale of forty Miles.

Early New England settlements

The extent of colonization of New England in the late 17th Century is shown in a contemporary map, a woodcut printed in 1677 to accompany *A Narrative of the Troubles with the Indians in New England*, written by William Hubbard, a Massachusetts clergyman. The map was drawn with north at the right, south at the left. Towns were indicated either by their names, by the picture of a house, or by a number, which corresponded to a table in the book. The text also stated, "those that are marked with figures, as well as expressed by their names, are such as were assaulted by the Indians." The vertical lines on the map mark the original north-south boundaries of the Massachusetts Bay Colony, set in 1629. The northern boundary encompassed territories that later formed the royal colony of New Hampshire. The southern boundary passed through lands granted to the settlers at Plymouth, so a new border was drawn in 1664.

combine ourselves togeather into a civill body politick . . . which we promise all due submission and obedience." Then they called a meeting of all the passengers. Somehow, the Pilgrims were able to cool the anger of the dissidents and to persuade most of the men to sign the compact. Women were not asked to sign. (Three of the *Mayflower* passengers who are best known—thanks to a poem by Henry Wadsworth Longfellow—Myles Standish, John Alden and Priscilla Mullins, were Strangers, and the two men were among the signers.)

Exploring parties soon went to the mainland around Plymouth—named by Captain John Smith, who had been there earlier—and then, in late December, a work party went ashore and began constructing a settlement. There was fear of Indians—a number of them had been sighted in the area—and so tension was high when one of them walked boldly into the colony some weeks after work had begun. The settlers were astonished as well as relieved by his friendly greeting. "Welcome, Englishmen," the Indian said.

The explanation for an English-speaking Indian was simple enough. The New England coast had been familiar territory to English sailors, fishermen and fur traders long before the *Mayflower* set sail from England. In fact, another group of English colonists had attempted to set up a trading post at the mouth of the Kennebec River in 1607, but the bitter Maine winter had withered that ambition, and they had returned to England the following spring. It was these earlier visitors who had taught English to some of the natives, an act for which the newcomers could be deeply grateful. One of the Indians, who not only spoke English fluently but had made two trips to London aboard English ships, became the colony's interpreter and its adviser on hunting, fishing and corn planting.

Although the Indians posed no immediate threat to the Plymouth settlers, the first brutal New England winter did. The settlers were a relatively young group and a courageous one, but they were ill-equipped and had no experience in setting up a settlement in the wilderness. A winter arrival, of course, complicated matters enormously. Most of the small band huddled in misery aboard the *Mayflower*—her return voyage was delayed until April 5—while small shacks of wood and mud were put up ashore around a rough common house and fort. Fever and scurvy took a heavy toll. The settlers' records tell the tragic story:

. . . this day [December 24] dies Solomon Martin, the sixth & last who dies this month.

Jan. 29th, dies Rose, the wife of Captaine Standish. N.B. this month eight of our number die.

Feb. 21. Die Mr. William White, Mr. William Mullins, with two more; and the 25th dies Mary, the wife of Mr. Isaac Allerton. N.B. this month seventeen of our number die.

March 24. Dies Elizabeth, the wife of Mr. Edward Winslow. N.B. This month thirteen of our number die. And in three months past dies halfe our company. . . . Of a hundred persons, scarce fifty remain, the living scarce able to bury the dead.

Somehow the survivors hung on. They not only managed to support themselves but bartered for furs with the Indians at outposts on Cape Cod and as far away as the Connecticut River and Maine. After the first autumn harvest the settlers invited their friendly Indian neighbors to share a thanksgiving feast, thus beginning an annual custom and establishing one of the few holidays on the early New England calendar. Christmas was not among the holidays. It was, the Saints said, a "human invention" and a "corruption," a heritage from heathen days. As the colony became more firmly established, most of the Strangers, voluntarily or under pressure, accepted the Puritan faith, and the Plymouth Colony became almost wholly a Pilgrim settlement.

Meanwhile, in England other Puritans, though less radical than the Pilgrim sect, were also seeking to escape the persecution of the King and his bishops, and they looked to the New World as the place to found a "New Canaan" or "Israel." Puritanism was a movement "to purify" the Anglican Church of the trappings of Roman Catholicism that remained after the Reformation. The Puritans' objective was to strip the Church of elaborate rituals and liturgy, incense, vestments, stained-glass windows and, most important, the hierarchy of bishops —all of which they regarded as needless papal baroque acquired by the Roman Church over several centuries. The Puritans felt that each church, or parish, should be free of diocesan government and have plain services with Bible study, extemporaneous prayers—abandonment of the prayer book was advocated—and stern sermons on moral duty. In short, the Puritans wanted to worship as they believed congregations had done in the early days of Christianity. Most Puritans still hoped to achieve these reforms while remaining in the Anglican Church. The Pilgrims, or Saints, had lost that hope and no longer paid allegiance to the Church of England. Both groups, however, drew fire from the bishop-influenced English government. And the differences between the Pilgrims and other Puritans

What may be evidence of a pre-Pilgrim settlement in New England has been found in the Old Stone Mill in Newport, Rhode Island. Some historians and archeologists believe it was built as a fortified church by Norsemen in the 14th Century, but most experts hold that Governor Benedict Arnold erected it as a windmill around 1665.

became meaningless when the latter came to the New World; once beyond the reach of the bishops, all Puritan churches became independent.

In 1628 a group of Puritans, perhaps encouraged by the survival of the Plymouth Colony, obtained a patent for a fishing and fur-trading enterprise to be established on the north shore of Massachusetts between the Charles River, at what was to become Boston, and the mouth of the Merrimack River, the present site of Newburyport. Territorial rights extended inland indefinitely. A small colony with a Puritan congregational church was set up at Salem under the leadership of Captain John Endecott.

Financial control of this organization and ownership of its land grant were taken over the following year by a syndicate of richer and well-connected Puritans, most of them Cambridge University graduates, under the leadership of John Winthrop, a scholarly 40-year-old lawyer. Although Charles I was cracking down hard on Puritans at the time, Winthrop managed to get a royal charter for a commercial colony named the Massachusetts Bay Company. His plans for the company, however, were far from what the King probably had in mind.

Such charters for colonial companies usually remained in England, held by the stockholders, who did not themselves go overseas. Ultimate control was retained by the King. Because Winthrop and his fellow Puritan stockholders were really planning their colony in Massachusetts as a religious refuge for themselves as well as for their followers, they established their company's headquarters in New England and brought their charter with them —thus quietly breaking ties with London. This permitted the settlers to establish a self-government more independent of the Crown than that of any other American colonists.

The colony founded in 1630 by the Massachusetts Bay Company was the first strong Puritan settlement in New England. The earlier pioneers at Plymouth and Salem had been few in number and weak in resources, but Winthrop's colony was well organized and, fed by Puritan discontent in England, grew in four years to a community of some 10,000 people, with several new towns spreading along the coast and inland from Boston, the first settlement. By 1700 the Massachusetts Bay Colony, which had absorbed Plymouth nine years earlier, had 80,000 settlers—15,000 more than the combined populations of New York, New Jersey, Pennsylvania and Delaware at that time. There were about 50,000 additional New Englanders in Connecticut, Rhode Island and New Hampshire, three Yankee colonies that were offshoots from Massachusetts.

In fact, Massachusetts might be a larger state today if Winthrop and the other founding fathers of the Massachusetts Bay Colony had governed their early settlers with more tolerance. But the Puritans, although they had come to Massachusetts to escape persecution, granted no religious freedom to doubters or to members of other faiths. In its early years the government was a strict theocracy; the Church ruled civic affairs, and the courts ordered punishment for religious and moral offenses as well as for breaking the civil law. Only Church members could vote or have a voice in town meetings. In 17th Century Boston a woman was hanged for being a Quaker, and a ship's captain, returning on the Sabbath from a three-year voyage, was put in the stocks for kissing his wife in public view on their front doorstep. Public floggings, stocks, pillories and ducking stools were used to chastise minor offenders. Even private wrongdoers, like Hester Prynne in Nathaniel Hawthorne's novel *The Scarlet Letter*, were forced to wear on their garments an initial letter indicating their offense—"A" for adulteress in her case.

Questioning, liberal-minded and nonconforming men and women found it almost impossible to live in this atmosphere of intolerance, and many of them left—either perforce or voluntarily—to establish self-governing settlements in other parts of New England, outside the jurisdiction of the Massachusetts Bay Company. Roger Williams, who infuriated the company on two counts, was ordered to leave. He not only advocated religious freedom but challenged the validity of the land title that the company had received from the Crown. The King could not convey the land, Williams said; only the true owners, the Indians, could do that. He was banished from Salem in 1636 for his theological and economic heresies and established a democratic colony with freedom for all faiths in Rhode Island.

A year later other offenders against Puritan orthodoxy were to join him. Anne Hutchinson, who was described by John Winthrop as a woman of "nimble wit and active spirit, and a very voluble tongue," set up a discussion center in her home in Boston. There sermons delivered by the town's ministers were subjected to intense and often highly critical analysis. Boston's men of the cloth, she held, were concerned with only the letter of the Mosaic law, not with its spirit, and as her following and influence grew, the church-state dignitaries became increasingly alarmed. Finally she was tried and found guilty of "traducing the ministers and their ministry." She was jailed and then expelled from Boston. She, her husband, their children and a number of her followers went to Rhode Island, where she helped to establish the town of Portsmouth. The Reverend John Wheelwright, Anne Hutchinson's brother-in-law and one of her most ardent supporters, was tried for "sedition and contempt of the civil authority." He, too, was found guilty and was banished. He moved to New Hampshire.

Connecticut's first towns—Hartford, Windsor and Wethersfield—were settled in 1635 by a large migration of families from the Boston area who departed voluntarily. Their leader, Thomas Hooker, disliked the Bay Colony's theocratic government in which only Church members had a voice, and he proposed "a general council chosen by all" to govern the new settlements. To orthodox Boston this was a shocking concept. The Reverend John Cotton, Hooker's close friend, said that God never ordained democracy "as a fitt government eyther for church or Commonwealth."

When the three towns drew up a constitution for Connecticut in 1639, however, universal suffrage was not included in the provisions. To vote, a citizen had to own property worth at least £30 and to obtain approval of the General Court. Moreover, there is some doubt that the court ever granted voting rights to non-Puritans. "Connecticut may have been more democratic in tone than Massachusetts, but scarcely so in fact," writes historian Richard B.

Morris, "and a government dominated by a select Puritan coterie ruled in relative calm throughout its colonial history."

Astonishingly, several towns were founded in Connecticut because men found the Massachusetts Bay Company's theocracy not too strict but too lax. Two of the original Puritan founders of the company, Theophilus Eaton and John Davenport, did not arrive in Boston from London until 1637. Dismayed by what they considered the overly flexible standards in the Bay Colony, Eaton and Davenport, along with the two shiploads of immigrants who accompanied them, sailed on to Long Island Sound where they established the colony of New Haven and a number of smaller settlements. For a quarter of a century these communities existed under an extraordinarily rigid church-state government based on John Cotton's code of laws, which were rooted in Mosaic law. (The Bay Colony had earlier rejected the code as too extreme.) In 1662 Charles II combined the Long Island Sound and Connecticut River settlements into one colony of Connecticut, much to the disgust of New Haven and its satellites.

Although New Hampshire and Maine were also lost by Massachusetts, the character of the Bay Colony's government played no part in the separations. Originally New Hampshire was a proprietary grant to Captain John Mason from the Crown. But he was an absentee landlord who ignored the colonists, and in 1641, several years after his death, the settlers requested that Massachusetts take jurisdiction over the area. In 1679 the King gave New Hampshire a charter of its own, making it a separate royal province. Maine was purchased by Massachusetts in 1677. The territory had also been a grant, this one to Sir Ferdinando Gorges, but neither he nor his heirs had done much to develop the region, and his grandson finally sold the Gorges rights to Massachusetts. The area remained a part of Massachusetts until 1820, when Maine was admitted to the Union as a state. Being a section of Massachusetts had never been completely satisfactory to the residents of Maine. At first Massachusetts had largely ignored the complaints, but war brought a move for separation to a head. Maine felt that it had been left undefended by Massachusetts during the War of 1812 when British forces seized and occupied all of the coast between New Brunswick and the Penobscot River. By now Massachusetts leaders were ready to relinquish their claim without argument. They decided that permitting Maine to become a state would be cheaper than governing that large and distant area.

Until Vermont declared its independence in 1777, it was claimed by both New York and New Hampshire. New York had tried to establish the Connecticut River as its eastern boundary in 1664. If this demarcation had been accepted, all of what is now Vermont—plus sizable sections of Connecticut and Massachusetts—would be part of New York. Some time later New York reached an agreement with Connecticut and Massachusetts on the present dividing line, 20 miles east of the Hudson River; but this left Vermont's status in doubt. When Benning Wentworth became royal governor of New Hampshire in 1741, he assumed that a northern extension of that same line and Lake Champlain formed the border between his territory and New York. On the supposition that Vermont was part of New Hampshire, Wentworth parceled out large land grants in Vermont that, before the Revolutionary War, were known as the "New Hampshire Grants."

But New York refused to give up Vermont and became embroiled in prolonged armed warfare, trying to govern that corner of New England. Ethan Allen's Green Mountain Boys fought a number of engagements with the Yorkers, as the New York forces were called by the Vermonters, until the Revolution began and all the colonies joined to battle a common foe, the British.

During the war, New Hampshire dropped its claim on Vermont, but New York refused to follow this example and managed to block Vermont's admission to the Continental Congress. In 1777 the highly indignant Vermonters set up an independent republic with its own coinage, postal system, foreign relations and other components of a sovereign power, and functioned as such for 14 years. The Vermont constitution was the first in America to outlaw all slavery and to grant universal suffrage to all men regardless of their economic status. Finally in 1790 the dispute was resolved; Vermont paid New York $30,000 for its claim and was permitted to join the Union the next year.

Not all the conflicts over New England territory were settled at the conference table; in the early days the opposition of the Indians to the loss of their land had to be dealt with bloodily. Except for a quickly quelled uprising of the Pequot tribe in 1637, there had been good relations between colonists and Indians for more than 50 years after the Pilgrim landing. But as the white population grew and more and more hunting ground was cleared for farming and pastureland, the Indians' resentment mounted.

In 1675 King Philip, chief of the Wampanoag

How a village was planned

The distinctive layout of the traditional 17th Century New England village —with its central, grassed common and its meetinghouse surrounded by homes built close together—can be traced to the needs and customs of the earliest settlers. The plan of Wethersfield, Connecticut, in 1640 is shown at right. Houses *(dots)* were grouped around the common (where all residents could graze their cattle) for, among other reasons, mutual protection against the Indians and because this was how villages were laid out in rural England. Wethersfield also built a fort for the village's further protection. Outside the village itself, in the Great West Field, the Great Meadow, and the Great and Little Plains, strips were allotted for cultivating crops, the larger strips often going to the more affluent residents. Later, the Naubuc Farms area, across the Connecticut River, was opened up for cultivation, and larger strips were allotted. Although most early New England villages were laid out this way, the practice was largely abandoned after the American Revolution as the region became more densely settled.

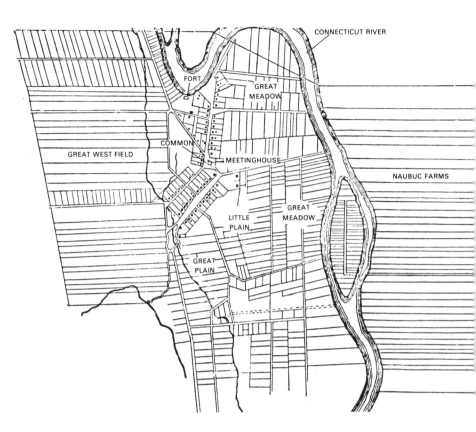

tribe that lived near Plymouth, held parleys with chiefs of other tribes in the region and convinced them that the Indians would be pushed out of the entire area unless they fought back. ("King Philip," whose real name was Metacom, was given the nickname by the colonists because of his regal manner and because he referred to England's Charles II as "my brother.") In the ensuing conflict, which was called King Philip's War, several thousand Indians and colonists were killed and a number of towns were wiped out. The bloodiest battle ever fought on New England soil was a three-hour clash in November 1675 between 1,000 colonial militiamen from Plymouth, Boston and Connecticut and some 3,000 Narragansett Indians on the frozen Great Swamp near present-day South Kingstown, Rhode Island. The colonists won a major victory. About two thirds of the Narragansetts were slaughtered or died in their burning wigwams; the colonists lost 80 men, including eight of their 14 company commanders. Finally in 1678, three years after the start of the war, the Indians sued for peace. A year earlier King Philip had been killed and his wife and nine-year-old son had been sold into slavery. The victory ended the threat to New England communities from Indians living in the area.

But the Indian problem as a whole was far from

ended. During the long wars between England and France from 1689 to 1763, in which the two powers fought for control of Canada and several other territories, Indians in Canada and on the northern frontier of Maine sided with the French. The reason was simple enough: the New Englanders were primarily homesteaders hungry for land, while the French were mainly concerned with fur trading and had little interest in establishing large settlements.

The French and Indian Wars, as the British-French conflicts in North America were called, took a heavy toll in New England, which received little military support from the mother country. Exposed frontier towns like Deerfield and Lancaster in Massachusetts, and Casco and Pemaquid in Maine, whose populations had been massacred or driven out in King Philip's War, were attacked again by the French and Indians a few years later. Deerfield, for example, a town of 125 persons, had been completely abandoned in King Philip's War and had remained deserted for seven years. Finally the community was re-established and held its first town meeting in 1686. Eighteen years later it was raided and burned by the French and Indians, who killed 49 of the inhabitants and carried away 111 others to captivity in Canada. All Indian harassment of New England finally ended in

1763 when the British gained control of Canada, ending the French and Indian Wars.

Despite the prolonged danger from Indians and the French, and the backbreaking toil of making a living from the poor, rocky New England soil, the energetic and serious-minded Puritan pioneers adapted themselves to their new world with impressive resourcefulness and ingenuity. They sought to have no economic dependence on England. The manual laborer and the mechanic became highly respected figures in Yankee society, and they made such things as tools, shoes, clothing, furniture, rope and firearms that colonists in the South had to import from Europe.

As early as 1637 a shipyard at Salem was building vessels to carry dried codfish to the West Indies and the Mediterranean. In 1643 there was a fulling mill in Rowley, Massachusetts, where homespun woolen was shrunk and tightened into smoothly finished clothing material. A few miles away at Saugus, a company headed by John Winthrop Jr., the Governor's son, was operating a successful ironworks by 1645. Three years after Harvard College was founded, in 1636, it had a printing press—the first one in the English colonies—performing the remarkable feat of turning out a Bible in the Algonquian Indian language. In 1647 Massachusetts passed a law, copied soon afterward by the Connecticut colonies, requiring every settlement with 50 or more families to have an elementary school and each community with more than 100 families to provide a public high school with courses in Latin, Greek and mathematics.

There were other differences between the early pioneers' life in New England and that of the first settlers in the South and the West. Most Yankee farms were small because the rocky slopes were hard to clear and till. As a result, one plow was usually enough to do all the plowing in a village. It was pulled by oxen because the work of plowing a previously uncultivated field full of stones and roots was too strenuous for horses. Since the farm work was so heavy and the roads so bad, horses were used almost exclusively for riding in New England before the Revolutionary War; in the rural areas there were no four-wheeled wagons or carriages, only clumsy two-wheeled oxcarts.

The smallness of the early New England farms made it possible for the families in rural towns to live closer together and to work more cooperatively than did the people of other sections of the country. A new township, usually only about six miles square, would be established by a group of families from an older settlement that was becoming crowded. They would build houses around a common, or village green, near their church and a town meeting hall, and clear privately owned fields and pastures on the land surrounding the village, helping one another with stump pulling, planting and haying. Other fields on the outer edge of the township would be community property where anyone could cut firewood or pasture his cattle. In the later years of the 18th Century, as the fear of attacks from the French and Indians lessened and the countryside was cleared of trees and became more populated, people began to build homes farther away from the center of the village.

Almost all of the bigger towns in New England before the industrial 19th Century were seaports; in colonial times, and for many years after the Revolution, most of the Yankee business and commerce were involved in the shipping trade. As odd as it seems today, the busy and prosperous ports in that era of smaller-draft vessels included not only Boston, Newburyport, Newport, Portland, Portsmouth, Providence and Salem, but such inland river towns as Norwich and Hartford.

The growing wealth and population of New England and the other colonies brought about a change in England's policy toward them in the late 1600s. In the earlier part of the 17th Century the colonies had been more or less ignored because they were small and economically unimportant. Now, however, they were a prize well worth exploiting, and England decided to exercise far greater control over them than it had done in the past. That decision marked a turning point in history. The effort to tighten the reins on the American colonies continued for about a century and resulted in the American Revolution, which severed all ties with the motherland. From the beginning the new colonial policy ran into difficulties. Imposing economic and political restrictions on colonies that had grown accustomed to running their own affairs inevitably aroused resentment.

New England posed an especially difficult problem for old England. Unlike the Southern colonies, which shipped raw goods to England in exchange for manufactured products, New England, having few natural resources except fish and lumber for export, was developing into a center of handicraft industries, some of which were actually competing with those of the mother country. Also, New England ships were competing with British ships in sea trade, and Yankee fishermen were proving more than a match for their British counterparts. Whaling was particularly profitable.

Between 1651 and 1696 the British Parliament

passed a series of shipping and trade laws—usually known as the Acts of Trade and Navigation—aimed at restricting direct commerce between the colonies and Continental Europe, thus increasing England's profits as a middleman. Certain articles grown or made in America could be shipped only to England or to its other colonies. A later act required that any goods from the colonies destined for any part of Europe north of Spain must first go to England for transshipment.

The simmering resentment of the colonists came to a boil with the passage of the Stamp Act in 1765—an imposition of stamp duties on newspapers, legal documents, ship's papers, licenses and other items. The angry response of the colonists brought about repeal of the act a year later. But in 1767 Parliament passed the Townshend Acts, which taxed such imports as tea, paints, paper and glass. Alarmed by the resistance, which was especially strong in New England, Britain increased its garrison in Boston. Simultaneously an anti-British political movement also grew, headed in New England by John Hancock, Samuel Adams and Paul Revere. On March 5, 1770, violence broke out. A Boston mob taunted a squad of British soldiers with insults and pelted them with snowballs until the Redcoats fired into the crowd. Three civilians were killed and two later died of wounds. The "Boston Massacre" intensified the hatred against British soldiers in all the colonies.

As it happened, the British government had repealed all Townshend Act duties, except the one on tea, on the very day of the "massacre," but the news did not reach the colonies for some weeks. Three years later the British gave the East India Company a tax advantage on tea that enabled the company to undersell American merchants. Sam Adams' Sons of Liberty, disguised as Indians—a ruse that fooled no one—boarded three ships at the Boston wharves and dumped 342 chests of East India Company tea into the harbor.

This act of defiance infuriated King George III. He immediately pushed through Parliament the so-called Intolerable Acts, which declared the port of Boston closed until the tea was paid for and until the King himself decided "that peace and obedience to the laws" were restored. As Edmund Burke protested, this shutting off of the city's food supply "dependent upon the Kings private pleasure" was a dangerous move, but George ignored the warning. The other colonies came to Boston's assistance, sending food and money to the blockaded port and calling together the meeting of the First Continental Congress at Philadelphia in September 1774 to discuss the crisis. All of the colonies except Georgia were represented. The congress voted to boycott British imports and to send a declaration of grievances to the King. If no redress was made, the congress was to meet again the following May. But a month before that deadline, the shots were fired at Lexington and Concord.

The New England Yankees who fought in that battle—and who forced the British back into Boston, leaving behind 73 Redcoats dead and 200 others wounded or missing—felt that they had taken up arms for a more important cause than any question of trade regulations, tea duty or taxation without representation. Self-government was at stake.

After the British forces under General Thomas Gage retreated to Boston on that grim April 19th in 1775, the city was besieged by a rebel army of 16,000 men from Massachusetts, New Hampshire, Rhode Island and Connecticut. On June 16 the Americans started to build artillery fortifications on the commanding high ground of Breed's Hill in Charlestown, across the Charles River from the North End of Boston. The next day, before the fortifications were completed, Gage sent a force of 1,550 men plus reserves of several hundred under Major General William Howe to dislodge the rebels by a frontal attack, with the aid of heavy gunfire from ships in the bay and batteries in Boston. Thousands of excited spectators watched the fighting from the church steeples and nearby hills of Boston. One of the onlookers, "Gentleman Johnny" Burgoyne, the British general who had recently arrived from England with Howe, described it later in a letter as "one of the greatest scenes of war that can be conceived." Twice the advancing British were driven back by the Yankees. Finally the defenders had to retreat under a third charge because they ran out of ammunition. Now commonly known as the Battle of Bunker Hill—the name of a higher slope behind the actual battleground—the engagement won the British only a defensive outpost of little value at a disastrous cost of lives and prestige.

"These people show a spirit and conduct against us they never showed against the French," Gage wrote after the battle to Lord Barrington, who headed the British War Office. "They are now spirited up by a rage and enthusiasm as great as ever people were possessed of, and you must proceed in earnest or give the business up."

But Gage and General Howe, who took over from him as commander of the British forces in Boston the following October, failed to profit from the

Evolution of the salt-box house

Soon after landing, New England settlers began building steep-roofed houses patterned after those they had known in England. The first houses were two-story structures *(top)* with one room (measuring about 16 by 18 feet) and a small vestibule on each floor. As settlers acquired the means to build larger houses, they developed the so-called "two-room plan" *(center)* that was essentially two smaller houses combined. Eventually, to get even more space, some families added a one-story structure to the back of their "two-room-plan" houses *(bottom);* later these back rooms were built as an integral part of the house. These larger houses were called "salt boxes" because they resembled colonial salt containers.

The method of construction was usually the same, regardless of the size. First a cellar was dug, the foundation laid, and a massive field-stone chimney erected, sometimes 10 feet by 12 in size. After all of the hand-hewn oak timbers had been notched for the frame, and wooden pins whittled to hold it together, the entire community would gather for a "raising bee." While the women prepared food for everyone, the men assembled the wall frames on the ground, then raised and joined them in one collective effort. This left the owner the lighter task of adding the clapboard walls and roof shingles and finishing the interior.

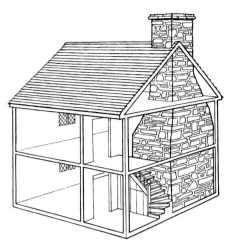

The simplest houses had one downstairs room, called the hall, used for living, cooking and dining. A staircase crowded next to the chimney led from the vestibule to another vestibule and an upstairs bedroom.

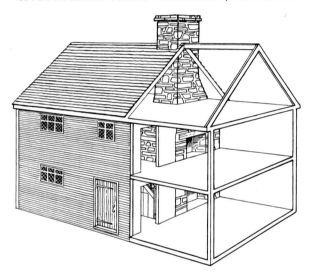

The "two-room plan" called for joining two of the basic houses —minus a second chimney. This provided the family with an extra bedroom upstairs, and a parlor in addition to the hall on the first floor.

The largest houses, the "salt boxes," had a separate kitchen, a pantry and another bedroom at the back in an addition called a lean-to, because its roof rafters leaned against the wall of the main house.

expensive lesson in Charlestown. Both men neglected to occupy another peak of high ground just outside the city, Dorchester Heights. Located immediately to the south of the town, this hill, because it looked down on the ships and docks in Boston Harbor, had even more threatening possibilities than Breed's Hill as a rebel gun position. George Washington, who took command of the Continental Army in Cambridge that summer, eyed Dorchester Heights and probably wondered why the British had left it unprotected. But Washington himself could not make use of the heights so readily available—he lacked the cannon that he would need to turn it into a position of command over Boston.

Washington's problem of getting the guns to drive the British out of Boston was solved the following winter by what was probably the greatest feat of endurance and courage performed in New England during the war—the hauling of 59 heavy pieces of captured enemy artillery over almost 300 miles of ice and snow from Fort Ticonderoga at the head of Lake George down the Hudson River Valley, across the thinly iced river and over the Berkshire Hills to Washington's headquarters in Cambridge. This herculean task was carried out by Henry Knox, a husky and jovial Boston bookseller who was later to become Secretary of War in the first President's Cabinet.

When Knox arrived at Cambridge with the cannon, Washington, who received him warmly, had good news for him; the Americans had just captured the British brigantine *Nancy*, which was loaded with artillery balls that fitted the guns from Ticonderoga perfectly—3,000 iron shots for the 12-pounders and 4,000 for the 6-pounders—as well as with 2,000 infantry muskets and 31 tons of musket ammunition.

Screened from British view by bales of hay in carts pulled by oxen, the cannon were hauled to the top of Dorchester Heights, on the present site of South Boston. The frozen ground on that early March night made the digging of earthwork emplacements for the guns impossible. Colonel Rufus Putnam built the works on top of the earth with fascines—bundles of sticks and straw covered with dirt—and with barrels of earth that could be rolled downhill at advancing British soldiers.

A captured deserter from the British ranks, who was with General Howe on the following morning, reported that the general looked up at the emplacements and exclaimed, "Good God! These fellows have done more work in one night than I could have made my army do in three months." Howe tried to bombard the fortified heights but found that his artillery could not be elevated enough to reach the parapets of the American position. He thought about storming the heights, but decided against such a move, possibly recalling what had happened at Breed's Hill. On the 17th of March the British evacuated Boston, sailing to Halifax with their entire garrison of some 13,000 troops plus about 900 local Tories.

The bombardment from Dorchester Heights was the last Revolutionary War engagement in Massachusetts, but about a year later the same type of untrained New England farmer militiamen who had fought so strongly at Lexington and Concord and at Bunker Hill wrote another chapter of Yankee spirit in the story of the struggle for independence. In the summer of 1777 General Burgoyne was moving a force of British and Hessians southward from Canada to connect with another British army under Howe, supposedly advancing up the Hudson River to Albany. They planned to split New England from the other colonies, thereby hastening the end of the war. Burgoyne sent two separate detachments of his spit-and-polish German mercenary soldiers, along with some Redcoats, Tories and Indian allies, into Vermont to make a raid on Bennington for cattle, horses and wagons. There they ran into a shirt-sleeve army of farmer-riflemen under the leadership of John Stark of New Hampshire.

When Burgoyne's forces had approached Lake Champlain from Canada in early June, the Vermont people had sent a hurried call for help to neighboring states. At the request of the New Hampshire legislature, Stark agreed to raise a force of militia and to fight the British, and in one week he recruited a band of 1,500 men. This was the tough group of homespun-clad Yankees who faced the Prussian leader, Lieutenant Colonel Fredrick Baume, and his advance party of some 700 men five miles west of Bennington on April 16, 1777.

Baume dug in and fortified his position meticulously, awaiting a second force of 550 German troops under Lieutenant Colonel Heinrich von Breymann, which was coming from his rear to give him support. Breymann might have arrived in time if he had not stopped his column every few hundred yards on the road to dress its ranks. "The bayonet, the butt of the rifle, the saber, the pike were in full play," one of Baume's lieutenants wrote later of the battle that ensued. "Our people wavered and fell back, or fought singly and unconnectedly, till they were either cut down at their posts . . . or compelled to surrender."

By the time Breymann's reserves finally arrived on the battlefield, the Americans were also reinforced. A fresh detachment under Seth Warner had arrived from Manchester. The enemy was routed. Stark's victory at Bennington was a considerable contributing factor in the surrender of Burgoyne at Saratoga two months later, the first great American triumph in the Revolution and generally regarded as the turning point of the war.

Historian Samuel Eliot Morison, a Yankee himself, points out that British soldiers fighting in New England during the Revolutionary War were mystified by a phenomenon that was entirely new to them—the eagerness of able-bodied civilian men all over the countryside to take up arms against an enemy. In Europe at that time an army could march safely through an enemy country until it encountered the hostile force of professional soldiers; townspeople either remained quietly in their houses or fled into the forests and mountains. They felt that fighting was for professional soldiers only. But in New England, Morison says, there were always men like Reuben Stebbins of Williamstown, Massachusetts, who had "not seen fittin' to turn out" until he heard the firing at nearby Bennington. "He then saddled his horse, called for his musket, and remarked as he rode off, 'We'll see who's goin' t' own this farm!'"

The faithfully restored interior of the oldest frame dwelling in Boston, built about 1676, appears as it did when Paul Revere occupied it. Revere was summoned from this house on the night of April 18, 1775, for his dramatic ride to Lexington and Concord.

A nation's birth recalled

Early American history is part and parcel of New England. Today a stroll through sections of Boston, Lexington, Concord or any of a number of other communities is like a walk through colonial days. The reason for this is the pride and dedication with which New Englanders have preserved their historic buildings and monuments. They have retained the dignity appropriate to the edifices in which great Americans were born, the American Revolution was fomented, historic documents were drawn and vital decisions made. By keeping these buildings as they were in the turbulent years of the nation's birth, New Englanders have maintained the aura of the colonial era. This pride in the past enables modern Americans to see in New England a cultural as well as a historical record of the time when the New World separated from the Old.

Photographs by Richard Meek

Historic Faneuil Hall, a Georgian-style masterpiece that served colonial Boston as an assembly hall and produce market, still performs these dual functions. In Revolutionary days, market prices were regulated downstairs while rebellion was plotted upstairs.

Its silence today broken only by tourist groups and an occasional public gathering, the upstairs meeting room of Faneuil Hall once resounded to the radical, rebellious cries of Sam Adams and his followers, while voices of moderation were shouted down.

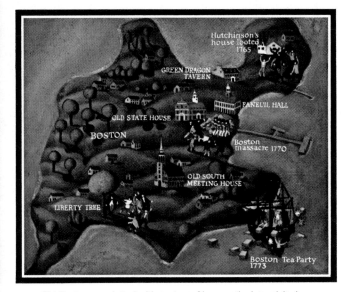

Old Boston was dotted with centers of insurrectionist activity in pre-Revolutionary years, as the map indicates. From the Liberty Tree, a tall elm that once stood in downtown Boston, patriots hanged Crown officials in effigy in protest over the imposition of the Stamp Act in 1765. Across town, patriots looted the house of Lieutenant Governor Thomas Hutchinson, who had attempted to enforce the act. Such patriots often gathered at the Green Dragon Tavern, handy to Faneuil Hall and the Old State House. From Old South Meeting House men poured forth to stage the Boston Tea Party.

Storm center for sedition

In the years just before the Revolution, some of the most significant acts of rebellion took place in Boston, a port city that was often first to feel the effects of revenue-producing measures imposed by the British, like the Stamp Act of 1765. Tension reached a height on March 5, 1770, when a group of British soldiers, taunted by an angry mob of colonists, fired into the crowd and killed five people. After this "Boston Massacre," the taverns, squares and meetinghouses were abuzz with sedition.

Most of the talk—and action—came from fiery Sam Adams and his followers, the Sons of Liberty. It was a group of Sons of Liberty who, on December 16, 1773, donned Indian disguises and dumped $90,000 worth of British East India Company tea into Boston Harbor. They were protesting the fact that the company had been permitted to ship its cargo from Britain without paying duties, enabling it to undersell American shippers. The jettisoning of the tea put the colonies on the road to war.

The oldest Georgian public structure in New England, the Old State House in Boston contained a merchants' exchange downstairs and meeting hall above. A place where politics and business mixed, it loomed large in colonial life: the Boston Massacre took place outside its doors and the Declaration of Independence was read from its balcony.

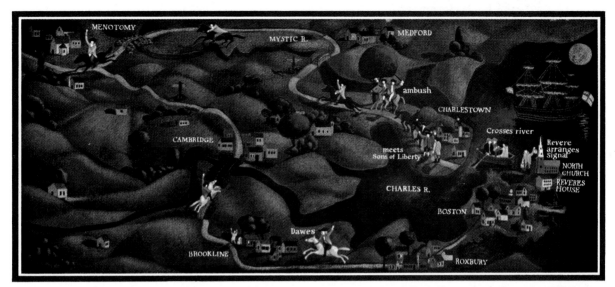

Out of Boston hurried Paul Revere on the night of April 18, 1775, following the route traced on this map and that on the following page. After signal lanterns were raised in the North Church, Revere was rowed across the Charles River, where he was given a horse by a group of Sons of Liberty. Revere then rode on toward Menotomy (modern Arlington), narrowly eluding a British patrol. Another rider, William Dawes, also set out to carry a warning to Lexington and Concord, but as a precaution was dispatched by a different route.

A midnight ride
toward a famous rendezvous

By the spring of 1775 the tide of revolution was running strong in Boston. The rebel leaders Sam Adams and John Hancock went into hiding in Lexington, 11 miles outside the city; preparing for an open clash, the colonials stored munitions in Concord, five miles beyond Lexington. On the night of April 18 the British moved to seize the stores. "Hardly a man is now alive," wrote Henry Wadsworth Longfellow in 1863, "Who remembers that famous day . . ." No one reported the events of the night less accurately than Longfellow. It is true that lanterns ("two, if by sea") were hung in the North Church to indicate that the British were embarking by boat—but the lights were not a signal for Paul Revere, as the poet said. Revere himself ordered the lanterns raised to notify patriots on the opposite shore, before he started on his historic ride.

The interior of the Old North Church remains as it was 200 years ago, when politically divided parishioners—British Army officers and colonists—prayed side by side. It became known as "Old" North Church after Longfellow so called it in "Paul Revere's Ride."

Soaring above today's surrounding buildings, the spire of the Old North Church was a logical place in 1775 to display signals warning of British movements. The spire was originally raised to this height to serve as a landmark for vessels heading into Boston Harbor.

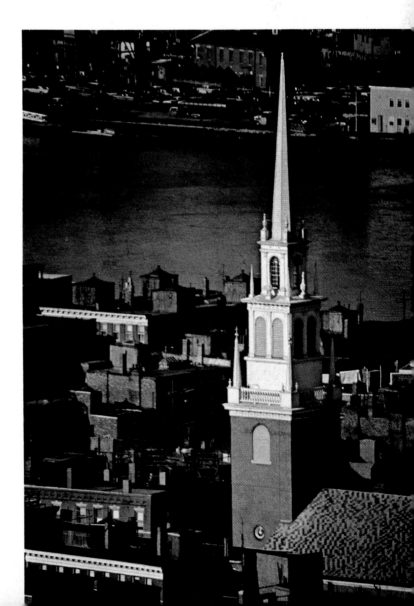

Plunging through the night, Paul Revere ended up in Lexington, arriving ahead of William Dawes. At the home of the Reverend Jonas Clarke, where Adams and Hancock were in hiding, he confirmed rumors that the British had taken the field. He and Dawes, joined by another rider, Dr. Samuel Prescott, then continued together toward Concord, only to encounter a British patrol. In the confusion, Prescott and Dawes escaped, but Revere was captured. Prescott rode on to alarm Concord. Revere was taken to Lexington and—inexplicably—released. While Minutemen hurried to Buckman Tavern to await the British, Revere fled with Hancock and Adams.

Buckman Tavern *(left)* was the headquarters of the Lexington Minutemen, where they nervously awaited news of the British advance toward their town. Rebels often gathered at the tavern, located on the town green, to discuss politics over a glass of rum.

In this room in the Lexington house of the Reverend Jonas Clarke, Sam Adams and John Hancock were awakened to receive news of the British advance. Built by Hancock's grandfather in 1698, the house had served the two patriots as a refuge for several weeks.

In peaceful surroundings, the first shots of war

Little towns like Lexington and Concord were strong for independence. Far from British troop concentrations in Boston, the farmers and traders were unafraid to store caches of munitions and supplies for the rebel cause. In them, nearly every able-bodied man served in the militia. But at dawn on April 19, when 700 British regulars drew up on Lexington Common after a march from Boston, the colonials were able to muster only some 70 Minutemen to face them. No one is today quite sure what happened next. It appears that the Americans were ordered to disperse and started to do so; then a shot fired by an unknown hand rang out. There was a rattle of musketry, the militia was routed, and eight Americans lay dead on the dew-dappled green. But they had gained time; when the regulars marched on to Concord, where a detachment exchanged fire with militia at North Bridge, they found few supplies to destroy. The return to Boston became a rout as farmers fired on the regulars from behind trees and stone walls. The Revolution had begun.

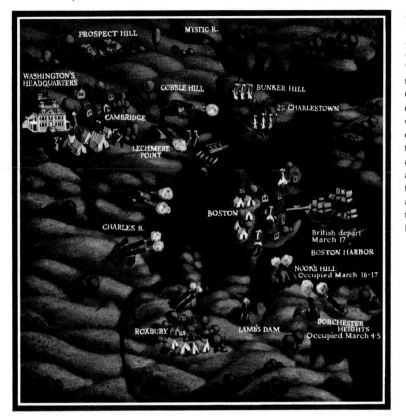

After George Washington had spent the latter part of 1775 and the winter of 1776 whipping the first American army into shape, he at last felt ready to engage the British garrison in Boston. The steps Washington took to accomplish this can be traced on the map. First, he reinforced the gun batteries at Cobble Hill, Lechmere Point and Lamb's Dam; he thus disguised his real plan—to fortify Dorchester Heights, where he emplaced cannon that could fire down on the city. Next, he stationed troops at Lechmere Point ready to take boats across to seize the city if the British attacked Dorchester Heights. Finally, he established a battery on Nook's Hill, only three quarters of a mile from Boston. This accomplished, the colonials were able to shell the city with impunity. The day after the fortification of Nook's Hill, the British abandoned Boston and embarked for Nova Scotia.

A handsome home for a general and a poet

In the early months of the Revolutionary War, Cambridge, Massachusetts, became the headquarters of the colonial army. It was a logical choice. Two-and-a-half miles outside British-occupied Boston, the town was a rebel stronghold. Pro-British sympathizers had been driven from it; militiamen had formed there on June 16, 1775, to march to the Battle of Bunker Hill—an engagement the British won, but at such cost in troops that it made them wary of attacking fortified American positions.

When George Washington arrived in Massachusetts to take command of the colonial troops, he established his headquarters in one of the handsomest houses in Cambridge, a Georgian mansion built in 1759. From July 1775 to April 1776 Washington lived in this elegant house, often riding to the hills overlooking Boston as he planned his strategy. From this headquarters he worked tirelessly to form an effective army from the ragtag, undisciplined militia. The house was to have one more illustrious resident; the poet Henry Wadsworth Longfellow lived in it from 1837 to his death in 1882.

The stately Georgian structure below, which Washington occupied in 1775 and 1776, was one of several estates set back from King's Highway (today's Brattle Street). Washington used the study *(left)* as his office when the house was his headquarters. The room, however, reflects the 19th Century décor in which it was furnished by Henry Wadsworth Longfellow, who lived in the house for 45 years. To the right of the fireplace is a chair made for Longfellow from the wood of the "spreading chestnut tree," under which stood the village smithy in the Longfellow poem. The standing desk on which he wrote a number of his poems is in the foreground.

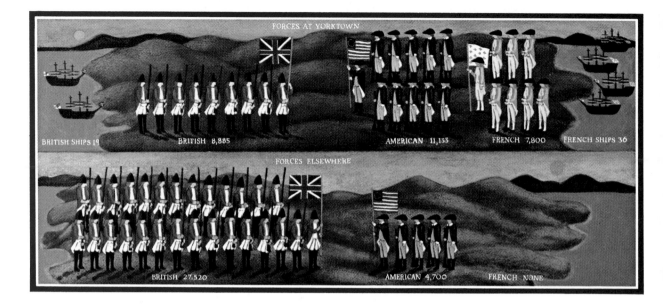

FORCES AT YORKTOWN

BRITISH SHIPS 19   BRITISH 8,885   AMERICAN 11,133   FRENCH 7,800   FRENCH SHIPS 36

FORCES ELSEWHERE

BRITISH 27,520   AMERICAN 4,700   FRENCH NONE

The overwhelming superiority in numbers enjoyed by the combined American and French forces at the decisive 1781 Battle of Yorktown in Virginia is indicated by the drawing at the left. The allied armies outnumbered the British by more than 2 to 1, and held a similar superiority at sea. Prevented from reinforcing and supplying the besieged troops at Yorktown by the French naval dominance in the area, the British were finally forced to surrender, losing about one third of their colonial army. The remaining British forces, mostly stationed in New York, were weary and dispirited. Yorktown proved to be the last major battle of the war.

High strategy planned in a modest tavern

In a simple house in Wethersfield, Connecticut, a meeting was held that led to the end of the Revolutionary War. After six years of fighting, the war had not been going well for the patriots. Washington's armies were bogged down north of New York City, and the French army had been stalled for a year in Newport, Rhode Island. In Wethersfield in 1781 Washington and the Count de Rochambeau, commander of the French forces in America, decided to combine their forces. Their first target was to be New York City. But, learning that a French fleet was en route to Chesapeake Bay, the two commanders marched south. In October 1781 the combined armies defeated the British at Yorktown, Virginia.

The house in which Washington and Rochambeau met in Wethersfield was built in 1752 by Joseph Webb. Known as "Hospitality Hall," the house appealed to Washington, who enjoyed comfortable accommodations.

In this quietly furnished room, Washington and Rochambeau settled plans to merge their forces. Halfway between New York and Rhode Island, Wethersfield provided a convenient conference location.

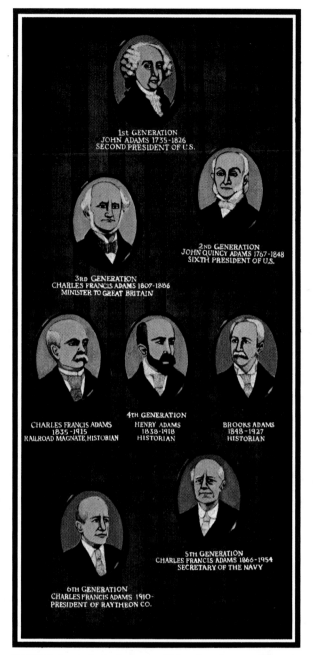

This family tree indicates the range of interests and accomplishments of the main line of the distinguished Adams family of Quincy, Massachusetts (Sam Adams, the Boston patriot, belonged to a collateral branch). John was a dynamic force behind the Declaration of Independence; John Quincy, after his term as President, served for 17 years as a militant antislavery member of the U.S. House of Representatives. The first Charles Francis also served in Congress. Of his sons, Charles Francis was President of the Union Pacific Railroad; Henry wrote an American classic, *The Education of Henry Adams;* and Brooks was a leading historical theorist. The next Charles Francis was a prominent businessman and public official, and the present Charles Francis heads the Raytheon Company, a major electronics firm with headquarters in Waltham, Massachusetts.

In these dignified early colonial houses *(top picture)* in Quincy were born the two Adamses who were to become Presidents. John Adams was born in the house in the background; his son, John Quincy Adams, in the other building. When John Adams was a young man, he used the room in the bottom picture as his law office; in it he helped draft the constitution of Massachusetts in 1779.

Ancestral homes
of a distinguished clan

New England is studded not only with houses in which vital military decisions were taken but with the ancestral homes of some of America's most illustrious families. Of all these New England clans the most extraordinary is the Adams family. Today in Quincy, Massachusetts, stand three buildings closely associated with the Adamses: the houses where John and John Quincy Adams were born and the 18th Century mansion that sheltered four generations of Adamses. These houses remain as solid as the Adams legend itself, monuments to a family that produced two U.S. Presidents as well as high-ranking public servants, writers and businessmen.

Called the "Old House" by the Adams family, this spacious colonial mansion in Quincy was originally built in 1731 and extensively added to over the years. John Adams bought it in 1787 and after his term as President retired here in 1801. John Quincy and his son Charles Francis used the house as a summer retreat, as did Charles's sons. In 1947 the house became a National Historic Site.

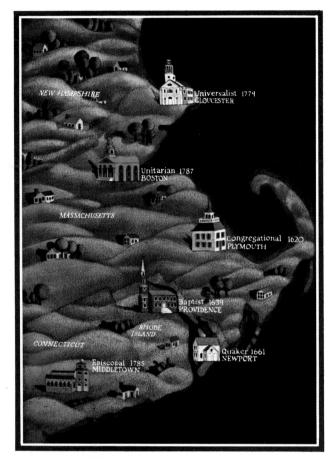

Stylized renderings of churches on the map at left indicate the number of important religious bodies that, in America, first came into existence in New England. Puritan separatists from the Church of England established the Congregational Church in Massachusetts in 1620. Roger Williams broke with Congregationalism to found the Baptist Church in Rhode Island. Quakers held their first Yearly Meeting in nearby Newport, and the Universalist and Unitarian Churches were founded in Gloucester and Boston. The Protestant Episcopal Church was the last to be established.

Tortuous beginnings
of an American religious group

Not all the colonists were anxious to sunder ties with England. Some remained loyal to the mother country and encountered oppression during the war. Members of the Church of England faced special difficulties. Not all were Tories, but the Church was the official religious body of the Crown, many of its clergymen were British sympathizers, and many early colonists had fled England to escape its restrictions. As the Revolution ended, many members of the Church sought to set up an independent American branch. Their efforts culminated in a decision, taken in 1783 in Connecticut, to attempt to obtain the consecration of an American bishop. The resulting Protestant Episcopal Church joined a number of new American religious groups, all of which sprang out of disagreements with either the previously dominant Congregational Church or the Church of England. The new bodies emphasized the diversity of religious belief that was to become a characteristic of the new nation.

In this room at the Woodbury, Connecticut, home of John Rutgers Marshall, 10 Episcopal church leaders met in 1783 and chose Samuel Seabury to seek ordination in England as a bishop. The Episcopalians had sent more than 40 men to England before Seabury —six had died during the voyage, and the others failed to win English recognition. With the Church nearly destroyed during the Revolutionary War, Seabury seemed doomed to failure. He did fail —in England. But he succeeded in obtaining ordination by prelates in Scotland, and in Middletown, Connecticut, in 1785, he was officially welcomed as the first American bishop.

Factories billowing smoke, lumber stacked for shipping, commercial craft plying the river—all reflect the economic prosperity of Providence, Rhode Island, around 1860. Industrial towns throughout New England were then enjoying a comparable boom.

4

The Great Epoch of Trade

New England's deficiencies were probably as important as its assets in making the region one of the world's great centers of trade, manufacturing and finance. The area's burgeoning economy in the late 18th and most of the 19th Centuries was largely the result of the pioneers' disheartening discoveries that New England's thin, rocky soil was unsuitable for large-scale farming and that there were not enough fur-bearing animals in the area to make trapping a substantially profitable enterprise. Faced with these disadvantages, the Puritan settlers had developed other means of livelihood. This course of action, dictated by necessity, became the foundation for New England's phenomenal economic structure in later years.

Commerce has been defined as "exchanging stuff for stuff," for instance, raw materials for finished goods, or one kind of manufactured article for another. When the European nations established colonies in North America, both the settlers and the mother countries assumed there would be a basic trade relationship between them: the colonies would ship such products as sugar, fur and fish and receive in return manufactured goods from the industries of Europe.

Certainly this was understood by the Puritans who organized the Massachusetts Bay Company in England. But when the settlers came to New England they discovered that their lands could not fulfill the traditional colonial role in the 17th Century European economy, and they soon realized that a different pattern of trade would have to be created if the settlements were to survive. Soon they turned to the sea and to lumbering, trade and handicraft industries.

This alteration of the original plan was not immediate, however. For about the first decade, the Massachusetts Bay Colony managed to survive as a farming community because the successive waves of newly arriving Puritans from England brought money and goods with them and were willing to pay high prices for the corn and cattle raised by established settlers on the small and laboriously cleared tracts of freehold land. Then, about 1641, immigration slowed down to a trickle. The growing strength of the Puritan rebellion in England against King Charles I—a rebellion that later developed into a civil war—encouraged most of the dissenters of the Anglican Church to remain at home. With the bottom falling out of its local farm market, New England turned toward the sea.

"Few coming to us, all foreign commodities grew scarce," Governor John Winthrop wrote in his journal in 1641, "and our own of no price. Corn would buy nothing; a cow which cost last year £20 might now be bought for 4 or £5, etc., ... These straits set our people on work to provide fish, clapboards, plank, etc., and to sow hemp and flax (which prospered very well) and to look out to the West Indies for a trade ..."

Trade with the West Indies was indeed one important answer. New England products, especially the Yankees' salted fish, were welcomed in the sugar-rich colonies of the Caribbean. Codfish soon became the mainstay of the Yankee economy. Soon after the Revolutionary War the Massachusetts legislature was to hang in the chamber of the House of Representatives—where it is still on display—a wooden replica of the "sacred codfish" as "a memorial of the importance of the Cod Fishery to the welfare of this Commonwealth." As early as 1676 an English observer, Edward Randolph, complained that Massachusetts, with a merchant fleet of some 430 vessels, had such a stranglehold on the West Indian trade that "there is little left for the merchants residing in England to import into any of the plantations."

Spurred on by such commerce, fishing and shipbuilding boomed in New England during the decades before the Revolution. The New Englanders sent their ships into French, Spanish and Dutch ports in Europe, the Caribbean and South America and sold their codfish in the West Indies and the Mediterranean, often clearing a 200 per cent profit on a single voyage. They developed a lucrative triangular trade route, shipping rum—distilled from West Indian sugar-cane juice or molasses—to Africa, where it was bartered for slaves who were carried to the West Indies and exchanged for money and for more sugar and molasses to be made into still more rum back home in New England.

All along the coast in those colonial days the port towns of Massachusetts grew and prospered, and busy shipyards thrived on the rivers. Boston, with a population of about 17,000 in 1740, was the largest town in the British colonies and had the busiest harbor in North America; a forest of masts lined its Long Wharf, which extended 2,000 feet into deep water from the foot of King (now State) Street. Salem, the home port of the ships belonging to the Derby family, was also prospering and, along with Marblehead, was sending codfish to the West Indies and the Mediterranean. Gloucestermen carried fish to South America, and Nantucket was already established as a deep-sea whaling center.

But the sea commerce of New England was by no means restricted to Massachusetts. Newport in Rhode Island and New London in Connecticut were concentrating on the rum and African slave trade and getting rich at it. Portsmouth in New Hampshire was an important shipbuilding town and was also sending lumber for hulls and white-pine masts and spars to Britain. Across the Piscataqua River from Portsmouth, at Kittery Point in the District of Maine, were the storehouses, lumberyards, shipyards and docks of Sir William Pepperell, the first native-born New Englander to be knighted by the British King, and one of the wealthiest merchant tycoons in colonial America. Pepperell owned some 2,000 acres of land along the Maine coast between the Piscataqua and the Saco Rivers. (The Lady Pepperell cotton mills, named after his widow, now manufacture bed linens in Biddeford.) Pepperell built ships and operated his own fleet of coastal and transoceanic vessels, bringing corn and tobacco from the Southern colonies, shipping fish and rum and lumber to Europe and the Caribbean, and bringing back dry goods, sails, cordage, sugar, wines and fruit. Sometimes he would sell both ship and cargo as a unit. In 1747 he built four warships for the British Navy. At his luxurious home at Kittery his walls were "hung with costly mirrors and paintings, his sideboards loaded with silver, and his park stocked with deer."

Down in Providence, Rhode Island, the Brown dynasty—founded by Captain James Brown and after his death taken over by James's brother, Obadiah, and James's four sons, Nicholas, John, Joseph and Moses—had established another trading empire before 1760. Along with their shipping business, the Browns bartered Rhode Island cattle and horses for Carolina rice, operated many rum distilleries, an iron foundry and a chocolate mill, ran a general merchandise store and carried on the largest wholesale candle business in the colonies. In New England's colonial era such Yankee merchants had very little working capital—there was not a single bank anywhere on the Atlantic Seaboard before the Revolutionary War, financial arrangements being made by individual lenders and investors—and so the question of how traders got started and how their holdings expanded is an interesting one. Shrewd trading with ship cargoes, and borrowing from acquaintances and relatives, provided cash. Also, the traders often operated on credit extended by British merchants. John Chamberlain in his history of American business, *The Enterprising Americans*, cites the case of Thomas Hancock, uncle of the John Hancock who was one of the signers of the Declaration of Independence. Hancock began as a bookseller in Boston in the 1720s after seven years of indentured apprenticeship to a bookbinder. To his stock of books he added tea, yard goods and cutlery, having imported such luxury items by sending overseas for barter a shipment of codfish, whale oil, whalebone and lumber.

"How did he get the wherewithal to buy the codfish in the first place?" Chamberlain asks. "Perhaps he would take hogs from farmers in exchange for Bibles, sending the pork on to Newfoundland and picking up fish from there to go to England for knives. Getting richer out of such huckstering, he might buy a 'piece of a ship' bound for Surinam (Dutch Guiana) to bring contraband [smuggled goods] home to Boston. Taking precautions, Hancock writes to his shipmaster before one such trip to Surinam: 'Closely observe, when you come on our coasts, not to speak with any vessels nor let any of your men write up to their wives when you arrive at our lighthouse.' In other words, slip in without any Empire customs officer seeing you."

Through such juggling and smuggling, Hancock accumulated enough wealth to build on the slope of Beacon Hill one of the finest homes in colonial Boston and to import yews and hollies to decorate his lawn. He handed down the house and his business to his nephew John, known as "The Prince of Smugglers," who joined Samuel Adams and John Adams in the Revolutionary movement; John Hancock was probably at least as much concerned with freedom of trade as with the freedom of man.

The outbreak of the Revolutionary War temporarily retarded New England's growing prosperity, as the British fleet closed down commerce with the

Ice harvested from the rivers and ponds of New England was a highly valuable cash crop in many parts of the region during the 19th Century. The ice was not only shipped to other parts of the United States but was also exported to tropical nations across the sea. In 1890 approximately three million tons of it were cut in Maine, a job that required the labor of about 25,000 men and 1,000 horses.

West Indies and stopped whaling and Grand Banks fishing. Shipbuilding slumped. During the war many Massachusetts shipowners, notably the Derby family in Salem, made money from privateering, sending armed vessels to sea under American government authorization to prey on British merchantmen. But business generally was poor. Even after the war ended, the depression continued in parts of New England. Several hard-hit ports, such as Newport, Newburyport and Marblehead—the last had been bigger and busier than Baltimore in 1765 —never regained their prewar commerce.

The resourceful Yankees refused to stay beaten for long. Cut off from much of their former business in Great Britain and the British West Indies, and no longer enjoying the wartime privileges that had been extended in French, Dutch and Spanish ports, the New Englanders sought longer and bolder trade routes to other parts of the world—Sweden, Russia, the East Indies and the rich markets of China.

George Cabot of the Beverly Cabots, who had left Harvard—apparently just before being requested to do so—to go to sea as a cabin boy, sent two of the first New England ships to the Baltic Sea in 1784, carrying tobacco, flour and rum and returning with Swedish iron and Russian sailcloth and hemp. The problem in dealing with the China market in the

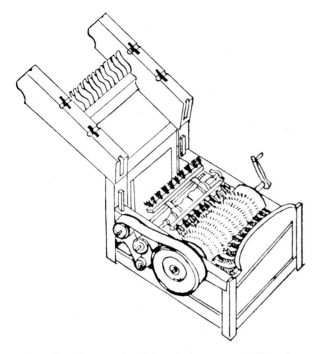

A machine whose use altered the nation's economy, Eli Whitney's cotton gin used spiked rollers to remove seeds from cotton fibers, readying them for spinning in a tenth of the manual-labor time. Soon after the machine's invention, cotton exports were booming, and a major base for New England's textile industry had been laid.

early postwar days, when money in New England was still scarce, was to find a bartering commodity that the Chinese mandarins wanted. The Boston merchants, who planned to send a vessel named the *Columbia* to Canton in 1787, heard that otter fur was a likely product for the Canton market, and so they routed the ship around Cape Horn at the southern tip of South America and sent it up the west coast of two continents to Vancouver Island in Canada. There agents for the merchants were to trade tools and knickknacks with the Indians for sea-otter furs, which would be carried across the Pacific to China.

The *Columbia*, built on the North River near Scituate in Massachusetts, was only 83 feet long and weighed only 212 tons—a small ship for the gales of Cape Horn, where no other North American vessel had ever sailed before—but she made the voyage to Vancouver safely. After spending the winter in the Northwest the *Columbia* continued to China, where the furs were traded for tea. So many other Yankee ships in later years followed the same route to China via Vancouver that the fur-trading Indians in the area began to call all white Americans "Boston men."

In Canton, Robert Gray, the Rhode Island-born captain of the *Columbia*, had found that 24 other

American ships had been there before him, all of them sailing an eastern course to China around Africa and across the Indian Ocean. Four of them were owned by Elias Hasket Derby, the shipping king of Salem, whose son, John, was also one of the *Columbia*'s shareholders. The China trade transformed Salem from a small codfish and coastal trading port into one of the wealthiest maritime centers of the Western world.

To make up trading cargoes for his larger ships to take to the Orient, Derby would fill the warehouses on Derby Wharf in Salem with iron, canvas, hemp, wine and lead brought by his smaller brigs and schooners from Russia, France, Sweden and Spain. He also collected flour, other provisions and tobacco from New York, Philadelphia and Richmond and molasses from the French West Indies. He imported shiploads of pepper directly from Sumatra, in what is now Indonesia; at a time when there was little refrigeration and when spice was needed to preserve meat, this made Salem the pepper center of the Atlantic.

While the China and East India trade was bringing affluence to Salem at the turn of the 18th Century, nearby Boston was handling more than one third of all the shipping in the United States. Along with a traffic in European and Oriental goods, the Boston merchants were back in business with the West Indies despite British efforts to keep them out. Britain's Captain Horatio Nelson, on guard duty in the West Indies, complained that Yankee captains would lie their way "through a nine-inch plank" in trumping up an excuse to land a cargo illegally, and the local planters, needing goods from North America, were always ready to claim that a Boston schooner had been forced to their shore "under distress." As a growing town of about 25,000 people in 1800, still unblemished by the smoke of factory industry or railroads, Boston was drawing virtually all of its sustenance from its wharves, warehouses and counting rooms.

Thus the rise of worldwide sea trade in the colorful Federalist era between the Revolution and the War of 1812 gave New England a new class of wealthy merchants with a more elegant way of life than their grandfathers had known in the rustic colonial days. In time, the salt-box houses of Salem's witch-scare years gave way to the Samuel McIntire-designed mansions, square and hip-roofed, with classic simplicity, among the finest residential structures in the United States. Charles Bulfinch gave Boston its handsome State House and many of the red-brick Regency-style homes on Beacon Hill, as well as the gracefully curved Tontine Crescent, the first such block of attached, or row, houses in America (they have long since been torn down to make way for stores and office buildings). Living in a formal luxury, with long dinners of many wine-washed courses in the late afternoons, and perhaps supper parties, balls or Federalist club meetings in the evenings, most of the merchants denounced the Jeffersonian Democratic-Republicans as dangerous radicals, followers of the Jacobin philosophy of the French Revolution. Emotionally and commercially pro-British, the majority of New England business-men were outraged when their shipping was disrupted by Jefferson's embargo on foreign trade in 1807 and by "Mr. Madison's War" against England in 1812. The Yankee rank and file, dependent on sea commerce, shared their opposition to the war.

In 1814, when the British extended their block-ade to the coast of New England and brought American shipping practically to a standstill, the Federalist-dominated legislature of Massachusetts summoned representatives from other states in the region to meet at a convention at Hartford to consider "their public grievances and concerns" and, perhaps, call a convention of all the states to revise the Constitution. Some of the more radical Feder-alists hoped that New England would form an in-dependent federation and make a separate peace with the British.

The Hartford Convention, after much delibera-tion, decided against any radical steps and let the Madison Administration off with a severe scolding. Such a defiant gesture at a time when Washington had been sacked and burned by the British drew ridicule from the rest of the country upon the New England Federalists. One cartoon published dur-ing the convention showed Massachusetts, Rhode Island and Connecticut leaping into the arms of the British King, George III, who is exclaiming, "O 'tis my Yankee boys! Jump in my fine fellows, plenty molasses and Codfish; plenty of goods to smuggle; Honours, titles and Nobility into the bar-gain—" In the next national election after the war, Madison's successor, James Monroe, who was also a Democratic-Republican, gave the Federalists an overwhelming beating.

After the War of 1812 the nation grew in prosper-ity and population, and New England's sea com-merce boomed again, far surpassing the foreign trade of earlier years. Although New York was by now the leading American port—in part because the opening of the Erie Canal gave that city direct access to the booming Midwest—and Boston had to settle for second place, the Yankees amassed wealth in the China trade undreamed of during the Federalist period. New Englanders and New Yorkers with their faster American-built vessels outclassed the slower British in the transatlantic freight and passenger competition. This superiority was maintained almost until the Civil War. The whaling fleets of Nantucket and New Bedford en-joyed a golden era until the discovery of oil in Penn-sylvania in 1859 slashed the market for whale oil. But Salem's East India trade went into a decline when the demands of the market began to require vessels with a capacity three times larger than the 200- and 300-tonners that Elias Hasket Derby had sent to Sumatra and Canton in the 1790s. Salem's harbor was too shallow for such big ships. Some of its merchant firms began to operate in Boston or New York. Marblehead, Newburyport, Newport, Providence and New London also lost importance as trade and passenger service more and more cen-tered on the big ports.

The greatest sailing ships in the history of the world, the fast and graceful three-masted, square-rigged Yankee clippers, were built in great numbers in New England and New York shipyards from about 1840 to 1860. Designed for speed rather than for cargo capacity, the clippers were catapulted to fame during the California Gold Rush that began in 1849 when they were used for fast delivery of merchandise around Cape Horn to San Francisco. There a bushel of potatoes brought $16, a dozen eggs cost $10, and lumber was being sold at a 1,000 per cent profit. The most famous and fastest clip-pers were designed and built by Donald McKay at his yards in East Boston, not only for the Gold Rush trade in California, but for service in the Brit-ish packet routes that ran from Liverpool to Aus-tralia when gold was discovered "down under" a few years later. Many of the McKay clippers, in fact, as well as clippers from Medford and New-buryport in Massachusetts, Portsmouth in New Hampshire, and the Maine shipyards at Bath, Kittery and Rockland, were built for New York and British owners and never sailed in New England waters after they were launched.

One of the first clippers built by McKay in East Boston was his *Flying Cloud*, about 230 feet long on her deck, 41 feet wide and 21 feet in depth, with a weight of some 1,800 tons. On her maiden voyage in 1851 the *Flying Cloud* made a trip from New York around Cape Horn to San Francisco in 89 days, smashing all previous records for sailing ships and setting a mark that was never beaten.

The clippers had no return cargo to pick up in California and so they usually went on across the Pacific to China, where the British merchants were

One of the best-known of the illustrious Concord coaches, the Deadwood Stage from South Dakota, is shown in 1895 outside the New England plant where it had been built nearly three decades before. "Buffalo Bill" Cody holds the reins. Although these stagecoaches are associated with the Far West, they were designed and built in Concord, New Hampshire, by the firm of Abbot-Downing. From 1827 to 1899 the company and its successors—J. Stephens Abbot and Lewis Downing parted for a period—turned out more than 3,000 coaches to haul passengers and cargo throughout America and in many foreign lands.

glad to pay them rates almost three times higher than those paid to their own slower British ships to carry tea to London. The *Flying Cloud*'s master, Josiah Perkins Cressy of Marblehead, picked up a cargo of tea in Canton and covered the 2,000 miles from there to Java Head—where the Java Sea joins with the Indian Ocean—in six days, nearly halving the previous record for the distance.

Cressy, like many Yankee sea captains, relieved the tedium of long voyages by taking his wife with him; crew members on a clipper never spoke to the captain, except in the line of duty, unless he spoke first, and he never mixed socially with his officers or men. The seafaring wives were sturdy women who often knew as much about navigation as their husbands. Mary Brown Patten of Boston was only 19 years old when her husband, the captain of *Neptune's Car*, fell ill from brain fever while fighting his way through a gale off Cape Horn in 1856. The first officer was in irons for insubordination and the second mate knew no navigation. Mrs. Patten took command of the 1,800-ton clipper for 52 days and sailed it safely to San Francisco.

But the clippers, one historian said, lasted on the maritime scene as briefly as if they had been "monuments carved from snow." Even if their disappearance had not been hastened by the new steamships and by the transcontinental railroad that enabled merchants to ship goods overland from the East to San Francisco, clippers were doomed by their high operating costs—they were heavily canvased and required large crews—and by their small cargo capacity, which made them lose money on routes where they could not collect inflated freight rates.

New England's tradition for building fine wooden sailing ships remained firm for some years after the demise of the clipper, but when shipping turned to metal-hulled, steam-driven ocean liners the region could never compete with the British, who had advanced metal and machine industries.

But the economic slack brought about by the gradual demise of shipbuilding was more than taken up by other enterprises. Even before the Civil War the wealth gained from shipping in the lush earlier days, particularly in the China trade and from whaling, had given Yankees the economic resource that they had sorely lacked in the immediate post-Revolutionary War years—investment capital for backing local industry and other business pursuits within their own shores. The quick fortunes made from sea commerce were too big to be reinvested solely in that same enterprise. Profits of more than $100,000 on a single voyage were quite common, and there were many trips to the Far East like the one made by the *John Jay* from Providence in 1794, carrying a $34,550 cargo of iron, rum, gin, pork, candles and tobacco to Bombay and returning two years later with $250,000 worth of tea. That was too much money to spend on more ships and longer wharves; some of it had to be put to use elsewhere.

One of the major investments for this wealth, and one that played a vital role in New England's vast industrial expansion during the 19th Century, was the network of railroads built in the region from about 1830 to 1860. The railroads broke New England's geographical isolation from the rest of the nation, broadened the domestic market enormously, facilitated the import of supplies to New England and eventually led to larger rail operations elsewhere. In time, such Western railroads as the Union Pacific, the Atchison, Topeka & Santa Fe, and the Chicago, Burlington & Quincy were controlled by New England capitalists. Much of New England's capital also went into America's first successful factories, the textile mills in Massachusetts and Rhode Island that started the industrialization of the region and changed its way of life.

For a period it had seemed that no one in New England, or anywhere else in the world for that matter, would be able to compete in textile manufacturing with Britain. In the late 18th Century an Englishman by the name of Richard Arkwright invented a power spinning machine, or frame. Until that time all spinning had been done by hand. Somewhat later, the Reverend Edmund Cartwright invented the power loom. The British government, immediately recognizing the enormous value of these inventions, especially if a monopoly could be maintained, forbade the exporting not only of the new textile machinery but of the plans for the machines. There were also strict laws against visitors making sketches of the equipment, and British workers with a knowledge of the processes were forbidden to emigrate.

In 1789 a young Englishman named Samuel Slater, who had served as an apprentice in a Derbyshire mill using Arkwright frames and knew its machinery intimately, somehow managed to make his way to the United States. Slater carried no sketches with him, for fear of punishment if they were found in his possession, but he had a detailed concept of how the spinning equipment worked. He heard that Moses Brown, of the wealthy Rhode Island shipping family, was trying without success to operate a cotton yarn mill. Slater wrote to Brown, told him of the information that was available and was immediately offered a position, and later a partnership in the business.

Working wholly from memory, but with the valuable assistance of an ironmonger and blacksmith named Oziel Wilkinson, Slater was able to build an entirely new system for spinning yarn. The new mill was built in 1790 in Pawtucket, and the Blackstone River furnished the power. At first the machinery refused to work; the cotton jammed in the carder teeth that were supposed to straighten the fibers before spinning. The angle of the teeth in the carder was one detail in Arkwright's machines that Slater had failed to memorize correctly. He studied the slope of the wires in a hand carder used by the wife of his chief mechanic and saw his mistake. After he patiently readjusted each of the thousands of wires in his carders, the spindles worked successfully— and America had its first real factory, performing work through water-powered mechanisms that formerly could have been done only by the hands of skilled artisans.

The cotton yarn from Slater's mill was "put out" to weavers who made it into fabric in their own homes or shops. But hand weaving could not compete with the new power looms of England, and the man who closed that gap was the gifted Francis Cabot Lowell. Lowell also used his memory to "smuggle" plans from Britain to New England, and his feat was even more impressive than Slater's. When illness interrupted Lowell's career in the mercantile business, he went to Manchester, England, in 1811 for a firsthand look at the new spinning and weaving machines. He memorized the designs of both. When he returned, the difficult task of translating his mental notes into machinery was accomplished by Paul Moody, one of the many unschooled engineering geniuses who somehow emerged from rural New England in the early 19th Century.

In 1814 the first New England textile mill that performed the entire process of converting raw cotton into finished cloth was opened by Lowell in Waltham, Massachusetts, near Boston. The Charles River supplied the power. Chartered as the Boston Manufacturing Company, the mill was backed by, among others, Lowell's brother-in-law, Patrick Tracy Jackson, who had grown rich in trade with the East and West Indies, and by Nathan Appleton, a wealthy Boston merchant who was Henry Wadsworth Longfellow's father-in-law.

The water power of the Charles River at Waltham soon proved inadequate for the mill's heavy volume of business. In 1822, five years after Lowell's untimely death at age 42, the stockholders established new factories near a 30-foot waterfall on the Merrimack River near the New Hampshire border. Around the mills they laid out a new industrial

Sewing circles were among the off-hours amusements offered the girls working in the textile mills in the newly created "company town" of Lowell, Massachusetts, in the 1820s. The workers were treated as young ladies and expected to behave as such. Cultural needs were not forgotten; there were concerts, lectures by such luminaries as Ralph Waldo Emerson, evening courses and music lessons. The boardinghouses where the girls lived were well chaperoned, and the rules required "temperance, attendance at religious services, neatness, punctuality, and early hours."

town that they named Lowell, after the company's founder.

Lowell became one of the first of the "company" mill towns that later sprang up everywhere in New England. For its time it was a remarkably enlightened place. The company's founder had not wanted to duplicate the injustices and hardships he had seen in British factories and had deliberately refused to hire child labor in the first plant in Waltham. Instead, he had recruited young people from New England farms and villages. This policy was continued in the new mills. The workers lived in company-owned rooming houses and three-decker tenements, shopped in company stores, worshiped in company-supported churches and were buried in company cemeteries. During its early years, Lowell was a labor utopia, admired by visiting sightseers from Europe, like Charles Dickens.

Because of the shortage of male labor before the deluge of immigration from Europe and Canada in the middle and later years of the century, most of the mill hands were young women from farms in Massachusetts, New Hampshire and Maine, who worked in Lowell for a few years and then went back home with their savings to get married. They stayed in comfortable and respectably supervised company dormitories whose cultural atmosphere

was somewhat like that of a college—their employers provided them with evening educational courses and domestic-science lessons, lectures by visiting authors, scientists and professors, and even a literary magazine, *The Lowell Offering*, which the girls themselves wrote and edited. But when the Lowell factories became pressed by competition from hundreds of other New England textile mills, and when Irish and French-Canadian laborers became plentiful, the community lost its campus atmosphere and took on the grim aspect of an overcrowded, overworked and underpaid industrial town.

In the late 1840s another company financed by shipping-rich Boston Yankees bought empty land and built the whole city of Lawrence, Massachusetts, as a textile center, naming it after their president and largest stockholder, Abbott Lawrence. The town was filled almost overnight with thousands of immigrant Irish and English millworkers. Scores of other cotton and woolen mills were spinning and looming in Rhode Island, Maine and in the faded port of Fall River in Massachusetts.

By 1860, when New England was producing nearly three fourths of the nation's cotton cloth, there were flourishing textile mills in Manchester, farther up the Merrimack in New Hampshire, where the giant Amoskeag mills—partly financed by Boston maritime money—were later to expand into the biggest cotton-textile operation in the world. The six-story red-brick buildings of Amoskeag lined both sides of the river for a mile and a half. By the early 1870s the company was turning out enough cotton cloth annually to "just about put a girdle about the earth."

As responsible for the industrialization of New England as Samuel Slater and Francis Cabot Lowell was Massachusetts-born Eli Whitney, whose earlier invention of the cotton gin—to separate the fibers from the seed—had greatly aided the industry. Whitney made an even more important contribution when he adapted to the mass production of guns the principle of manufacturing through the assembly of precision-tooled interchangeable parts. The idea of putting together thousands of guns from thousands of machine-made duplicate parts—instead of hand-fashioning one gun at a time—was developed in France but was never put into production. With some refinements of his own, Whitney used the process to fill a government order for muskets at his small factory in Hamden, outside of New Haven, in the early 1800s.

Samuel Colt studied Whitney's interchangeable-parts technique with the inventor's son, Eli Whitney Jr., before opening his own plant in Hartford

The water of Cape Cod Bay joins that of Buzzards Bay as the last barrier in the Cape Cod Canal is ceremoniously removed in 1914, and a short, safe seacoast route opens for New England commerce. The canal, cut across the strip that joins the cape to the Massachusetts mainland, provided a long-deferred sea passage between Boston and the south. As early as the 17th Century, Pilgrims in Plymouth argued the need for such a route to avoid the long and dangerous trip around the cape. In 1776 George Washington added his voice to those demanding a canal because it would "give greater security to navigation against the enemy."

A number of attempts at construction were made over the years, but all failed. Finally New York financier August Belmont took over and digging began in 1909. The U.S. government bought the canal in 1928 and dropped the previous tolls. Now some 17,500 vessels use the canal annually.

and giving the pioneers of the Old West one of New England's most history-making inventions, the revolving, cylinder-firing pistol, better known as the Colt revolver. The principle of interchangeable parts also resulted in the establishment of New England's mass-produced clock industry, which helped give Connecticut's Naugatuck Valley world fame as an industrial area. The production of Elias Howe's sewing machine, first demonstrated in Boston in 1845, depended on the interchangeable-parts concept, as did the manufacturing of standardized machinery for mass-producing shoes. Until the time of the Civil War, shoes had been stitched in homes or small shops. The rise of shoe factories all over New England during and after the war followed Lyman R. Blake's invention at South Abingdon, Massachusetts, of a process for mechanically sewing soles to uppers. Mass-produced shoes provided the Yankees with another great field of industrial employment and management profit.

A complete list of the many significant inventions and technical developments that came out of New England minds during the 18th and 19th Centuries would make almost unbelievable reading. The inventions in Connecticut alone include vulcanized rubber by Charles Goodyear; the stone crusher of Eli Whitney's nephew, Eli Whitney Blake, which

revolutionized road building; the Rogers Brothers' method of silver-plating flatware; Ithiel Town's wooden-lattice truss bridge; and the measuring instrument invented by Francis A. Pratt and Amos Whitney that was accurate to .00001 of an inch.

There was similar creativity in other states. One of the first railroads in America, powered by horses, was built in Quincy in 1827 to bring granite from quarries for the Bunker Hill Monument. Samuel F. B. Morse, the inventor of the telegraph, was a native of Charlestown, Massachusetts; Alexander Graham Bell invented the telephone in Boston with the financial support of the Forbes China-trade and railroad wealth. The first American gasoline automobile was driven by Frank Duryea in Springfield, Massachusetts, in 1893.

Banking, which in its modern sense was nonexistent in New England until after the Revolutionary War, became big business during the 19th Century. When banks were formed in the region in the late 1700s and early 1800s, they grew with astonishing speed and played an important part not only in the economic development of New England, but in the nation's westward expansion.

The first to make its appearance was the Massachusetts Bank, established in Boston in 1784. Its founders said that they had learned through "the

Experience of many Nations that well regulated Banks are highly useful to Society, as they promote Punctuality in the Performance of contracts, increase the medium of Trade, facilitate the Payment of Taxes, prevent the Exportation of, and furnish a safe deposit for Cash. . . ." Apparently "the Experience" was an influential teacher; a number of other banks soon opened their doors in New England.

Because, except for brief intervals, there was no uniform paper currency in the United States until 1863, the issuing of bank notes that served as the paper money of the times was a major function of these early financial institutions. The notes were backed only by a bank's assets, and therefore their acceptability as currency was dependent upon the people's confidence in an institution's stability. In this period of great expansion throughout the nation, many banks in other parts of the country overextended themselves and collapsed. Few Yankee bankers, however, made this error. Not only did they operate their institutions conservatively, but New England's banking regulations were among the most stringent in the United States. Thus, there was great public trust in currency issued by New England banks.

The banks, of course, were vital in financing New England's growing industries, but their financial activities were not restricted to the northeast corner of the nation. As previously stated, New England capital pioneered the building of railroads in the West; it also financed copper mining in Michigan and flour mills in Minnesota. The banks' rate of growth makes such far-flung operations understandable; by 1838 about one third of the nation's banks and more than a quarter of all the bank capital in the U.S. were centered in the region.

Insurance, New England's other great financial empire, rose from the sea. It originated in Boston and Hartford late in the 18th Century when groups of merchants agreed to share the financial loss if a ship belonging to one of them was attacked by pirates or was lost in a storm. In time the loose partnerships of underwriters formed themselves into insurance companies. Expansion into other fields—fire, casualty and life insurance—took place largely in the 19th Century. The earliest known printed insurance policy in America was drawn up on February 8, 1794, by the company of Sanford and Wadsworth in Hartford, giving a local homeowner, William Imlay, £800 of fire insurance for one year at the rate of .5 per cent. (The pound continued to be used as a monetary unit for many years after the Revolution.)

Hartford became nationally recognized as "the insurance capital of the United States" by surviving the huge financial drain brought about by the disastrous fires that swept New York City in 1835 and Chicago in 1871. When Eliphalet Terry, President of the Hartford Fire Insurance Company, heard the news of the New York fire, he hurried to the Hartford Bank and obtained a promise of unlimited backing. He then dashed to Manhattan in a sleigh through the below-zero December weather. Finding most of the New York insurance companies ruined by the 700-building blaze, Terry announced that his concern would pay in full every claim made on one of its policies. He also mentioned that he was ready to accept new business and was promptly swamped with applications, which almost balanced his losses from the fire. After the Chicago fire it was Marshall Jewell who stood up on a packing box and announced that Hartford's Phoenix Insurance Company was ready to pay off every policyholder immediately.

New England would have been even more powerful economically if its states had not been so isolated geographically from the coal and iron ore that built the industry of the Middle West. When steelmaking became the key to industrial growth, New England fell behind the rest of the nation. Larger calamities were still to come, however. In the 1920s the region's economy was dealt a direct and devastating blow when a combination of technological advances and wage differential between areas of the U.S. all but shattered the textile industry. Cotton mills in the South had been providing serious competition since the 1890s. And when synthetic fabrics were introduced in the 1920s, the Southern textile manufacturers saw that synthetics would cut into the cotton market and began to produce the new products. The Yankees stubbornly continued to produce cloth only from natural fibers. Even more serious was the growing disparity between wages paid in New England and the South. As a result, many textile manufacturers closed their New England mills and began operations in the Southern states. New England's once dominant position in the industry was gone, and it has never been regained.

But in the age of electronics after World War II, New England revived again as it did in the era of worldwide sea trading after the Revolution and in the rise of its water-powered factories after the Civil War. And with the coming of the Space Age, the land of the Puritans, which Alfred North Whitehead in 1942 described as the capital of the world of modern learning, may be on the threshold of its greatest renaissance.

Well-wishers line the deck and other guests assemble on shore to cheer the launching of the Yankee clipper *Glory of the Seas* in Boston Harbor in 1869. In the foreground, wearing a top hat, is the ship's designer, the famous clipper builder Donald McKay.

Ships, machines and rich Yankees

During the 19th Century, New England became a prodigy of industrial growth, productivity and economic strength. The region's cargo ships helped the U.S. command the seas; its goods reached world markets; its banks and insurance companies steadily acquired greater power.

Unwittingly, the Yankees had been preparing for the new age for generations. Finding the area's soil unfit for large-scale farming, they had early turned to shipping, business and handicraft industries for a livelihood. Thus they had both the outlook and the skills needed in the industrialized 19th Century. In addition, the region had three natural resources of huge value: good ports, lumber for shipbuilding and water power to run machines. The time, the people and the place were perfectly geared for one another, and New England made the most of its opportunities.

The proud sailing vessels that made history

The great fleet of New England-built sailing ships were the fastest vessels on the seas for much of the 19th Century. Even the merchant marine of Britain, traditional ruler of the waves, could not match the speed of Yankee liners. Most renowned of all New England vessels was the trim, beautiful Yankee clipper. Clipper ships were in their glory in the 1850s, years of the California Gold Rush and the booming Orient trade, when shippers paid high premiums for fast delivery. But in the post-Civil War years the development of the steamship made commercial sailing vessels obsolete, and New England lost much of its importance as a shipbuilding center.

Captain Wylie R. Dickenson entertains his wife and daughter about 1895 in his cabin aboard the *Aryan*, the last full-rigged wooden sailing ship built for commerce. In the 19th Century the master of a sailing vessel would often take his family with him on his voyages.

HELMSMAN

SHIP'S CARPENTER AND FIRST MATE

Life aboard the Yankee clipper *Great Admiral* was hard and dangerous for the officers and crew, but the men took pride in knowing their ship could show her wake to any other type of sailing vessel afloat. Although less extreme in design than earlier clippers, the *Great Admiral* was built for speed. Cargo space was sacrificed to provide a trim hull. The craft was heavily sailed and required a large crew to handle the canvas under the orders of a captain always driving to cut sailing times. Early in the 19th Century, crews consisted primarily of Yankees, but by 1877, when the pictures at right were taken, recent immigrants were manning the ships.

STEWARD IN CHARGE OF CABINS

SEAMAN AND SECOND MATE

A lonely figure on the poop deck, Captain
Walter Mallett surveys the complex rigging of
his square-rigged bark, *Guy C. Goss*, in harbor
at Bath, Maine, in 1879. Maine continued to
build such great sailing ships after the trade
had languished elsewhere in New England.

Prosperity from looms in the factory towns

Factories as well as ships contributed to New England's flourishing economy in the 19th Century. Soon after the invention of the spinning machine and the power loom in Britain, New England became the nation's prime textile manufacturer. But building the first machinery taxed Yankee ingenuity. Because Britain not only forbade the exporting

UNBALING RAW COTTON FOR THE CLEANING MACHINE

DRAWING, OR STRAIGHTENING, THE FIBERS BEFORE SPINNING

REMOVING BOBBINS OF NEWLY SPUN YARN

EXAMINING THE FINISHED COTTON CLOTH

of machinery but would not even let plans be sent out, men like Francis Cabot Lowell went to England, memorized the designs and thus "smuggled" them to New England. By 1860 the region was producing about 75 per cent of all cotton goods made in the United States. Great mills soon converted many quiet communities into busy manufacturing towns.

Women weave cotton thread into finished cloth on the giant power looms of the Pacific Mills in Lawrence, Massachusetts. The entire process of converting raw cotton to fabric was done in these mills. A large proportion of the work force consisted of women and children.

Using production methods devised in the late 18th Century—the assembling of machine-made, interchangeable parts—Springfield Armory workers in Springfield, Massachusetts, produce rifles on a mass basis. The armory has made guns for the U.S. Army since 1795.

Adapting old skills to new machines and methods

When machines were invented in the late 18th and the 19th Centuries to mass-produce clocks, shoes and firearms, it was no happenstance that New England became (as it remains) one of the world's great centers of these industries. Yankees had been making these products on a handicraft basis ever since colonial times. There was, therefore, a large supply of skilled craftsmen who could adapt quickly to the age of machinery and mass production.

Another factor that helped the growth of the new mechanized industries in New England was the absence of trade guilds. In Europe the guilds and certain other groups feared the machines would throw men out of work, and sabotage, strikes and boycotts were common. Without such handicaps, the new methods flourished in New England, forming the basis for modern assembly-line production.

"Pulling-over" machines stretch part of a shoe over the last, or wood form, at the Stetson Shoe Company in South Weymouth, Massachusetts, around 1900. Shoemaking was an ancient skill in New England; the first shoemaking shop in America opened in Lynn, Massachusetts, in 1635.

With samples of their work displayed behind them, employees of E. Ingraham and Company, clockmakers, assemble outside the factory in Bristol, Connecticut, in the 1880s. The country's first mass-produced, machine-made clocks were turned out in New England in 1808.

Making money with money in banking and insurance

New England's success in shipping, manufacturing and commerce during the 19th Century nourished, and was in turn nourished by, the area's burgeoning banks and insurance companies. Thanks to Yankee shrewdness and conservatism, stability and growth went hand in hand. In a period when bank failures were commonplace elsewhere in the nation, New England banks remained solid. The insurance companies, first formed to share the risks of sea voyages, soon expanded their activities and wrote accident, life and liability policies. Today New England remains one of the great financial centers of the world.

At work in a skullcap, Stephen Holbrook Rhodes, president of Boston's John Hancock Mutual Life Insurance Company from 1879 to 1909, examines some papers as an aide stands by. The company, founded in 1862, today has assets of well over eight billion dollars.

Tellers, clerks and bookkeepers freeze in position for a photograph taken at the First National Bank of Boston in the late 1800s. Founded in 1784, the First National, like other New England banks, grew rapidly with the region's expanding economy.

5

Decades
of Immigration

They are all descendants of Englishmen and, of course, are united by all the great bonds of society—language, religion, government, manners and interest." Timothy Dwight, President of Yale College, wrote that description of the people of Boston in 1796, but the observation would have been equally accurate about any New England town from the early 17th Century until almost the middle of the 19th. For more than 200 years the homogeneous structure of New England's population remained unchanged. Oddly enough, the toppling of the structure began as the result of a potato blight in Ireland, some 3,000 miles away.

The blight struck Ireland in the mid-1840s, and during the next five years an estimated one million persons died of starvation. The famine also triggered one of the greatest mass emigrations in history; between 1846 and 1851 about 1.6 million Irishmen left their native land. The vast majority headed for the United States, and a high percentage of them came to New England. The change in the pattern of population there was rapid and drastic.

Bystanders cheer on the marchers in South Boston's Saint Patrick's Day Parade. In this celebration, dear to the local Irish-Americans, Boston politicians of all nationalities and parties become Irishmen for a day and march in honor of Ireland's patron saint.

In many areas the once-dominant Yankees were soon outnumbered.

The sheer number of newcomers was, in itself, sufficient to upset the status quo and to create gigantic problems. But seriously aggravating the situation was the fact that language was the only one of the "great bonds of society" that the immigrants shared with the older residents—and even the language had an unfamiliar lilt. The Roman Catholic religion of the Irish, their concepts of government, their manners, interests and attitudes were totally at odds with those of the Yankees. Under the circumstances conflict was inevitable.

Boston had a population of 115,000 in 1845. During the next 10 years, more than 150,000 poverty-stricken Irishmen poured into Boston Harbor. But that was only part of the migration. Another huge contingent of emigrants from Ireland crossed the Atlantic at a lower fare by traveling as ballast aboard empty cargo ships heading for Canada to pick up lumber. After landing at New Brunswick or Quebec, these immigrants traveled by rail or simply walked down to New England.

Most of the Irish who came to New England at this time settled in the seacoast cities, especially in Boston, which was then smaller in area and even more crowded than it is today. These people had no money to travel farther inland, and besides, they were determined, after their tragic experience on the farms of Ireland, to make their living as city dwellers. Unfortunately, these uneducated peasants were ill-equipped for urban life. With no business experience or mechanical skills to offer, they could find only the lowest-paying manual jobs as dock workers, pick-and-shovel laborers or domestics. Not unexpectedly, the only homes they could afford were in cellars, shacks and hastily built tenements in the slum districts.

There were some more affluent and adventurous Irish immigrants in that pre-Civil War period who pushed on in small groups from the seaports to the younger and still growing towns of the Great Lakes area and the Mississippi Valley. There assimilation was relatively easy and peaceful. But in the older, stricter and well-established New England society, the Irish newcomers were both a burden and a threat. And their alien—and hated—religion and strange Celtic ways stirred up dormant feelings of distrust and prejudice that have subsided only in recent years.

The Yankees were not unique in their antipathy. In New York, Philadelphia and all the other communities that felt the impact of mass immigration, the newcomers also faced hostility and discrimination, severely limited job opportunities and dreadful living conditions. However, the confrontation between Yankees and Irish was especially bitter. Both peoples were proud and unbending, and because their beliefs, aspirations, customs and viewpoints were diametrically opposed, the frequent contacts between the two groups created not understanding but friction.

Neither the Yankees nor the Irish Catholics viewed tolerance of other religions as a virtue. The early Puritans had founded Massachusetts as a Biblical commonwealth—the "American Israel" it was often called—and had viewed themselves as the chosen people, "the sifted grain." From the beginning, they considered those who differed as enemies; Quakers and Baptists were persecuted, and Roger Williams was driven from Massachusetts for his advocacy of religious tolerance. The religion most feared and hated by the Puritans, however, was Roman Catholicism. The Puritans had gained their name as a sect in England because they had wanted to "purify" the Anglican Church of all remaining taints of popery, and they had left England because they failed. Over the years this bias gradually lost its vigor, and peoples of other religions, including Catholics, were cordially accepted. But in pre-1850 New England the members of other faiths were comparatively few. When the tidal wave of Irish Catholics struck the region, all of the old prejudices were resurrected.

The Irish were no less militantly intolerant. "A *Christian* Protestant . . . is a contradiction in terms," said one of their spokesmen. Non-Catholics were religious outcasts and should, if necessary, be forced to mend their ways. "No man has or can have a *religious* or a *moral* right to be of any religion but the true religion," editorialized a Catholic journal of the time. On one point, however, the publication saw eye to eye with the Yankee Protestants: "Every religion by its very nature is intolerant of every other, and condemns itself, if it is not."

Religion was not the only chasm that separated Yankees and Irish. British ancestry was a source of pride to the Yankees. They remained "solidly and steadily English, settled down into an English mold and hardened into it." The Irish immigrants, because of England's centuries of exploitation of their homeland, despised everything British and even after settling in the U.S. continued to send money back to the old country to help finance rebellions against the Crown. Yankees were the leaders of the antislavery movement; the Irish, fearing competition for jobs from freed Negroes, were proslavery. The Yankees believed in a fluid society that permitted a man of ability and drive to move upward economically and socially. The Irish preferred strict class lines. Judith O'Rourke, a washerwoman quoted in the *Boston Pilot*, an Irish Catholic publication, reflected this viewpoint when she scoffed at the idea of sending her children to high school and college. She expressed the hope that her sons would "grow up honest good men, like them that's gone afore them, not ashamed of their station, or honest toil." The Yankees had faith in the perfectibility of man and thus were basically reformers who supported such movements as women's rights and the improvement of prisons. The Irish were suspicious of reform and usually fought it. These were only a few of the areas of conflict between Yankee and Irishman. The *Pilot* summed up the situation when it stated that "cooperation for any length of time in important matters between *true* Catholics and *real* Protestants is morally impossible."

The Yankees used all their considerable power to disparage the Irish, to discriminate against them, and to hold them down economically and politically. The Irish were portrayed as drunkards and criminals, as spawners of illegitimate children and as people who preferred taking charity to working. They were considered subversives whose only loyalty was to a foreign pope; all secrets, personal or state, they might learn were supposedly passed on to him via the confessional. Even non-Yankees came to accept this image of the Irish. For example, Boston Negroes, themselves discriminated against, did not want Irishmen as neighbors.

Vehemently anti-Catholic political organizations with patriotic-sounding names began to flourish in New England in the early 1850s. One such association was the Order of the Star-Spangled Banner, better known as the "Know-Nothing Party" because the members replied, "I know nothing," when asked about the activities of the order. By 1854 the Know-Nothings were strong enough in Massachusetts to elect a governor and to control both houses of the state legislature as well as Boston's city council. One of the first acts of the new governor was to disband the Irish military companies—primarily marching societies, but viewed by the Yankees as a threat to law and order; the Know-Nothing Boston council also blocked the Jesuits from buying land in the city's North End as a site for their proposed Boston College. Because the Know-Nothing office-holders were inexperienced, and therefore inept, in government, most of them were not re-elected. The anti-Irish sentiment did not diminish, however. In 1857 the Massachusetts legislature made ability to read and write a prerequisite for voting, and two years later a bill was passed that denied voting rights to a foreigner until two years after naturalization. Both measures, of course, were aimed primarily at reducing the political power of the Irish.

In the years that followed, as other immigrant groups arrived, they met less open hostility than had the Irish of the famine years, because their movement to New England was more gradual and orderly, and because they came at a time when the region's expanding industrial economy was better able to absorb them.

The boom of manufacturing after the Civil War drew a steady stream of French Canadians into such industrial towns as Manchester in New Hampshire, Lewiston and Biddeford in Maine, and Pawtucket and Woonsocket in Rhode Island. There was also a considerable influx of English-speaking Canadian Protestants, most of them from Nova Scotia and the other Maritime Provinces.

Between 1880 and the beginning of World War I, another great tide of immigration came from Europe—Italians, Poles, Lithuanians, Scandinavians, Germans, Russian Jews, the seafaring Portuguese, who settled in the fishing ports of Massachusetts and Rhode Island, and more Irish. Many of these newcomers were Roman Catholics, thereby increasing the Yankees' suspicion and distrust. Most of the German and Scandinavian Protestant immigrants, whose religion would have made them more acceptable to the Yankees, were affluent enough to travel beyond New England to the more promising farmlands of the Middle West.

By the time these immigrants began arriving in the closing decades of the 19th Century, the original Irish contingent was the only large group of foreigners that had been on the New England scene for a period of more than 30 years. Shunned socially and economically by the Yankees, naturally clannish and politically skilled, and clinging to their suspect Catholic religion, they had established a tight and securely entrenched "New Ireland" of their own.

"At the end of the last century," an Irish Bostonian wrote in the 1950s, "the Irish were in about the same position as the Mexicans of San Antonio are today." Actually, by 1900 the Boston Irish comprised about half of the city's population, had elected an Irish mayor and were about to elect a second one, and were becoming one of the most powerful ethnic groups in city politics in America. The newcoming Italians, Slavs, Russian Jews and French Canadians found that the long-established Irish in New England were almost as aloof and as difficult to deal with as the chilly Yankees.

However, even by the turn of the century there was still no rapprochement in Boston between the Yankee Protestants and the Irish Catholics. Boston newspapers before World War I segregated social items about Yankees and Irish Catholics on different pages of the Sunday society sections. The satiric jingle, "And this is good old Boston/The home of the bean and the cod/Where the Lowells talk to the Cabots/And the Cabots talk only to God," was first recited by an Irishman, John Collins Bossidy, at a Holy Cross alumni dinner in 1910.

Although the Irish improved their economic position and moved upward from the pick and shovel into business, the professions and politics, they and all other newer immigrant groups had a harder struggle to gain a social foothold in New England than did their counterparts in other sections of America. In Yankee territory they faced the closed door of an older society, jealously proud of its genealogy and historic traditions. The proper Yankee wanted no intimacy with any outsider whose family prestige, firmly based on events of the past, could not compare with his own.

"The Irish who went to Chicago and St. Louis . . . had the advantage of growing up with their city," William V. Shannon wrote in his political and social study, *The American Irish*. "Those who went to New York and Philadelphia encountered wealthy classes that were fluid and diverse in their makeup, and less directly continuous with the past. The Irish who went to Boston could not have been worse off, psychologically speaking, unless they had gone to Charleston, South Carolina."

Action bred reaction. The strong anti-Yankee resentment of the Irish was as hot and as easily aroused as their anti-British fervor. Football games between the Irish of Boston College and the Yankee Protestants of Harvard were discontinued after World War I, partially because of unusual roughness of play on the field and violence among spectators in the stands. The games have never been resumed. The Irish parents of Joe McKenney, the outstanding high-school football star in Boston in 1923, were indignant when Joe said he had been offered a scholarship at Harvard. "You'll go to a Catholic college like Boston College, or you'll go to work," his mother told him. He was in a Boston College uniform that fall.

Promising football material was not the only loss suffered by the Yankees in their war with the Irish. Early in this century a Protestant church in the Irish district of Roxbury caught fire, and the Irish firemen were somewhat leisurely about answering the alarm. As they made their unhurried way toward the blaze, an Irish ward leader called to a group of his constituents standing on a corner near the church, "What kind of Catholics are you, anyway? Why aren't you down the street enjoying the fire?"

By 1900, Irish politicians were powerful, especially in Boston, but the same Yankee Brahmins who guarded New England's social heritage also continued to control the wealth. As recently as 1945, when John Gunther was doing research in New England for his *Inside U.S.A.*, he found that in predominantly Irish Catholic Boston only four out of the 30 Chamber of Commerce directors were of Irish descent, no large department stores were Irish-owned, and not one Irishman was a member of the executive body of the New England Council, the region's business-promotion organization. A Boston woman of Irish lineage who now lives in New York heard someone at a cocktail party talking about the cobblestone pavement in Louisburg Square on Beacon Hill. "Those aren't cobblestones," the woman said with deep feeling. "Those are Irish heads."

Inevitably, time—with a strong assist from a family named Kennedy—has brought about a major change in the Yankee-Irish relationship. Joseph P. Kennedy, the father of President John F. Kennedy,

was one of the first Irishmen to get a foothold in New England's banking and financing world on Boston's State Street. The Ambassador, as his son's White House associates called him, often remarked that as a youth he was more aware than most Irishmen of the condescension with which the Yankee Brahmins looked down on his class of people because he was more closely involved with them in college and in his early days as a Boston financier. His grandfather was a refugee from the Irish famine who settled near the Cunard Line docks in East Boston in 1849, but in the next generation, Patrick J. Kennedy, Joseph's father, became a Democratic political leader in the same neighborhood, owned three saloons, a wholesale liquor business and a coal company. Unlike other Irish boys, who went to the Jesuits' Boston College or Holy Cross in Worcester (if they were able to go to college at all), Joe Kennedy enrolled at Harvard and became a member of the prestigious D.U. Club and Hasty Pudding.

After his graduation from Harvard in 1912, Kennedy again moved away from the Irish world and into a more exclusively Yankee domain when he began his career in banking. Irish bankers in Boston were then as scarce as Irishmen with Brahmin inlaws. Kennedy's father-in-law, the peppery and outspoken John F. Fitzgerald, who was Boston's mayor at that time, asked the president of a leading bank in the city why he had no Irishmen on his board of directors.

"Well," the banker said uneasily, "a couple of the tellers are Irish."

"Yes, and I suppose the charwomen are, too," Fitzgerald said.

In 1914 Joe Kennedy, at age 25, became the youngest bank president in the United States when he raised $45,000 and gained control of the Columbia Trust Company in his East Boston neighborhood. The next step up for him was to become a utility-company director.

Twice in the next few years Kennedy's name was proposed for membership on the board of trustees of the Massachusetts Electric Company, and both times he was turned down. Then in 1917, about the time that his second son, John F., was born, he was finally elected. The company's chairman admitted to him that he had been rejected earlier only because he was an Irish Catholic. Kennedy's election caused a major stir on State Street.

After breaking through the first barrier, Kennedy went on to another important position, the managership of the stock department in the Boston office of Hayden, Stone Incorporated, a New York investment house. But, as he said later, he could never feel that he belonged in the inner circle of the Adamses, Cabots and Forbeses. Although he was now theoretically accepted by the Yankees who had opposed his utility-company trusteeship, he was always conscious that his Irish roots and his religion marked him as an oddity. In 1926 Kennedy, already a trader on Wall Street, moved his family to New York, making his departure in grand and defiant Irish style. He chartered a Pullman parlor car, brought it to a railroad siding near his suburban Brookline home, loaded it with his children and their nursemaids and belongings, and carried them directly to the Riverdale section of New York City, where he had bought a new house.

By the late 1950s, when the Kennedy family had gained great wealth and national prominence and their son was moving toward the Presidency, a Boston political supporter hailed them proudly as "our first Boston Irish Brahmins." However, except for summer vacations on Cape Cod, none of the Kennedys had lived in Massachusetts since their father had moved them away in the private railroad car. As a Senator from that state, and as President, John F. Kennedy maintained as a voting address a small apartment on the unfashionable side of Beacon Hill, but he seldom slept there. When he returned from wartime service in 1945 and decided to run for office in the Congressional district of his ancestors, he knew few people in Boston outside of his relatives and the professors who had taught him at Harvard. He reminded one political commentator of the typical British upper-class politician, the Oxford-educated scion who leaves his London society life to try for the House of Commons from a remote constituency in Yorkshire where his forefathers had a castle and where his name is well known, but where he, himself, is a stranger. (However, Senator Edward Kennedy has been a resident of Boston since the early 1960s.)

In 1957, three years before he became President, John Kennedy, then a U.S. Senator, was elected to Harvard's Board of Overseers. His father, remembering the Massachusetts Electric Company, was more impressed by this honor than by any of his son's political successes. Somebody asked the Ambassador some time later if he thought a Catholic could ever occupy the White House.

"If a Catholic like Jack, and an Irish one from Boston at that, can get elected as an overseer at Harvard," the elder Kennedy said, "he can get elected to anything."

Despite the Kennedy record, most Irish doubt that they will ever become completely assimilated

James Michael Curley *(left)* and John F. "Honey Fitz" Fitzgerald, Boston's most colorful Irish mayors, show Democratic solidarity at a 1928 meeting. Fitzgerald, the grandfather of the late President John F. Kennedy, was elected mayor in 1905. Curley, who served four terms as mayor between 1914 and 1950, was jailed for fraud during his last term but retained office while in prison.

in the New England environment. The terms of their present-day coexistence with the Yankees, however, are far different in character from the earlier impasse when the two contingents, in the words of Oscar Handlin, seemed to have "no more contact than if 3,000 miles of ocean rather than a wall of ideas stood between them." Many of the old antagonisms were buried with the late James Michael Curley, the Irish Mayor of Boston who advanced his colorful political career by ridiculing the Yankee Brahmins. "The term 'codfish aristocracy,'" Curley often declared, "is a reflection on the fish. . . . [The Yankees] got rich selling opium to the Chinese, rum to the Indians, or trading in slaves" —an oversimplified but not completely erroneous observation. Significantly, it was in the same month that Curley died, November 1958, that John F. Kennedy, the complete antithesis of traditional, Curley-type Irish Catholic politicians, was re-elected to the Senate from Massachusetts with the support of the staunchly Yankee Republican Boston *Herald*. In his remarkable victory Kennedy rolled up the largest plurality in the history of the state and swept such Brahmin communities as the town of Beverly, which elected a Democrat to a major office for the first time in its history.

Perhaps even more indicative of the softening of

attitudes on both sides of the Yankee-Irish conflict was the nationally televised performance of Mozart's *Requiem* during a Mass for the late President Kennedy in 1964. The Mass was said in the Roman Catholic Cathedral of the Holy Cross, and the *Requiem* was played by the Boston Symphony Orchestra, one of the Brahmins' most cherished institutions, and sung by a 180-voice chorus that included the Harvard Glee Club. The performance was given at the suggestion of Henry B. Cabot, president of the symphony's board of trustees, and he and his Proper Bostonian associates were in attendance. To both the Protestants and the Catholics of New England, it was a moving and precedent-shattering event.

In today's New England the largest non-Yankee ethnic groups besides the Irish are the Italians and the French Canadians or, as many of the latter prefer to be called, the Franco-Americans. Like the Irishmen before them, the Italian immigrants had avoided farm life in the New World and had congregated—usually close to the Irish—in the larger manufacturing cities of Massachusetts, Rhode Island and Connecticut. The Italians and Irish had few cultural bonds in common except religion, and they competed fiercely for jobs and in politics. Many of the Italians sided politically with the Yankees and became Republicans; the Irish were almost solidly Democratic.

The old rivalry still flares up socially and politically. A few years ago the Republican Governor of Massachusetts, John A. Volpe, who is of Italian extraction, was a guest of honor at an Irish political corned-beef-and-cabbage luncheon on St. Patrick's Day in South Boston. A lively controversy in the local news at the time concerned parking restrictions around the State House. While discussing it in a talk before the large gathering, one Irish politician turned to Volpe and, recalling the stereotype of the Italian barrel-organ player, said, "And if you don't watch out for those no-parking signs, Governor, they'll haul away your hurdy-gurdy."

The Italian immigrants had felt cut off from the main current of New England community life because of the language barrier, but their children soon overcame this handicap. The same cannot be said for the French Canadians, who live mostly in the smaller manufacturing towns of northern New England and the mill cities of Rhode Island. They still cling proudly to their French tongue, send their children to Catholic schools where French is spoken, attend churches with French services and read French newspapers. In cities like Lewiston, Maine, or Manchester, New Hampshire, most merchants have at least one French-speaking clerk.

Consequently, the French-speaking population in New England, although strong in numbers, has always been isolated from its neighboring ethnic groups. In recent years, however, their insulation has been weakened. Some families have simply come to the conclusion that it is quixotic to hold to French as a first language in an English-speaking nation. Television has also played a part in the change. "More and more of our teenagers today, thanks to TV, are refusing flatly to speak French," a French Canadian in Biddeford, Maine, said recently. "Our older folks are shocked, but there isn't much that they can do about it." Another factor in the change is the financial inability of many of the French communities to support a complete parochial school system. In the absence of Catholic high schools, students attend public schools where all instruction is in English.

The political and economic lot of the French Canadians in the northern New England mill towns today, where they work for relatively low wages, is somewhat similar to the situation of the Irish at the turn of the century; the Franco-Americans have political control of certain communities because they are the majority of the population, but almost all local banks and large business concerns are in the hands of the Yankees.

The metamorphosis of any group from second-class to first-class citizenship in the United States always requires time, but the transformation has eventually taken place. Perhaps two incidents, one important, the other insignificant, illustrate the change in attitude that has occurred in recent years. One took place in 1966 when, with considerable support from the Republican Brahmins of Massachusetts, Edward Brooke became the first Negro in the history of the United States to be elected to the United States Senate by popular vote. The second incident shows that the prejudices of the Yankees' old enemy, the Irish, may also be eroding. Not long ago the son of a Boston Irishman was offered a choice of scholarships at both Catholic and non-Catholic colleges. Recalling the McKenney family's cold rejection of their son Joe's opportunity to go to Harvard in 1924, the father hesitantly approached his own aged father for a word of guidance. "Young Matty has a chance of going either to Boston College, Holy Cross or Harvard, Dad," the younger man said. "Which one do you think he ought to take?"

The elderly Irishman stared at his son in disbelief. "You *amadawn!*" he shouted, using the Gaelic epithet for a simpleton. "Harvard, of course!"

A bearded Irish patriarch, Captain John Fulham, skipper of a Boston fishing boat, joins his family in an 1890s portrait. Penniless on arrival in 1864, Captain John and wife Ellen *(seated, left)* founded a prosperous family line still flourishing today *(pages 108-109).*

A vigorous heritage from many lands

Nowhere in the nation is the colonial heritage more revered than in New England. Yet there are few regions where peoples of other than English stock play a more vital role or comprise so large a proportion of the population. Large-scale non-English immigration into New England began with the Irish of the 1840s, who fled from famine at home to settle in the U.S., especially in Boston, as unskilled laborers, scorned by the native Yankees. Other groups—the French of Canada, the Italians, the Portuguese—came later in the century, lured by jobs in the region's factories. The newer arrivals also faced prejudice and like the Irish had little to offer but a desire to work. But this has served them well, for in a few generations each group has secured a significant measure of prosperity and acceptance, as the family-album pictures on the next eight pages demonstrate.

Founder of the clan, John Fulham is shown in a detail from the portrait on page 107. In the 1890s John was better off than most of the Irish; his fishing boat earned enough money to keep his daughters out of domestic service—the fate of many Irish girls. John's line is traced *(below, right)* through his youngest son.

An Irish family in food processing

Of all New England's many ethnic groups the Irish-Americans are the oldest and most completely assimilated. So strong was the tide of mid-19th Century Irish immigration into Boston that by 1855 almost 29 per cent of the city's residents were Irish-born. Hated, derided and discriminated against by the Yankee majority, subject to vile attacks upon their customs and their Roman Catholic religion, the Irish huddled together in slum ghettos. They worked at menial jobs, scrimped and saved until, by the turn of the century, they began to be powerful enough to make their weight felt. First in politics and then, more slowly, in business, they entered the mainstream of New England life. One of their own, John Kennedy, became President, and many have achieved success similar to that of the Fulhams.

THE FULHAM FAMILY

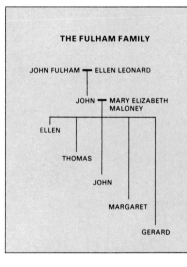

Builder of a family fortune, John N. Fulham advanced his education after high school by attending night courses in bookkeeping at a Boston business school. By 1912 he was in a position to buy the Haskins Fish Company, a wholesale firm, and in 1913 John married Mary Elizabeth Maloney *(right)*, from the respectable suburb of Winthrop,

where the newlyweds took up residence. Already John's achievements indicated continuing financial and social success and a life far different from the circumstances his parents knew. All of John's five children were educated at private schools, although careful attention was paid to teaching the three boys the intricacies of the fish industry.

Third generation

Consolidators of a family fortune, John N. Fulham's three sons—Thomas *(left)*, Gerard *(center)* and John—pose in 1958 with the then Senator John F. Kennedy at a Boston fund-raising breakfast. Taking over their father's faltering business shortly after World War II, the brothers soon returned it to prosperity. Among their innovations were advertising—a radical step in the tradition-bound New England fishing industry—and the packaging of frozen-fish products to be sold throughout the nation under the three brothers' "Four Fishermen" label *(top)*. The fourth fisherman in the name stood for the customer. By opening new markets, this effort helped shore up the entire Boston fishing industry. In 1947 Tom Fulham *(on right, upper left)* was on hand for the first regularly scheduled shipment of fish from Boston to the Midwest. The brothers are now counted among Massachusetts' leading citizens and have held many important posts: one has been Chairman of the State Board of Natural Resources. But tradition remains strong. All are active church members, and their sister, Sister Mary Vianney Fulham *(upper right)*, heads a Roman Catholic college in New Hampshire.

First generation

The very model of a modern clothing merchant, Arthur Henri Benoit *(right)* came to Maine from St. Dominique, Quebec, as a factory hand in the late 1870s. By 1906, when this portrait was taken, he was already prosperous. The card below announces his employment at Webber's clothing store in Saco, Maine, where he was so successful that he was soon made a partner in the firm's Westbrook, Maine, store *(third building from the right, below)*. In 1893 Benoit became sole owner of that store, and soon he owned several others, including the biggest men's store in Portland.

ARTHUR BENOIT
A l'honneur d'informer ses amis et le public Canadiens en général, qu'il est entré au service de

MR. C. H. WEBBER,

❀ MARCHAND ❀ DE ❀ HARDES, ❀

NO. 55 RUE MAIN, SACO.

On me trouvera au magasin, les Mardi, Jeudi et Samedi soirs.

Une vesite est respectueusement sollicitée.

Son and heir Henri Benoit sticks to business as manager of his father's Portland store in 1917. Already the family was showing a marked disposition to break away from the restrictive customs of the Franco-American community. Henri attended a junior college in Buffalo, New York, at a time when few Franco-Americans pursued higher education. Later he served in the American Army and was discharged as a lieutenant after World War I. Perhaps most unusual of all was Henri's marriage outside the ethnic group, for in 1919 he wed an Irish-American girl, Katherine Walsh.

A French family in the clothing business

Of all New England's ethnic groups, one of the largest, most widely dispersed and least assimilated are the French Canadians—or Franco-Americans, as they prefer to be called. Although many families came to New England a century ago, there are still areas where French is more commonly heard than English. In part this arises from the determination of the French to maintain their culture. Yet even among them, assimilation is taking its toll, a fact reflected in the decline of the French press in New England. In 1912 there were seven French-language dailies; today not one remains. One highly assimilated and successful family is the Benoits, shown here.

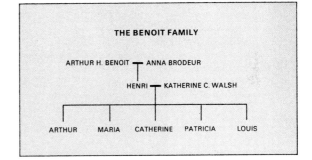

THE BENOIT FAMILY

ARTHUR H. BENOIT — ANNA BRODEUR

HENRI — KATHERINE C. WALSH

ARTHUR   MARIA   CATHERINE   PATRICIA   LOUIS

On a happy occasion, Arthur H. Benoit, grandson of the firm's founder, confers with his father, Henri, during a celebration of the company's 75th anniversary in 1965. Indicative of the Benoits' rapid assimilation is the fact that both Arthur and his brother Louis are graduates of Bowdoin College in Maine, once a Yankee stronghold.

BUSINESS AS USUAL – THE GREATER BENOITS

Responding to the postwar economic boom, the Benoits in 1947 enlarged their Portland store, adding a number of departments, including a women's wear section. Today the Benoits operate Maine's largest chain of men's clothing stores and are active in a variety of charitable, political and financial affairs. Their ties with the Franco-American community have all but vanished, and Henri's children have married into prominent non-French families.

First generation

Trained as a wigmaker for royalty, James Pettine *(above)* came to the U.S. in 1896 and found little demand for his skill in Providence, Rhode Island. Entering an allied field, James became a barber and later went into the real-estate business where he made and lost a fortune. Meanwhile he married Alvina Caruolo *(right),* another Italian immigrant. Their only child, Raymond, was born in 1912, and by the time the youngster was of school age the Pettines' fortunes had so improved that they moved from Providence's "Little Italy" to an exclusive suburb.

Austere and resplendent in his Italian Army physician's uniform, Dr. Dominico N. Golini poses for a portrait shortly before emigrating to the United States in 1902. After arriving in Providence he became the first Italian to pass the state medical examination and began his practice in the Italian community. In 1905 Dr. Golini wed Carlotta Manente *(right),* a cultured and well-educated Italian immigrant. After the doctor's death in 1913, his widow became a prominent physician. The couple's daughter, Lidia, became the wife of Raymond Pettine in 1941.

The rapid rise of the Italian-Americans

The flood tide of Italian immigration—from 1880 to the mid-1920s—was late to rise and slow to recede. But so vast were the swarms of Italians who came to southern New England that even today they form the largest foreign-born group in both Rhode Island and Connecticut. Most of the new immigrants found jobs in New England's factories and sought protection from bias in the festering ghettos called "Little Italys." But in the span of two generations many Italian-Americans, like the Pettine-Golini family shown here, have lifted themselves to respected positions in politics, the professions or business.

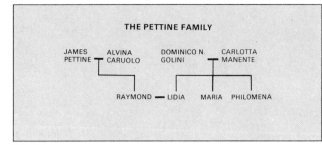

THE PETTINE FAMILY

JAMES PETTINE ⊤ ALVINA CARUOLO   DOMINICO N. GOLINI ⊤ CARLOTTA MANENTE

RAYMOND — LIDIA   MARIA   PHILOMENA

Second and third generations

A lifetime ambition is realized as Raymond Pettine (center) is congratulated in 1966 by Chief Judge Edward W. Day after being sworn in as a federal judge in the U.S. District Court for Rhode Island. Beside the new judge is his wife, Lidia, and their daughter, Lydia. Judge Pettine's interest in the law stretches back to his childhood when a cousin, a successful criminal lawyer, regaled him with tales of courtroom battles. Mrs. Pettine is a choreographer of note and a founder of the American Festival Ballet.

113

The cohesive tradition of the Portuguese-Americans

Of New England's smaller ethnic groups, the Portuguese stand out as one of the most cohesive. Living mostly in Massachusetts and Rhode Island, Portuguese-Americans, like the Nunes family shown on these pages, generally sought out a rural life, though others became fishermen or factory hands. Much of the farm produce of both Rhode Island and Cape Cod is still raised by Portuguese-Americans. Devoted Roman Catholics, the Portuguese have tended to form congregations along ethnic lines, and the Church has helped maintain their traditions.

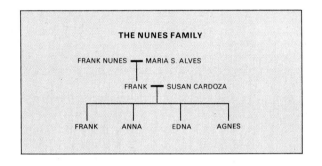

THE NUNES FAMILY

FRANK NUNES — MARIA S. ALVES

FRANK — SUSAN CARDOZA

FRANK   ANNA   EDNA   AGNES

Second generation

Standing beside his Model T Ford, Frank Nunes Jr. poses with his bride, the former Susan Cardoza, during their honeymoon in 1918. It was Frank Jr. who built his father's farm into a dairyman's show place. He was also a partner with his two brothers in a successful automobile agency in Newport, Rhode Island, and had interests in several other fields. So prosperous was Frank Jr. that he was able to go into semiretirement in 1949, at the age of 52. Thereafter he devoted himself to the life of a gentleman farmer and to his four children and 19 grandchildren.

Shortly after arriving in New England from Portugal in 1891, Frank Nunes *(seated, lower picture)* poses with a friend. His future wife, Maria Alves, is seen at left in the top photograph. Frank and Maria were married in 1895 when he was still a farm laborer earning $15 a month—a modest wage even in those days. By 1912, however, he was the owner of a 10-acre farm in Middletown, Rhode Island, and five years later he bought a 50-acre farm that he left to his children.

Rhode Island's Public Utilities Administrator, Frank L. Nunes *(left)*
checks a new dialing system with a telephone company official.
Father of five and a former treasurer of Middletown, Rhode Island,
Nunes is proud of his heritage and boasts that neither he nor his
children have anything but Portuguese blood. However, he maintains
excellent relations with all ethnic groups in Rhode Island, and in
1964 a Jewish organization named him "Man of the Year."

6

Building
the New Boston

A familiar story in Boston concerns the visitor who asked two elderly Proper Bostonian ladies at the Friday afternoon symphony concert where they bought their formidable, old-fashioned hats. "We don't buy our hats," one of the dowagers said. "We *have* them."

Like its old ladies' hats, Boston itself remained comparatively unchanged for many decades, as did the satellite city of Cambridge, whose problems are in many ways similar to Boston's. Even in the 1950s, after other big American cities had begun to rebuild and expand, the downtown section of the Hub of the Yankee Universe looked much the same as it had at the turn of the century when the last horse-drawn streetcars were still running in the Back Bay. The only skyscraper rising above the low red-brick skyline was the Custom House tower, built in 1915. And that was there only because Boston's ordinances, which prohibited the erection of tall buildings, could not be enforced on a project of the federal government. Although new homes, new shopping centers and new industry, especially in

Beacon Hill's stately old houses and churches, above a graceful sailboat on the Charles River, contrast sharply with such new structures as the State Street Bank Building *(background)* to retain the "old Boston" that gives the city its aura of historical charm.

electronics, were blooming in its outer suburbs, the city of Boston had lost 100,000 of its more affluent population between 1949 and 1959; many of the elegant town houses on Commonwealth Avenue and Beacon Hill had been turned into rooming houses and kitchenette apartments or taken over by tax-free educational institutions, and slum districts were spreading.

One cause of Boston's stagnation was its inhabitants' reverence for the past, which had stymied many well-meaning attempts to jar the city out of its old ways; for although the city's wealth of historical sites and colorful neighborhoods had helped to give Boston its special charm and atmosphere and to make it a favorite city for tourists, they had also caused many Bostonians to feel that any changes at all would hurt their town. But a more deep-seated cause was the wall of antagonism between the Yankee bankers on State Street, who controlled its business capital, and the spendthrift Irish politicians, such as the late notorious James Michael Curley. Curley liked to boast of the time that he had forced the First National Bank of Boston to give the impoverished city a loan by threatening to open water mains that would have flooded the bank's basement vaults. The antagonism between the Yankees and the Irish had produced

The man-built city

More than half of present-day central Boston is built on land created by earth-fill projects. The dark area at right, superimposed on a modern map of the city, shows the relative size of the 783-acre peninsula when the Puritans arrived in 1630. Major reclamation was begun in 1799, when 60 feet were shorn from a peak near Beacon Hill to fill in part of the shoreline for the building of Charles Street. Between 1807 and 1824 much of Beacon Hill itself was shaved off to add 50 acres in the cove adjoining Copp's Hill. In the 1830s most of the shallows seen to the right of the narrow Boston Neck were filled. The largest project was the reclamation of the flats of Great Bay started during the 1850s, which created one of the city's most fashionable residential areas—Back Bay. The last trace of the original waterfront was covered up in the 1860s, when the remainder of Town Cove was filled in.

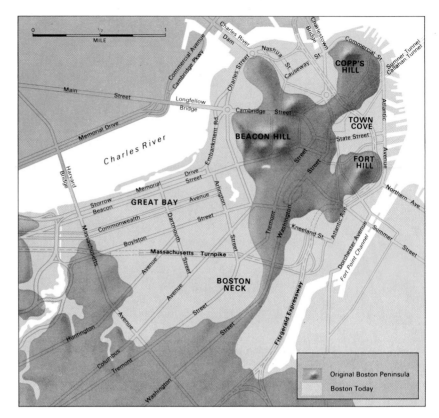

economic lethargy throughout the city, and the governmental mismanagement had caused the tax rate to climb until it was about the highest of any city in the nation.

By 1959 Curley, who had been able to hold office even while doing time for fraud in a federal penitentiary, was no longer mayor. Yet the streets of Boston were still being cleaned by hand-pushed brooms instead of by mechanized equipment, and the Yankee banking community was still in no mood to help the Irish municipal government avoid bankruptcy. The situation, however, was not as bleak as it seemed. Ever since the 1930s many Yankees and Irishmen had been working hard at narrowing the gulf that separated the two groups. The atmosphere was right for a viable rapprochement. What was needed was an entirely new kind of mayor, one who could win confidence and bring peace between State Street and City Hall.

Such a mayor, and an Irish one at that, came into office in a wheel chair in 1960—40-year-old, hard-driving John F. Collins, a polio victim who had worked his way through law school and who had big ideas about rejuvenating the city. One of his first moves was to cut some 1,200 jobs from the payroll and to enforce economy measures that enabled him to lower the tax rate. This radical departure from

past policy and his ambitious plans for the future won Collins the strong support of the Yankee Brahmin leader Charles A. Coolidge, president of Boston's Chamber of Commerce and a former member of the Harvard Corporation. Another of Collins' major allies was Monsignor Francis J. Lally, who became Chairman (unpaid) of the Boston Redevelopment Authority in 1961. Monsignor Lally's assistance was especially valuable. As editor of *The Pilot*, the voice of Boston's Roman Catholic Diocese, he carried considerable weight with the Irish-Catholic population of the city.

With the help of Coolidge, Monsignor Lally and other civic-minded citizens, Collins broke down the previously almost impenetrable barrier that had separated City Hall not only from the Yankee financial community but also from the Yankee-supported academic world of Harvard and M.I.T., an invaluable economic resource ignored by previous Boston mayors. Older Irish politicians were surprised a few years ago when Collins, on behalf of the city of Boston, gave an official luncheon honoring the several Nobel Prize winners who live in the Boston area. "Can you imagine Jim Curley giving a luncheon for Nobel Prize winners?" one of them said. "A luncheon for Pat O'Brien, or maybe for Mae West, yes, but not for Nobel Prize winners."

Even more surprising was the honorary degree that Collins received from Harvard in 1964, the first ever awarded to a mayor of Boston. The citation hailed him for giving "the old Hub a new spin."

Out of the new spin of the Hub and the friendly spirit of cooperation between its business, academic, professional and political people have come many exciting developments. With federal financial aid to supplement state and private investment, Boston in the early 1960s launched a massive and dramatic urban-renewal and neighborhood revitalizing campaign that may total two billion dollars in cost by 1975. The federal government picked a location in the area as the site of its new $50 million NASA Electronic Research Center. But much of the renewal was generated locally. During the 1950s the city's leading industrial real-estate developers, a firm with the richly Boston-sounding name of Cabot, Cabot & Forbes, had drawn many plants from the downtown district to industrial parks on Route 128, the belt expressway on the outer edge of the metropolitan area. Now the same firm turned back to the city, building in partnership with M.I.T. the research-and-development center of Technology Square near the NASA lab site on the Cambridge side of the Charles River, investing in downtown apartment- and office-building projects and buying the Ritz-Carlton, Boston's elite hotel. But the biggest and most stunning of all the changes brought to Boston in its sudden rebuilding in the 1960s were the new Prudential Center in the jaded Back Bay section and the huge Government Center complex that began rising high beside old Faneuil Hall at the downtown end of the city.

All this was accomplished by means of vigorous leadership from City Hall. When Collins became mayor in 1960, he lured Edward J. Logue to Boston from New Haven, where Logue had gained national fame for his role in the extensive rebuilding of that city. The first task Collins and Logue faced was that of clearing the way for the construction of the $175 million Prudential complex, a Boston version of New York's Rockefeller Center. For five years the Prudential Insurance Company had been ready to start the project, but it had been locked in fruitless negotiations with the city and state over taxation problems. Collins and Logue pushed the deal through quickly with a tax arrangement that had been set up by Collins' predecessor, John Hynes, a man with sound ideas but with little ability to bring them to fruition. The Prudential Center, instead of being taxed on the basis of its assessed valuation, was allowed to pay the city of Boston 20 per cent of its gross rental income,

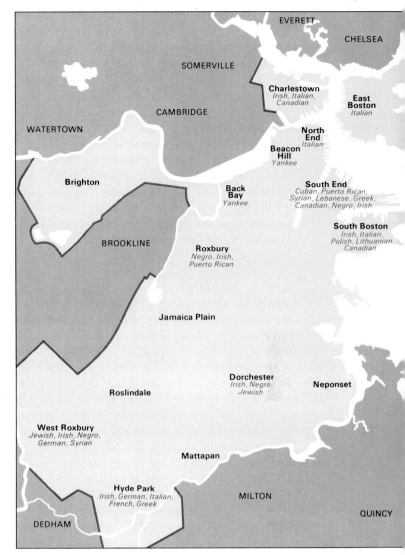

Mass migration during the 19th and early 20th Centuries transformed Boston, once the domain of English-sired Yankees, into a typical American "melting pot." The accompanying map of the city and the suburbs (the city proper is colored in green) shows where the various ethnic groups are concentrated. Although many Yankees remain on Beacon Hill or in the Back Bay section, most of them have departed to the suburbs. The rest of the city is largely given over to the Irish—by far the largest category—and to Italians, Poles, Jews, Lithuanians, Canadians, American Negroes, Syrians and others. The Irish, who first began coming to Boston in the 1840s, huddled in the North End section where they had landed. But as their economic condition improved, they moved to other sections. Today Italians are the dominant group in the North End.

with a guarantee of three million dollars a year.

In return, Boston obtained the massive Prudential Tower of 52 stories, completed in 1965 as the tallest skyscraper in the United States outside of New York and Chicago. It looms above staid Copley Square and the dome of the Christian Science Mother Church in the Back Bay, with a view of New Hampshire's mountains from its upper floors and with a downtown extension of the Massachusetts Turnpike's expressway from New York State passing underneath it. The glass-enclosed "Skywalk" on the 50th floor has become a prime tourist attraction. The gleaming tower is the centerpiece of a resplendent arrangement of plazas, arcades and new buildings, including the 29-story Sheraton-Boston Hotel (the first new big hotel built in Boston since 1927), twin 26-story apartment houses, and the city's War Memorial Auditorium, an elaborate convention and exhibition hall with a theater seating 5,800 people—all built above what used to be the passenger train yards of the Boston and Albany Railroad.

The boldest step taken by Collins and Logue was the Government Center project at the old downtown heart of the city, where Paul Revere lived two centuries ago. The concept for the project had been developed during the administration of Mayor Hynes, but little progress had been made in implementing the idea until Collins took office. To clear the site for the Government Center, 60 heavily built-up acres had to be leveled—among them the famed old honky-tonk district of Scollay Square and its most famous landmark, the Old Howard burlesque theater favored by many generations of sailors, soldiers and Harvard students. The new overall plan for this large area, designed by the Chinese-born New York architect I. M. Pei—later to become the architect of the John F. Kennedy Memorial Library in Cambridge—replaces 22 old streets with six new ones, two of them broad and sweeping avenues leading to a central plaza with an ultramodern new City Hall at its core and tall federal and state government buildings, private office buildings, a motel and a 2,000-car parking garage around its perimeter. The Government Center will also have a Catholic chapel designed by José Luis Sert, dean of Harvard's Graduate School of Design. (The chapel will be named for St. Botolph, a Seventh Century English monk who was originally called "The Boat Helper" because his prayers for men at sea were reputed to be most effective. Years of careless pronunciation by Englishmen corrupted "Boat Helper" to "Botolph" and finally to "Boston," the name given to

the town in Lincolnshire, England, and then to the settlement in Massachusetts.) Of this daring venture in bedrock urban renewal, which will tear out a whole section of the city and replace it with an entirely different one, Logue says, "Whoever thought Old Lady Boston could do it?"

A main goal of the planners is to attract many of the recently departed higher- and middle-income families back to downtown homes, within walking distance of their work. To serve them, new apartments are going up. One spectacular high-rise project, also designed by Pei, is underway on the Atlantic Avenue waterfront near the spot where Donald McKay's clippers unloaded their Oriental cargoes before the Civil War; here the accent is on convenience—a $40 million spread of apartment towers with a 1,500-car garage, an aquarium, a motel, shops, restaurants and marinas. Many of the people living here will work in another new Boston skyscraper, the nearby 34-story State Street Bank Building, which was built by British money on almost the same spot where British tea was dumped into the harbor by enraged colonists in 1773.

As author John P. Marquand's Bostonian hero George Apley said about marriage, urban renewal can be a damnably serious business, and this is particularly so in a tradition-cherishing city like Boston. Collins and Logue have run into heated opposition from private citizens and rival Irish politicians alike. In the shadow of Harvard Stadium, a huge billboard was erected with the message "To Hell with Urban Renewal." Some of the homeowners on sites to be cleared threatened a shooting war if the wreckers came, and protested that "our press, our priests, our politicians have deserted us." Much of the opposition came from people with a deep regard for Boston's past. Local historians remember uncomfortably that Boston's priceless Old State House, built in 1713 by the colonial government, was almost torn down in 1881 because the land at the head of State Street had become valuable. Chicago quickly offered to move the building to Lincoln Park on Lake Michigan. Blushing furiously, the Boston city fathers called off the wreckers.

Even the Boston underworld has a tender regard for relics of the city's past. After the trial of the bandits charged with the famous 1950 holdup of Brink's, Incorporated, prosecutor Garrett H. Byrne recalled that the robbers' original plan required entering the company's armored-car garage through sewer pipes. The proposed route, however, was blocked by an obstruction under Faneuil Hall, the historic scene of protest meetings in Revolutionary times. One of the gang suggested clearing the sewer

The Freedom Trail

Boston's Freedom Trail (indicated by the white line on the map) provides a walking tour of a number of notable historic attractions. Among the 15 sites along the route are the Boston Common, the training ground of the militia as early as 1634; the State House, where the charter of the Massachusetts Bay Company and other historically important documents are on display; the Park Street Church, scene of early antislavery speeches; King's Chapel, completed in 1754; the Old South Meeting House, where a meeting was held that triggered the Boston Tea Party; the Old State House, seat of the colonial government and near the site of the Boston Massacre; Faneuil Hall, the "Cradle of Liberty," where the revolutionary town meetings took place; the Paul Revere House, built in the 1670s; and the Old North Church, where the lanterns were hung to signal British troop movements. The trail is a mile and a half long and takes about two hours to traverse.

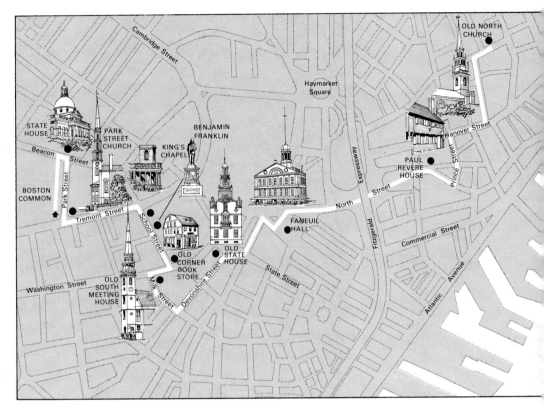

main by a charge of explosives. A leader of the mob exclaimed, "You mean to say you'd take a chance on blowing up Faneuil Hall? Faneuil Hall, *the Cradle of Liberty?* Nothin' doing. The sewer is out—we go in from the street."

Bostonians' regard for the objects and traditions of the past has not always forestalled change in the city. In the 19th Century, repeated upheavals—physical and social—took place. Large-scale building vastly expanded Boston's area, while successive waves of immigration altered the character of neighborhoods—and both types of alterations have contributed, in one way or another, to the colorful atmosphere and associations that lure visitors to tour all parts of modern Boston.

The most drastic physical change of the past was the great enlargement of the central city—the peninsula between the Charles River and Boston Harbor that the Bostonian calls Boston. (He refers to other sections within the city limits by district names—South Boston, East Boston, Charlestown, Roxbury, Jamaica Plain, Dorchester, West Roxbury, Roslindale, Hyde Park.) More than 60 per cent of today's downtown Boston is man-made land, created between 1804 and the Civil War. The earlier peninsula, small, pear-shaped and hilly, was almost an island, connected to the mainland at

Roxbury along the present route of Washington Street by only a thin strip of land known as the Neck, which was often underwater at high tide.

The original city was later filled out by cutting down and leveling most of its hills, but until long after colonial times the encircling shoreline skirted the west slopes of Beacon Hill and the edge of the Boston Common, America's oldest city park, where General Howe's British Redcoats drilled while they were besieged by Washington's troops during the winter of 1775-1776. Even the city's beautiful Public Garden was a watery marsh until 1850. Thus all of 18th Century Boston, the old section dating back to the Revolutionary War, was crowded into the small area between the Common and the North End, where the signal lanterns were hung in the Old North Church steeple at Paul Revere's direction. Consequently the historic shrines that the tourist wants to see—and which helped give rise to so much of the opposition to the recent changes—are within easy walking distance of one another. The Boston authorities have marked out such a foot-tour route, known as the Freedom Trail, which covers many highlights of the city's colorful past in only a mile and a half's walk.

Beginning on the Common, the Freedom Trail first passes the handsome Park Street Church, where

Few men made greater contributions to early post-Revolutionary Boston than the architect Charles Bulfinch, whose Massachusetts State House *(right)* on Beacon Hill remains an outstanding example of the so-called Federal style. From 1787 to 1817 he designed some 50 public and private buildings in Boston. His works as an architect were equaled by his efforts on the Board of Selectmen: he introduced the city's first street lighting—whale-oil lamps—and enlarged the public-school system.

the fiery abolitionist William Lloyd Garrison delivered his first antislavery speech in 1829. Boston, the hotbed of the Revolutionary War, was also the hotbed of the Civil War; one of its heroes is Robert Gould Shaw, scion of a Yankee Brahmin family. Shaw's mother, after proudly watching him march out of Boston at the head of a Massachusetts regiment of Negro troops, wrote joyously, "What have I done that God has been so good to me?"

Next to the Park Street Church on Tremont Street is the Old Granary Burying Ground, another stop on the Freedom Trail, where the tourist will find the graves of John Hancock, Samuel Adams and Paul Revere. Looking down on the burying ground are the stately windows of the Boston Athenaeum, one of the country's finest private libraries and a stronghold of Yankee culture, incorporated in 1807 by the Anthology Society, a literary club. A plaque at the Beacon Street entrance to the building reads, "Here remains a retreat for those who would enjoy the humanity of books." One of the library's past directors, the late Mark A. DeWolfe Howe, used to claim that one windy day, when an old porkpie hat blew off the head of a Beacon Hill lady, it rolled along Beacon Street until it came to the Athenaeum's entrance, where it made a sharp right turn up the steps. Among the Athenaeum's cherished customs, now discontinued, was afternoon tea. Its peculiarly Boston menu, recorded in Cleveland Amory's book *The Proper Bostonians*, listed tea with three crackers for three cents (two cents extra for cheese) and tea with one plain cracker and cheese and one sweet cookie for four cents. Walter Muir Whitehill, the bearded scholar who now serves as the Athenaeum's director, was asked recently why the tea serving had been stopped. "Because too many writers like Amory were cracking cute jokes about it," he said.

After passing the Athenaeum the Freedom Trail turns down School Street, formerly the site of the country's first public educational institution, Boston Latin School, and leads to King's Chapel and City Hall. King's Chapel, its interior probably the finest example of colonial design of any church in New England, was the Episcopal place of worship for the early British governors in Boston and later became the first Unitarian church in America. At the foot of School Street, on the corner of Washington Street, stands the small, gambrel-roofed, three-and-a-half-story brick building of the Old Corner Book Store, built in 1712, and frequented later by Hawthorne, Longfellow, Emerson and James Russell Lowell. It has happily been restored to its original appearance by the *Boston Globe*, which uses the old store as a downtown office.

A turn north on Washington Street takes the traveler to the Old State House and the scene of the Boston Massacre. The Freedom Trail leads on to Faneuil Hall, the "Cradle of Liberty," which is still a marketplace as it was in colonial days, with meat, grocery and produce stalls on its lower floor. From Faneuil Hall the Freedom Trail passes under the moving traffic on the elevated John F. Fitzgerald Expressway, named for the mayor of Boston who was John F. Kennedy's maternal grandfather, and leads the tourist to Paul Revere's house in the North End. This is the only 17th Century wooden house still standing in Boston. It was built in the 1670s, about 100 years before Revere moved into it, and its style of architecture is Elizabethan, the overhanging second story and small casement windows with diamond-shaped panes of glass resembling the houses known to the Puritans in England. Few of Boston's older homes have survived because the city was swept in its early years by a series of great fires; the last big blaze, in November 1872, destroyed 65 acres of buildings in the area between Washington, Summer, Milk and Broad Streets, then a residential neighborhood and later rebuilt as a business and retail shopping district.

The Freedom Trail comes to its end a few blocks away in the North End at the Old North Church and the nearby Copp's Hill Burying Ground, from which British guns fired across the water toward the slopes of Charlestown during the Battle of Bunker Hill. The Old North Church, made famous by Longfellow's poem about Paul Revere's midnight ride ("One if by land and two if by sea"), is also Boston's oldest church. It was built in 1723, and the eight bells in its steeple are inscribed: "We are the first ring of bells cast for the British Empire in North America." Its pews have brass plates bearing the names of 18th Century merchants and sea captains. The surrounding narrow streets of the North End were once lined by fine homes of seafaring families, but these were later replaced by tenements during the busy days of Irish immigration. Now the North End is Boston's crowded but pleasant Italian neighborhood, with an atmosphere like Mulberry Street on New York's Lower East Side. Despite its congestion and run-down buildings, sociologists have advised Boston's urban-renewal planners to leave it alone; dislodging the families of Italian descent who have lived there happily for many years would destroy a solid neighborhood.

The North End's changing ethnic patterns offer an interesting sidelight on Boston's social history.

Oliver Wendell Holmes, like many other 19th Century Boston Brahmins, wrote as an avocation. A doctor of medicine and dean of the Harvard Medical School, he is remembered mainly as an author. *The Autocrat of the Breakfast Table*, a collection of sketches that first appeared in the *Atlantic Monthly*, is probably his best-known work.

Not far from the early colonial home of Paul Revere are the tenements where John F. Fitzgerald and his daughter, Rose Kennedy, the late President Kennedy's mother, were both born during the neighborhood's Irish period. Near the old home of the Fitzgeralds on Hanover Street is the funeral parlor where the bodies of the anarchists and convicted murderers Nicola Sacco and Bartolomeo Vanzetti were viewed after their execution in 1927, when the district had become solidly Italian.

Further sociological and historical insights on Boston can be gained by looking briefly at some of the districts away from the downtown area. Across the mouth of the city's Inner Harbor from the North End, in the Charlestown Navy Yard, is another proud relic of Boston's past, the U.S. frigate *Constitution*. Better known as "Old Ironsides," she rides at anchor and receives hundreds of visiting tourists every day. The dock where the *Constitution* rests as the oldest man-of-war in the Navy is the same place where she was launched in 1797, when the Navy Yard was the site of Edmund Hartt's shipbuilding yard. Behind her masts the granite Bunker Hill Monument rises from the heights of Charlestown, where Boston's bloodiest Revolutionary War battle was fought.

Charlestown and the waterfront peninsula of

In intellectually oriented 19th Century Boston, Louis Agassiz, the world-famous Swiss zoologist and geologist, became the current social lion when he was brought to the city for a series of lectures in the winter of 1846-1847. Crowds of 5,000 were not unusual when he appeared at Tremont Temple. Later he became a professor at Harvard, where his teaching influenced a generation of scientists.

South Boston on the opposite side of the city are two sections of Boston that have remained solidly Irish since before the Civil War. Most of the men in the two communities have worked on the Boston Harbor docks for many generations as longshoremen. A few years ago when the undefeated football teams of South Boston High School and Charlestown High School were about to meet in an eagerly awaited game, one of the coaches observed, "Not a ship in the harbor will go out today." South Boston, which has nine Catholic churches within its area of two square miles, claims that it has produced more Catholic priests and nuns than any locality of its size in North America. Among its notable native and adopted sons are Richard Cardinal Cushing, Boston's archbishop, Speaker of the House of Representatives John W. McCormack and Ohioborn Frank "Danky" Daniels, the oldtime vaudeville performer who originated the favorite Boston Irish greeting, "Shake the hand that shook the hand of John L. Sullivan." (Sullivan, the great heavyweight boxer, was a Boston boy.) South Boston Irish rose up in Anglophobic furor when a Boston City Council member suggested in 1941 that sand from England, being carried as ballast in freighters returning empty from wartime British ports, could be spread on the local beaches. A veteran member

of the neighborhood's L Street Brownies, the hardy exercise enthusiasts who plunge into South Boston's Old Harbor every day of the year, declared that he would never swim again if he had to walk across English sand to get to the water.

Old Bostonians say that if a street in the city is reasonably wide and straight you can be sure that its neighborhood was covered with water not long ago; the broader and more modern thoroughfares such as Commonwealth and Massachusetts Avenues, which contrast sharply with the North End's narrow colonial lanes and Beacon Hill's constricted Federalist side streets, are on the younger land in the Back Bay and the Fenway, both of which were added to Boston shortly before the Civil War when the size of the downtown peninsula was more than doubled in acreage. The enlargement of Boston during the Victorian era was brought about because the city's population was being swollen by immigration and increasing business and prosperity. During the 19th Century the population jumped from 24,937 to 560,892, continually forcing the city to create new living space.

The stylish new neighborhoods, west of the Common and the recently landscaped Public Garden, were settled at a time when the city's Yankee Brahmin wealth, parlayed from the sea trade into textile manufacturing and Western investments, had created an affluent society with the leisure to indulge itself more and more in cultural pursuits. With the rise of Back Bay social life, such institutions as the Boston Symphony Orchestra, the Boston Museum of Fine Arts and the small but choice Isabella Stewart Gardner Museum at Fenway Court were founded.

The Boston Symphony, established in 1881 by Henry Lee Higginson, is still one of the most highly regarded orchestras in the world and has one of the longest seasons of any city symphony—33 weeks at Symphony Hall in Boston and eight weeks in the summer at Tanglewood in the Berkshires. In the spring its members perform at the famous Boston Pops concerts in the same hall, presenting informal programs to an audience that is seated at small tables and served refreshments with the music. After the Pops season ends and before the Tanglewood concerts begin, some of the musicians move to the Hatch Memorial Shell for the annual summer series of free outdoor music on the Esplanade beside the Charles River Basin at the foot of Beacon Hill.

Another unique fixture on the Boston cultural scene is Fenway Court, the Italian palace assembled on the Back Bay's landscaped river road by

Mrs. John Lowell Gardner from bits and pieces of *palazzi* picked up in Venice and Rome. Mrs. Gardner, better known as "Mrs. Jack," was one of old Boston's most celebrated characters. An heiress from New York who was married in 1860 to the son of one of Boston's last East India merchants, she set out to show a thing or two to the Boston society that had frowned on her flashy behavior; she strolled on Tremont Street with a lion cub on a leash, scrubbed the steps of the Church of the Advent as penance in Lent, and had her portrait painted by John Singer Sargent in a dress that so daringly revealed the lines of her figure that her husband refused to allow it exhibited during his lifetime. Mrs. Gardner built her palace when she was a widow of about 60, filling it with now-priceless Renaissance art—most of it selected for her by Bernard Berenson, then a young, unknown Harvard student—and she left it to the public as a museum with the stipulation that nothing in the building, not even a drape or a piece of furniture, could be moved or changed after her death. Mrs. Gardner's art collection includes Titian's masterpiece, *The Rape of Europa*, and works by Rembrandt, Vermeer, Raphael and Cellini. Her palace, built under her personal supervision, is an exquisite artistic work in itself, with flowers blooming all winter under the high glass roof of its inner courtyard. Mrs. Gardner herself continued to live in it, after opening it as a museum, until she died in 1924 at the age of 84.

Socially today Boston is not the staid and provincial city that it was in Mrs. Jack Gardner's day or in the much later time when Joseph P. Kennedy moved his young family to New York because, as he often said later, he did not want his daughters growing up where they would not be invited to join the debutante clubs. In the old Boston, among the Irish and the Italians as well as among the Yankees, any outsider faced a coldness memorialized in many stories and customs. On spring nights in the Harvard Yard, students used to shout, "Rhinehart!" The cry, according to one legend, mocked a student named Rhinehart who came from a small town in the Midwest and knew nobody in Cambridge because he had not attended a New England prep school. Trying to make himself known to the other students, he would turn on the lights in his third-floor room at night, slip downstairs and hide in the shadows of the yard, shouting at his own windows, "Oh, Rhinehart—are you in, Rhinehart?" Eventually he was discovered and so humiliated that he left college.

Several Bostonians say that the breakdown of

the barrier of mistrust between the financial community of Yankee State Street and Mayor Collins' City Hall that opened up a new spirit of enterprise in Boston is a reflection of a larger reaction against provincial clannishness that has taken root generally among ethnic, economic, political and religious groups in Massachusetts in recent years. They point out that Harvard University made a drastic break from its Yankee traditions when it selected Nathan Pusey, a native of Council Bluffs, Iowa, as president in 1953; every previous president of Harvard had been a New Englander. Edward Brooke, elected U.S. Senator from Massachusetts in 1966, is not only a Negro but an outsider who has a District of Columbia background. Two of the leading figures in the Boston business world, Ephron Catlin Jr., Senior Vice President of the First National Bank of Boston, and Eli Goldston, President of the Eastern Gas and Fuel Associates, are from Missouri and Ohio, respectively.

"When I first came here in 1956," recalls a New Yorker who heads the Boston bureau of a national newsmagazine, "I noticed that the whole city seemed to be divided into tight compartments of people who didn't speak to each other. I was told that it had always been that way in Boston. Not only was there a wall of silence between the bankers and the politicians but neither of them knew the labor-union heads. The Irish and the Italians didn't know each other and the Jews and the Lithuanians were strangers to everybody. And then, all of a sudden a few years ago everybody loosened up and started to get acquainted. I don't know which came first, the chicken or the egg—did the compartments break down when the city started rebuilding and business began to boom, or was it the other way around? I suspect the latter, but, in any case, Boston has gotten over being retarded."

There are many theories about the cause of the new spirit of friendliness in Boston. A most conspicuous breaker of barriers is ecumenical-minded Cardinal Cushing, who is friendlier with the Cabots and the Lowells than any Catholic archbishop or bishop of Boston before him, and who seems to spend as much time appearing at synagogues and Protestant churches as he does at Catholic Communion breakfasts. Two prominent Bostonians, Charles Coolidge and Erwin D. Canham, editor of the *Christian Science Monitor*, attribute a major share of credit for the closer understanding between businessmen, politicians, bankers, labor chiefs and academic leaders to a series of Citizens' Seminars on local problems held in recent years at Boston College, the Jesuit institution at Chestnut Hill that

has grown since World War II into one of the largest Catholic universities in America. Coolidge points out that a number of Boston's leaders in various fields became acquainted with one another for the first time at the Boston College seminars and have remained friendly since.

Some concept of the novelty of such democratic round-table discussions on the Boston scene may be gained from a story told at one of the seminar sessions by John "Red" Moran, the local leader of a longshoremen's union. He said that he had been shaving that afternoon before the mirror in the kitchen of his tenement flat in South Boston when his mother came in and asked him with some concern why he was home from his work at the docks so early in the day.

"I've got to go out to Boston College to give a talk with Ralph Lowell, the State Street banker, and some big-shot professor from M.I.T.," Moran explained.

His mother bowed her head and began to weep. Moran put down his razor and anxiously asked her what was wrong.

"Oh, my God, you're drinking again!" she said.

The new air of tolerant understanding, says the Boston Athenaeum's Walter Whitehill, a discerning observer of the Hub scene, is a feedback from Boston's broadened role in modern higher education.

"Our universities have always strongly influenced this community of ours," Whitehill says. "In the old days, Harvard and M.I.T. were predominantly Boston schools for Boston boys, and so was Boston University. Boston College was a small daycollege for Boston Irish Catholics only, and Brandeis hadn't been born yet. Now all of these universities draw more brilliant young men from all over the nation, and all over the world, and the rise of this town as a center for scientific research and development brings another whole new group of brainy people here, the like of which we never had before. As a result, Boston itself becomes more cosmopolitan and more progressive in its thinking— and we find ourselves with a new Prudential Tower, and a new Government Center rising from the demolished Scollay Square."

The more tradition-loving Proper Bostonians feel that such a disruption of their old red-brick skyline is a stiff price to pay for progress. When the Prudential Center was opened, a reporter asked a Boston attorney with the Old Guard name of Faneuil Adams what he thought of it. "I think the tower is perfectly horrible," he said. "It's much too tall. But," Faneuil Adams added quickly, "I think all this building is saving the city."

A descendant of John Adams', Boston society *doyenne* Abigail Adams Homans reflects upon a family memento. Her published memoir, *Education by Uncles,* lovingly evokes the world of late-19th Century Boston—of balls and belles and lazy summers by the sea.

The special world of Boston's elite

Some have called them Boston Brahmins, but perhaps Oliver Wendell Holmes's phrase "man of family" describes more aptly the members of that circle who have indelibly stamped their names on Boston's cultural and economic life. For a century and more not taste, nor wealth, nor scholarship, nor wit—alone or in combination—was sufficient to gain entry into the charmed circle. The background of a rich family long-established in Boston was the main requirement.

Today such rules have been relaxed, but the traditions of the "good families" continue—ties with Beacon Street, support for the Boston Symphony and the Massachusetts Historical Society, a Harvard education, and most important of all, a strong commitment to public service that has made such names as Adams, Saltonstall, Lodge, Lowell and Peabody known to all America.

The focal point
of traditional Boston

Although Beacon Hill today looks much as it did a century ago, it now serves primarily as a home away from home for most of Boston's elite. Comparatively few Brahmin families still live on Beacon Hill—most of them have moved to such suburbs as Chestnut Hill and Milton—and their former town houses, like many of those on West Cedar Street *(above)*, now shelter foundations and private clubs. Boston gentlemen retreat to these clubs in the midst of a busy day for a quiet lunch and genteel conversation.

Cobblestones, such as were formerly found all over Boston, still form the paving along Beacon Hill's Acorn Street *(right)*. This kind of pavement seemed appropriate to a late-17th Century visiting British journalist, for he wrote that "their streets are like the Hearts of the Male Inhabitants, paved with pebbles." The small houses along Acorn Street date from the early 19th Century and many were built for the coachmen of prominent families who resided nearby. Today most of these houses are occupied by white-collar families.

An archetype Bostonian, Samuel Eliot Morison

Admiral, historian, retired Harvard professor, yachtsman, twice winner of the Pulitzer Prize for biography—these are but a few of the titles descriptive of Samuel Eliot Morison, shown at right with his wife, the former Priscilla Barton, in the drawing room of their Beacon Hill home. He is the archetype of the Boston "man of family," combining in his person wit, grace, vigor and intellectual competence of the highest order. A man of tradition, he recalls with pleasure an upbringing in "an atmosphere where scholarship, religion and social graces were happily blended." He is a man able to wear a flowing cloak to a symphony concert without self-consciousness; a man who can glory in his heirloom-filled home—the house in which he was born in 1887—without seeming pompous. Yet he is also a man of action. In typical fashion, when working on his Pulitzer Prize-winning biography of Columbus—*Admiral of the Ocean Sea*—Morison was not content merely to examine his subject as depicted in dusty records; instead he made four trips aboard yachts to retrace the voyages of the great discoverer. Serving as a Navy historian during World War II, he continually sought out action so that he might be history's witness as well as its scribe. Now retired from both the Navy and the classroom, Admiral Morison remains a prolific writer. He has achieved with superb nonchalance a goal much admired by the Boston Brahmin: a life of active scholarship combined with dedicated public service.

Members of the Massachusetts Historical Society, the oldest such organization in America, hear guest speaker George Kennan, a former Ambassador to the Soviet Union, give a talk. The society is one of the most exclusive of Boston's historical groups, limiting its resident membership to 150. Although no dues are levied, members are expected to contribute both funds and scholarship. Since its foundation in 1791 the society has published more than 200 works on American history written or edited by its members.

A symphony patron, stern and resolute, enters her limousine after a Friday afternoon concert by the Boston orchestra. In the background, another elderly lady—clad in "sensible" Bostonian garb—walks with a younger and somewhat more modishly dressed companion. Traditionally the Boston Symphony is the highest cultural shrine for a lady of family. It is her checkbook that helps the orchestra meet its deficit, and she would almost as soon miss a family wedding or funeral as one of the Friday performances.

The ladies in flowing gowns, their escorts in white tie and tails, glide across the Sheraton Plaza's ballroom *(above)* in a ritual reminiscent of the turn of the century. The periodic Waltz Evenings are a first-family tradition in Boston, but outsiders also attend. The walls that once surrounded Brahmin society are disappearing, and many families that once would have been excluded are now welcomed.

An elegant setting
for scholarly pursuits

In solitary splendor, save for a few statues and busts of classical mien, a scholar studies a book in old Boston's sanctum sanctorum, the Athenaeum. Its 443,000 volumes, including an outstanding collection of works published in the Confederacy, make this institution justly renowned among the world's great private libraries. It was founded in 1807 by members of a Boston literary club for men, and at one time ownership shares were closely held. Today, however, almost anyone interested in buying a share can usually find one for sale. Other changes have come with time. No longer in force is an 1849 rule that barred women from certain sections containing books considered too worldly for feminine eyes, an order promulgated after the trustees had decided that it was not "desirable that a modest young woman should have anything to do with the corrupter portions of polite literature."

Proper schools
for proper people

There was a time when the educational path of a well-born Boston child was fully charted. A girl would go to a prestigious academy such as the Winsor School, whose students, like those shown below, were expected to take part in such body-building sports as lacrosse. Most girls did not go on to college, but those who did chose Mount Holyoke, Radcliffe or Wellesley. For the boys, the path was narrower still. After attending a proper prep school, Harvard was the only acceptable goal, and a centuries-old family connection with the university almost assured the boy's acceptance, regardless of his academic qualifications. Today the situation is changed. The three young Saltonstalls (shown at right in the Harvard Yard) —brothers Stephan *(left)* and Thomas *(right)* with their cousin James—had to compete for admission with students from all over the United States. Many young men from Brahmin families cannot meet the new entrance requirements, but Harvard remains the training ground of choice for most gentlemen of Boston.

7

The Legacy
of Intellectualism

For more than three centuries New England has led the nation in educational and scholarly achievement. Partly as a consequence, it has produced more outstanding writers, philosophers, critics of the status quo, poets, nonconformists, rebels, and other men and women of intellectual vigor than any other section of the country, and has made such names as Harriet Beecher Stowe, Noah Webster and Henry Wadsworth Longfellow familiar to every schoolboy.

There have been those who believe that New England's intellectual verve has been gradually disappearing since the last decades of the 19th Century. Certainly a decline did seem to set in at that time. The creative peak had come in the pre-Civil War decades of Emerson and Thoreau, which have been described by Alfred North Whitehead, the philosophical scholar, as one of the great ages, "not yet as famous as it deserves to be." That period of flowering was followed by what the literary historian Van Wyck Brooks called New England's Indian Summer, still productive, but declining from

In full academic regalia, scholars parade to the 1964 inauguration of Kingman Brewster Jr. as the 17th President of Yale University. Founded in 1701, the third college in the colonies, Yale continues to contribute to the brilliant intellectual history of New England.

natural inspiration to contrived planning, the October season when the Nathaniel Hawthornes gave way to the Henry Jameses. Yet instead of shriveling back into bare branches, the region kept putting out new shoots, producing in recent decades another impressive list of literary luminaries.

If there was a low point in New England's intellectual and literary history, it came in the 1920s and 1930s, when Boston, and by implication all of the region, became nationally notorious for its banning of books and censorship of the theater. A number of other cities were equally prissy at the time, but Boston, as the "American Athens," received the most attention and ridicule. In 1927 Boston authorities ordered the withdrawal from sale of 68 books, including the works of H. G. Wells, Sinclair Lewis, Ernest Hemingway and Sherwood Anderson. By no mere coincidence, Massachusetts in the same year was denounced by intellectual liberals everywhere because it persisted in sending to the electric chair two Italian-born anarchist agitators, Nicola Sacco and Bartolomeo Vanzetti, whose conviction for a payroll robbery shooting seemed to many observers to be more influenced by ideological prejudice than courtroom evidence. Both the book banning and the denial of clemency to Sacco and Vanzetti were encouraged by profound

139

distrust of radicalism; any rebellious departure from the conservative conventions brought instant retaliation from both the staid, Protestant Yankee Brahmins and the reactionary Irish Catholic clergy and city government—one of the few instances of agreeable collaboration between those two otherwise dissident factions. Boston's Watch and Ward Society, a supposedly benevolent Brahmin organization that had assumed responsibility for the city's morals, could always count on the help of the Irish mayor and the city censor in having a book banned or a play closed.

The aberration of the 1920s and the 1930s has long since faded, along with much of the prickly distrust between the Yankees and the Irish in other matters. But the climate it fostered prevailed long enough and with sufficient strength to leave in the minds of many Americans a derogatory taint on the word "puritan"—with the lower-case "p"—since the anti-intellectual moves were reputed to spring from "puritan" instincts among New Englanders. That this should have occurred was particularly ironic in view of the fact that it was New England's original Puritans—with a capital "P"—who were responsible for initiating the region's magnificent intellectual saga that has endured for well over 300 years.

The literary historian Moses Coit Tyler described the Puritan intellectual atmosphere in *A History of American Literature*. "In its inception," he wrote, "New England was not an agricultural community, nor a manufacturing community, nor a trading community: it was a thinking community; an arena and mart for ideas; its characteristic organ being not the hand, nor the heart, nor the pocket, but the brain. . . . Probably no other community of pioneers ever so honored study, so reverenced the symbols and instruments of learning. Theirs was a social structure with its corner-stone resting on a book."

Only six years after the founding of the Massachusetts Bay Colony in 1630, the settlers took money from their own treasury to establish a college—Harvard. By the end of the 1700s there were colleges in all the other New England states—Yale in Connecticut, Brown in Rhode Island, Vermont in Vermont, Dartmouth in New Hampshire and Bowdoin in Maine.

The Puritans had brought their appreciation of learning with them from England. In the first generation of colonists there was a ratio of about one college-trained scholar, usually from Oxford or Cambridge, to every 40 or 50 families. The clergy, in particular, was well educated; throughout the colonial period some 95 per cent of the ministers had college degrees. But the colonial colleges, although established primarily to educate the clergy, were not merely theological schools. In fact only about half the graduates in the first two generations that attended Harvard joined the ministry. The Puritans wanted all their leaders, including the ministers, to have a broad, liberal education. "The learned class was indeed an order of nobility among them," says Tyler.

In their enthusiasm for liberal education, however, the Puritans, who adhered to strict dogma in both religious and temporal matters, were forging a two-edged sword. Inevitably a certain percentage of educated men and women in any such rigid society develop a tendency to question, to analyze and frequently to attack the precepts of the established order. Roger Williams and Anne Hutchinson, for example, caused major disturbances in the Massachusetts Bay Colony through just such heretical questioning. A scholarly clergyman and skillful writer as well as a noncomformist, Williams sadly described his banishment from the colony as "the day of our last farewell, the day of the splitting of this vessel, the breaking of this bubble, the quenching of this candle."

Not all the early Puritan ministers, of course, were rebels against the Church-state. There were, for instance, Increase Mather and his more famous son, Cotton, who supported the theocracy in their sermons and their writings. Cotton Mather, the author of some 450 books and pamphlets, wrote the popular *Magnalia Christi Americana*, an ecclesiastical chronicle of New England, in which he argued that the history of Massachusetts demonstrated the workings of the will of God. His earlier work *Memorable Providences relating to Witchcraft and Possessions* helped to fan the hysteria of the Salem witch trials, although he himself had grave doubts about some of the proceedings.

Cotton Mather's belief in the power of witches, shared by almost all clergymen of the time, went hand in hand with his scholarship in science. He was the first native-born American to be elected to the Royal Society, England's most distinguished body of scientists. Increase Mather was also a historian—he wrote *A History of the War with the Indians*, an account of King Philip's War—and a writer on witchcraft—his *Cases of Conscience Concerning Evil Spirits* was an attack on the court for having admitted the "spectral evidence" given by the young girls who were the witnesses in the Salem trials. Both men contributed to higher education in New England: Increase served as the president of

Harvard; Cotton was among the founders of Yale.

Like nearly all other early New England authors, Increase and Cotton Mather wrote only to teach. Literature meant to be read for pleasure or to evoke an emotional response was frowned on. Fiction was viewed as frivolous, and little of it was produced. But poetry, especially if it taught a moral lesson, did not fall into this category; the first book published in the English colonies in North America was in verse—the Bay Psalm Book, The Whole Booke of Psalmes Faithfully Translated into English Metre.

Some of the 17th Century New England poets enjoyed considerable success. For example, Michael Wigglesworth's *The Day of Doom*, a volume published in 1662 that dealt with Judgment Day, became a "bestseller" in the colonies. The book enjoyed public favor for at least a century; by 1760 some 10 editions had been published.

Not all popular poets of the time, however, adhered to religious themes. There was, for instance, Anne Bradstreet, a Puritan wife who wrote poetry about her day-to-day life, but also voiced her annoyance with the less-than-flattering attitude of many men toward the female mind. She expressed her feelings with a nice touch of wit in her poem in praise of Queen Elizabeth:

> *Now say, have women worth? or have they none?*
> *Or had they some, but with our Queen is't gone?*
> *Nay masculines, you have thus taxt us long,*
> *But she, though dead, will vindicate our wrong.*
> *Let such as say our Sex is void of Reason,*
> *Know tis a Slander now, but once was Treason.*

Another literary sport of the 17th and early 18th Centuries was Edward Taylor, a Puritan minister in Westfield, Massachusetts, and probably the greatest poet of New England's colonial period. Taylor, who was the only one of his contemporaries to write in the style of the witty English metaphysical poetry, published little in his lifetime, but he left a considerable body of work along with a request that it not be printed after his death, a request that was fortunately ignored. Although Taylor dealt with religious themes, he treated them with a passion and intensity uncommon in American poetry at the time:

> *Shall I not smell thy sweet, oh! Sharons Rose?*
> *Shall not mine Eye salute thy Beauty? Why?*
> *Shall thy sweet leaves their Beautious sweets upclose?*
> *As halfe ashamde my sight should on them ly?*

By the early decades of the 18th Century, the intense, all-encompassing fervor of the Puritan faith began to abate, especially in the seaboard towns. Regular church attendance was still a requisite for respectability, but religion no longer dominated the minds of New Englanders as it once had. This trend was not allowed to go unchallenged. Theologian Jonathan Edwards of Connecticut, who shared in the contemporary interest in scientific and cultural developments, was in religious matters as strict a Calvinist as any of his Puritan ancestors. He rejected any softening of Calvinism's doctrines, and in 1734 and 1735 he conducted a major revival. But by mid-century his rigid orthodoxy had alienated his followers at Northampton, Massachusetts, and he was dismissed as pastor. He took over a smaller congregation in Stockbridge, Massachusetts, where he wrote his theological masterpiece, *The Freedom of the Will*, in which he presented ethical and metaphysical arguments supporting determinism, the belief that all events are determined by previously existing causes.

In his attempts to restore an earlier piety, Edwards was fighting a war that could not be won. With increasing wealth came a growing concern for the amenities of living, including reading for pleasure. New England writing reflected the change. Now writers were free simply to entertain, to explore new areas in the world of ideas and to evoke emotions without the need to incorporate a moral lesson. Also, as readers became more sophisticated, purely literary values took on added importance.

With the birth of the colonies' first successful newspaper, the *News-Letter*, in Boston in 1704, and the rapid proliferation of periodicals that followed, writers had a new outlet for their work. Until that time there was not a single newspaper in all of England's North American possessions. In 1690 Benjamin Harris had attempted to found one, *Publick Occurrences*, also in Boston, but the publication had been closed down after only four days because Harris had failed to get permission for his venture from the governor and his council.

Many of the early newspapers published poems, essays and humorous pieces along with news items. Boston-born Benjamin Franklin's first literary efforts appeared anonymously in the *New-England Courant*, a journal owned by his half brother James. And at least one play became newspaper fare: although theatrical performances were forbidden in Boston at the time, *George Barnwell*, a play by the London dramatist George Lillo, was printed serially in the *New England Weekly Journal*.

As England tightened its control over the colonies in the 18th Century, newspapers began giving

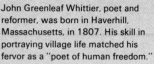

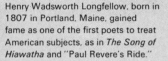

more and more space to political debate over the actions of the mother country. An even more important literary factor in the gathering storm, however, were the pamphlets that were being published in vast quantities throughout the colonies. These pamphlets, says one historian, were "the corpus of literature of the American Revolution—a couple of thousand little books with their pretentious and formidable titles, intended for instant circulation, designed to change men's minds, addressed to urgent problems, sometimes touching the universal issues that confront men everywhere, any time, in civil society."

Among the most prolific of the radical group of pamphlet writers in New England were James Otis, Josiah Quincy, and John and Samuel Adams. Otis was probably the most influential. A successful Massachusetts lawyer, he had written a textbook in Latin, in verse form, and another in Greek, before converting his pen into a weapon against England. In one of his early pamphlets, *The Rights of the British Colonies Asserted and Proved*, published in 1764, Otis attacked Parliament and asserted that supreme power resides "*originally* and *ultimately* in the people*," a sentiment that was to be echoed in the Declaration of Independence. However, he urged the colonists "to behave like men, and use

the proper legal measures to obtain redress." But a year later his *Considerations on Behalfe of the Colonists* had a more radical tone: "Revolutions have been. They may be again." In still another pamphlet, Otis coined one of the great pre-Revolution rallying cries, "No taxation without representation." In historian Tyler's words, Otis gave "a conservative and law-respecting race, a conservative and lawful pretext for resisting law, and for revolutionizing the government."

To be sure, not all the pamphleteers were radicals. Samuel Seabury, a Connecticut clergyman, was one of a number of writers who supported the Crown. With his loyalist tracts signed "A. W. Farmer," Seabury drew fire from young Alexander Hamilton. Often such antagonists engaged in lengthy and heated debate in print. Unless a reader kept up with the exchange of pamphlets, he would soon lose the thread of the argument.

By 1774 a blizzard of pamphlets was coming off the presses in New England. Opinion was hardening into three firmly held viewpoints: the Right, made up of the extreme loyalists who gave full support to the Crown; the moderate Center, which favored changes in the relationship between England and the colonies but wanted to maintain the traditional ties with the mother country; and the Left, which demanded independence and finally won it.

Immediately after the Revolution, there was a lull in pamphlet writing, but as the now-independent Americans prepared to establish a government of their own, the battle of words was joined again between the Federalists, who argued for a strong central government, and the Antifederalists, who wanted a loose confederation of sovereign states.

One of the pamphleteers for the Federalist cause was the Connecticut-born lexicographer Noah Webster, who was to win fame throughout the states for his *A Grammatical Institute of the English Language*, published in three parts between 1783 and 1785. The first part of this series later became his *Elementary Spelling Book*, which was to be a standard textbook in the United States for decades; by 1850, seven years after his death, when the population of the United States was less than 23 million, about a million copies of the speller were being sold annually. Webster in 1828 published *An American Dictionary of the English Language*, a monumental work that broke with British lexicography and made him the prime influence in standardizing American spelling and pronunciation.

During the closing years of the 18th Century, writers began to be concerned with other subjects besides politics. In 1789 William Hill Brown, the son of a Boston clockmaker, wrote the first American novel, *The Power of Sympathy*. In subject matter, at least, the book seems closely akin to many of the modern novels now available at a corner drugstore, for it dealt with seduction, incest, abduction, rape and suicide. "The diction employed by Brown is decorous to the point of obscurity," says one historian, "and the episodes are only obliquely described; but between the lines lie the very elements against which moralists were inveighing as likely to inflame the passions if not corrupt the heart."

New England also produced some playwrights during the last decades of the 18th Century. Among them was Boston-born, Harvard-trained Royall Tyler, an outstanding jurist who wrote *The Contrast*, the first American comedy to be produced in this country. The play, which opened in New York in 1787, was an immediate success. The dialogue was nimble, and the lusty plot—involving an English cad with evil designs on various American women —was designed to please anti-British sentiment (the Englishman lost out on all counts).

But in the history of New England's intellectual community, everything that happened in the 17th and 18th Centuries seems only a quiet, if necessary, prologue to the sweeping and brilliant drama of the 1800s. As a backdrop, there was the great expansion of higher education. During the 19th Century, some 75 additional senior colleges and about a score of junior colleges opened their doors in New England. Among the senior colleges were such outstanding institutions as Middlebury, Amherst, Wesleyan, Tufts, the Massachusetts Institute of Technology, Bates and the University of Massachusetts. Women were not neglected in this vast expansion; the century saw the establishment of such colleges as Mount Holyoke, Wellesley, Smith and Radcliffe. All of these new institutions along with the older ones provided a favorable climate for the remarkable intellectual achievements of 19th Century New England.

Just the first generation born in New England in the 19th Century would, by itself, have made the 1800s remarkable. The years 1800 to 1820 saw the birth of such renowned writers as Ralph Waldo Emerson, Nathaniel Hawthorne, John Greenleaf Whittier, Edgar Allan Poe, Oliver Wendell Holmes, Harriet Beecher Stowe, Henry David Thoreau and James Russell Lowell. Historians of great talent, such as George Bancroft and John Lothrop Motley, and men destined to become famous editors, such as Orestes Brownson and Charles Dana, came into the world in those years. Also born in New England during this same period were influential reformers like Elizabeth Peabody, William Lloyd Garrison and Henry Ward Beecher, men and women who would provide the intellectual leadership for fundamental changes in the social and political structure of the nation. New England even provided this richly gifted generation with someone to perpetuate its more pungent thoughts: John Bartlett, who was to compile the invaluable reference book *Familiar Quotations*, was born in Plymouth in 1820.

Dividing these New Englanders born between 1800 and 1820 into categories is convenient but somewhat misleading. Almost all of the reformers wrote extensively; likewise, many of the writers, editors and historians were ardent reformers. Certainly Harriet Beecher Stowe, famous as an author, was one of the country's most effective fighters against slavery.

The New England into which these future intellectual leaders were born was a far different place than it had been even half a century before. With the coming of the machine age and the growth of world trade, the region was going through an astounding industrial and commercial expansion. Great family fortunes were being established. Far more people were traveling and absorbing the culture of other lands. Extensive libraries, containing the best of European literature, were common to

many homes—and their books were avidly read.

Many of the wealthy and well educated, at least, were abandoning the strict, uncompromising religion of their forefathers in favor of a tolerant, more relaxed Unitarianism. Boston, in particular, must have shocked the ghosts of the settlers with its permissive attitude toward worldly literature. "Even the young girls . . . read *Tom Jones*, Smollett and *Tristam Shandy*, as if they had never heard of a Pilgrim Father," says Van Wyck Brooks in *The Flowering of New England*. "In every house one found the standard authors, Hume, Gibbon, Shakespeare, Milton, Dryden, the *Arabian Nights*, *Don Quixote*, Sir William Temple's works in folio, a set of Hogarth's original plates, perhaps, or two or three first editions of Pope, books that were worthy of their calf bindings, on shelves that might have been carved by Grinling Gibbons, surmounted by marble busts." There were even a few sybarites in the city. Harrison Gray Otis, a former U.S. Senator and mayor of Boston, "at the age of eighty, after forty years of gout, breakfasted every morning on *pâté de foie gras*. Every afternoon, at the Otis house, ten gallons of punch evaporated out of the Lowestoft bowl that was placed on the landing."

But it was nourishment for the mind that made Boston famous. In 1803 a number of the town's leading intellectuals, including John Thornton Kirkland, president of Harvard, and John Lowell, a lawyer and writer, joined in forming the Anthology Society to encourage a national literature and began to publish the *Monthly Anthology*. The first literary magazine in the country, its pages carried the works of such men as Daniel Webster, Aaron Bancroft and Alexander Everett. In 1815 the *Monthly Anthology* became the *North American Review*, an outstanding quarterly that survived until 1940 under the editorship of such luminaries as Jared Sparks, Edward Everett, James Russell Lowell and Henry Adams.

Almost all American writing was still being treated with lofty condescension in England, but one book by a New England author had to be read by every British seafarer who wanted to be abreast of the best modern navigation techniques. That book was *The Practical Navigator* by Nathaniel Bowditch. This amazing man, whose formal schooling ended at age 10, was one of the great mathematicians of his time. He studied navigation while serving as a crew member on five long sea voyages and was able to find some 8,000 errors in the most authoritative book on the subject then available. Bowditch's own book, published in 1802, saved countless lives of men at sea and, in revised form,

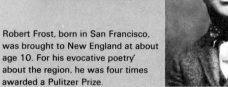
is still being used by mariners all over the world.

The scholarly study of science, earlier stimulated so powerfully by Benjamin Franklin, was also getting a firm foothold at Yale during the early years of the 19th Century. In 1802 Benjamin Silliman, a native of Connecticut, and an outstanding chemist, physicist and geologist, became Yale's first professor of chemistry and natural history. In 1818 he founded the *American Journal of Science and Arts*, a publication that played an important role in stimulating scholarly interest in science in the United States.

However, at Harvard, and in the Boston area generally, the concern was mainly with letters. A young Massachusetts poet from a small village in the Berkshires, William Cullen Bryant, was causing quite a stir with "Thanatopsis," "To a Waterfowl," "Inscription for the Entrance to a Wood" and "The Yellow Violet," all written before he was 21. And in 1829 a Salem-born 25-year-old writer named Nathaniel Hawthorne published his first novel, *Fanshawe*. That book was a failure, but he was to gain a solid reputation after the publication of *The Scarlet Letter* and *The House of the Seven Gables* in the early 1850s.

In the 1830s a major religious and literary revolution bearing the name Transcendentalism struck New England. The movement was based broadly on the concepts of the 18th Century German philosopher Immanuel Kant, especially on his *Critique of Pure Reason*. Kant's argument, briefly, was that the three great problems of metaphysics—God, freedom and immortality—could not be solved by speculative thought, and that their existence could neither be proved nor disproved on theoretical grounds or by scientific demonstration. He called this the "Transcendental Dialectic." However, he said, without belief in their existence there could be no morality. Thus, a categorical imperative became the center of Kant's ethics: "Act as if the maxim from which you act were to become through your will a universal law of nature."

To a number of the ministers of New England, troubled by the rationalism of Unitarianism and the commonly expressed belief of its followers that "character is more important than creed," Transcendentalism appeared as a means of reform. It also appealed to some prominent writers living in or near Concord, Massachusetts, and they applied it to literature. Emerson and Thoreau were the major spokesmen. Outsiders called the group the "Transcendental Club" or the "Concord group."

The Transcendentalists held the concept, common to the Romanticists of Europe, that the human intuition was the highest form of knowledge. They glorified individualism, believed God was within each man and found harmony in all things in nature. To propagate their ideas, the Concord group established a magazine, *The Dial*, that was published only between 1840 and 1844 but in those few years generated hot controversy in New England's intellectual community.

Emerson, a former Unitarian minister, was probably Transcendentalism's most effective voice. He wrote with rare skill, and in three books—*Essays*, *Representative Men* and *English Traits*—he expressed his beliefs in simple and concrete words that many readers found highly persuasive. Thoreau, a sometime naturalist, surveyor and laborer, was more of a humorist than his close friend Emerson, and his approach to Transcendentalism was considerably more earthy. Thoreau was also a rebel and militant nonconformist. In his essay *Civil Disobedience*, which was to exert significant influence on 20th Century revolutionary movements at home and abroad, he expressed an anarchistic attitude toward government, holding that if a government is guilty of an injustice "of such a nature that it requires injustice to another, [you should] break the law [and] let your life be a counter friction to stop the machine." In his most famous work, *Walden*, based on his experiences and thoughts when he lived in a hut close to Walden Pond outside Concord, he urged modern man to simplify his demands so that he could "suck out all the marrow of life."

Among the lesser figures in the Concord group were Bronson Alcott, one of the great leaders of educational reform who advocated the integrated mental, physical and spiritual development of children; Orestes Brownson, a clergyman and writer; and Margaret Fuller, an author and ardent feminist: her *Woman in the Nineteenth Century* did much to spur the movement for women's rights both during and after her time.

The ideas of reformers and nonconformists were especially attractive to young New Englanders, and in this respect the college-age group of the late 1830s and early 1840s resembled many of their counterparts of the 1960s. They despised their parents' preoccupation with making money and refused to take any interest in business. They held the view that "the great art of being a merchant is to look wise and ride in a carriage," and scoffed at the idea of being a "mere" lawyer. They disdained the authors their fathers esteemed, and they made fun of the colleges and professors. "Poetry was the only life for them," says one historian, "or painting, or contemplation, if they had to starve in a garret or a hut."

The romantic voice of this generation was Henry Wadsworth Longfellow. The young people avidly read his "Footsteps of Angels," "The Light of Stars," "The Reaper and the Flowers" and "Hymn to the Night" and rejoiced at his insight into their feelings. Though Longfellow today is remembered more for sentimental doggerel like his *Hiawatha*, he was revered then by youth all over the world. Says Van Wyck Brooks, young men ". . . up and down the Hudson and the Mississippi, in England, Scotland, Holland, in far off Russia, beside the Neva as beside the Danube, heard the trailing garments of the night, shared these reveries of the New England springtime that Longfellow was putting into words. . . ."

A spirit of rebelliousness was felt by more people than merely the young in the 1840s, however. In the latter part of that decade, there were revolutions in Europe, worldwide unrest and a surge of demands for change in nations on all parts of the globe. The crusade for reform was especially strong in New England, and several of the Transcendentalists were among the leaders of various movements. It was a broad-scale assault on the status quo. Women's suffrage, the rights of labor, temperance, modification of dress, "scientific" diets—all had their fiery advocates. Anarchistic, socialistic and communistic communities, such as Fruitlands and Brook Farm, were established; Thoreau and Alcott were strong supporters of these "utopias."

Most important of all the reform movements in New England was the drive to abolish slavery in the United States. Among the leaders of this dangerous cause—its spokesmen were often the target of mob violence—were Theodore Parker and Elizabeth Peabody, both Transcendentalists; Wendell Phillips, the most radical of the lot (he advocated not only freedom, but land, education and full civil rights for Negroes); Massachusetts Senator Charles Sumner, a powerful abolitionist voice in Congress; and that eloquent Congregationalist preacher from Litchfield, Connecticut, Henry Ward Beecher.

Editors and writers were also in the front line of the battle. William Lloyd Garrison published *The Liberator*, probably the most influential of the abolitionist papers. One of the most popular of his contributors was John Greenleaf Whittier, whose poems were quoted by abolitionists everywhere. Later his *Liberator* poems were published in book form under the titles *Poems Written During the Progress of the Abolition Question*, *Voices of Freedom* and *Songs of Labor*.

But the literary work that had greatest impact for the abolitionist cause was a novel, *Uncle Tom's Cabin*, written by Harriet Beecher Stowe, a shy, gentle woman who was Henry Ward Beecher's sister. Published serially in the *National Era*, an abolitionist paper, and then as a book in 1852, *Uncle Tom's Cabin* became an immediate international sensation. More than 300,000 copies of the book were sold in the United States in its first year, and it was translated into 37 languages abroad. "In all the history of the printed book, the Bible alone had appeared in so many versions," says Van Wyck Brooks. G. L. Aiken did a dramatization of the novel, and numerous companies took the play to all parts of the North. *Uncle Tom* was still being produced in the early part of the 20th Century. Mrs. Stowe's characters, "Uncle Tom," "Topsy" and "Simon Legree," became parts of the language. Although the novel was no diatribe—in fact, Mrs. Stowe was warmly understanding of the South's problems—she probably did more than any other single person to arouse the conscience of the nation against slavery. When President Abraham Lincoln met her some years later, he said, "So you're the little woman who wrote the book that made this great war."

Meanwhile there was plenty of writing being done in New England that was not concerned with slavery. Delightful and amusing sketches by Oliver Wendell Holmes were appearing in a new Boston-based magazine called the *Atlantic Monthly*, edited by James Russell Lowell. Later these pieces were collected into a book that was published under the title *The Autocrat of the Breakfast Table*. Holmes was another of the many part-time writers who flourished in New England. He began his career as a practicing physician, then went to Dartmouth as professor of anatomy and physiology, and later became dean of the Harvard Medical School.

Early in the 1860s the *Atlantic* scored another great coup with the publication of *The Man Without a Country* by Edward Everett Hale, a Boston minister. The Civil War was then raging, patriotism was high, and Hale's powerful story of the Army officer forever banished from the homeland he had betrayed and denounced struck a highly responsive chord with the public. Philip Nolan, the protagonist, became as well established a folk figure as Rip Van Winkle.

About the same time, the *Atlantic* was also publishing the poems and short stories of Louisa May Alcott, Bronson Alcott's daughter. The Alcotts were chronically in financial straits, and Louisa had decided to ease the situation with her writing.

She was brilliantly successful. After serving as a nurse in the Civil War, she published her popular *Hospital Sketches* in 1863, but even she must have been astounded by the enthusiasm that greeted the appearance of *Little Women* some five years later. It was one of the most popular books for girls ever written. The Alcotts' money worries were over. *Little Men* and *Jo's Boys*, sequels to *Little Women*, all enjoyed big sales, as did her other books.

In the post-Civil War years of the 19th Century, the enthusiasm for crusades in support of great causes abated in New England's intellectual community. Not that there was any lessening of dedication to learning or enthusiasm for writing. Bret Harte, a writer from the West who visited Cambridge, remarked that a man could not shoot in any direction without bringing down the writer of two or three volumes. A woman who lived in Cambridge said that social conversation with a neighbor never posed a problem. If the talk lagged, all she had to do was ask the gentleman how his book was coming and a detailed answer was certain. When one little girl asked another, "Your grandfather is a poet, is he not?" the second youngster replied with some surprise, "Why, yes, isn't yours?"

Boston accepted unself-consciously its right to be known as the Athens of America, so much so that few natives bothered to use the term any longer. The city's pre-eminence in American letters remained unquestioned. Every serious writer in the United States aspired to appear in the pages of the *Atlantic*, for then his name would be known to other authors and to editors all over the country. As Brooks has reported, "Boston excelled in the machinery of culture, as well as in culture itself."

One young author who had come to Boston from another city wrote to a friend, "The humblest man of letters has a position here which he doesn't have in New York. To be known as an able writer is to have the choicest society open to you. . . A knight of the quill here is supposed necessarily to be a gentleman. In New York—he's a Bohemian!—outside of his personal friends he has no standing."

New Yorkers, who generally had a less-than-enthusiastic view of Boston, grumbled that one had to face a test to get into the Hub city and, if one passed, was awarded a kind of degree when one departed. Because of the city's cultural reputation, visiting lecturers found appearances there a nervous strain. Even Mark Twain, a hardened veteran of the lecture platform, admitted that the experience was unsettling. A Boston audience, he wrote, was comprised of "4,000 critics."

Despite their feverish interest in culture, Proper

Bostonians were also immensely interested in making money. In theory, at least, prosperity was always achieved through hard work, honesty and other homely virtues, and one New England writer, Horatio Alger, made a fortune perpetuating this legend in his books for boys. Beginning with *Ragged Dick*, published in 1867, Alger wrote about one hundred novels, all of which argued that industry, tenacity and bravery not only were good for the soul but also had a magnificent effect on the bank account.

While Alger cheered the status quo, a frail New Hampshire woman by the name of Mary Baker Eddy gave the strongly entrenched religious and medical communities a severe shaking in 1875 when she published her *Science and Health* and then went on to establish the Christian Science religion that was based on the precepts of her book. A major tenet of the new religion was complete reliance on "the scientific system of divine healing" and concomitant rejection of medical science. Despite a lifetime of poor health, she lived until she was nearly 90 and continued to exercise a strong influence over the Church until her death.

In sharp contrast to Mrs. Eddy's fame was the sheltered life of one of the era's most important women in the world of writing. Emily Dickinson, daughter of a distinguished Amherst, Massachusetts, lawyer who clung to the old traditions of Puritanism, was a recluse for most of her life. She was, however, a poet of enormous talent, and during her 56 years she scribbled more than one thousand poems on scraps of paper and on backs of envelopes. Only three were published while she was alive, but some five years after her death, in 1886, the first collection of her works was printed. Other volumes of her work continued to appear as late as the 1950s. A number of critics regard Emily Dickinson as the best of the women poets born in the United States, and the techniques she developed had a profound effect on poets who followed her.

The late decades of the 19th Century also saw the full blossoming of the brilliant talent of Boston-born Henry Adams, one of the brightest stars in the New England galaxy of writers. Adams, who was an editor of the *North American Review* and a teacher of medieval history at Harvard, had written two biographies and two novels before the publication—from 1889 to 1891—of his monumental, nine-volume *History of the United States*. He is best-known, however, for his masterly autobiography, *The Education of Henry Adams*, one of the true classics of American literature, which was first printed privately in 1906 but not published for the general public until 1918, the year of his death.

Despite such promising work, the closing years of the 19th Century seemed to many critics the end of New England's intellectual dominance. Said Barrett Wendell of Harvard, "We are vanishing into provincial obscurity. America has swept from our grasp. The future is beyond us." The great writers seemed to be dying off: Lowell, Whittier, Francis Parkman, Holmes—all died in the early 1890s. Oliver Herford, a witty and humorous writer, described New England as "the abandoned farm of literature." The anti-intellectual wave that was to culminate in the 1920s and 1930s would soon get underway.

But those who tolled the bells for New England culture were premature. The 20th Century saw the region's colleges and universities acquire new prestige and witnessed the advent of a new generation of distinguished writers who took their place in the forefront of the world's literature. Among the modern voices were the poets Edward Arlington Robinson, e.e. cummings, Edna St. Vincent Millay, and Amy Lowell and Robert Lowell—both members of James Russell Lowell's family and striking proof that the old Puritan literary blood strain was still vigorous. Towering over them all was that giant of contemporary American poetry, Robert Frost. Though born in San Francisco, Frost spent most of his life in New England and became one of the region's most respected and popular citizens; his eloquent, tight-lipped verse is as sturdy and as doggedly simple as a Vermont stone wall. Another adoptive New Englander whose work became well known throughout the country was John P. Marquand, author of a number of novels, including *Wickford Point* and *The Late George Apley*, which portray the manners and morals of the Boston area with a skill that has not been surpassed.

Nor did all New England philosophers die with the 19th Century. Cambridge-born John Dewey became one of the most brilliant and controversial thinkers of the early 20th Century. His formulations of the principles of a democratic and industrial society and his revolutionary ideas on education are still influential.

Far from running down, New England's intellectual clock, as Van Wyck Brooks once observed, is still ticking soundly. The elder Oliver Wendell Holmes once paid tribute to Boston's cultural accomplishments in a statement that could apply to the entire Yankee region: it was a place, he said, that "had opened, and kept open, more turnpikes leading to free thought and free speech and free deeds than any other city in the country."

Men of ideas
and action

In an age when the nation's dependence upon a deep reservoir of knowledge in its colleges and universities is greater than ever before in history, New England continues to hold its centuries-old position as one of the world's great centers of intellect and talent. Men from the region's institutions of higher learning are contributing to every aspect of contemporary life, from atomic research to foreign policy, from advising private firms to establishing their own enterprises. New England's intellectual heritage dates back to the Puritan pioneers. Acutely aware that scholarly men of action are a basic requisite for the advancement of a civilization, the early settlers founded Harvard, the first of many colleges they were to establish. The men trained in and associated with these New England institutions are among the nation's most valuable assets today.

As Chairman of the Massachusetts Institute of Technology Corporation, James R. Killian Jr. presides over one of the most prestigious sources of highly trained scientists in the world. The portrait above him is of Richard C. Maclaurin, a former MIT president.

Photographs by Alfred Eisenstaedt

One of the great men of photography, Dr. Harold E.
Edgerton, Professor of Electrical Measurements
at MIT, is framed by his most famous invention,
the strobe light. This electronic flash has made
possible stop-motion photography, enabling men
to observe in pictures movements too fast for their
eyes to see. Other inventions that have sprung
from his research are underwater acoustic devices
and cameras, which aid oceanographic studies.

Edward Mills Purcell, Professor of Nuclear Physics
at Harvard and co-winner of the Nobel Prize in 1952
for his work in atomic science, stands beside a map
of interstellar hydrogen clouds, of which he is a
co-discoverer. The discovery that these clouds
emit radio waves of a particular frequency has
enabled scientists, with the use of radio telescopes,
to map distant parts of the universe. Dr. Purcell
is also active in international scientific affairs.

Exploring and exploiting scientific frontiers

In and around Cambridge, Massachusetts, site of both Harvard University and the Massachusetts Institute of Technology, are laboratories staffed by one of the largest concentrations of scientists in the nation. Their research spans the spectrum of scientific inquiry, ranging from deep-sea exploration to cosmic communication. Although much of the work done by these experts is "pure" research, i.e., without a particular concern for any direct application, the modern scientist is also likely to be ready to put his knowledge, talent and experience to immediate use for industry and government. The achievement of such men, it has been said, "shapes the life of every human presently inhabiting the planet, and will influence the destiny of generations to come."

A Harvard professor of chemistry, George Bogdan Kistiakowsky is primarily concerned with pure research in his field, but he has also made notable contributions to national defense and to private business. During World War II, he worked on the Manhattan Project that built the atomic bomb, and later served as Special Assistant to the President for Science and Technology. He has been a consultant to several private companies.

Jerome B. Weisner, provost of MIT and former director of its Research Laboratory of Electronics, has been described as "a combination of the practical and the theoretical man of science." The combination has worked well for the U.S. His work in the laboratory led to techniques that made possible the Distant Early Warning network, the "DEW line" chain of radar stations in the upper part of the Northern Hemisphere.

From the laboratory to the market

In addition to serving as a reservoir for research scientists, New England has become a center for scientist-businessmen marketing laboratory-developed products. Equipment for the U.S. space program, computers and electronic equipment are among the commodities made in the region. Such industries constantly require the services of faculty scientists. To permit easy discourse between business and university, a science-oriented industrial park has been erected near the Harvard and MIT campuses.

Scientist-businessman Arthur Kantrowitz helped bring U.S. space missiles safely back to earth: a former Cornell professor, he became director of the AVCO Corporation's Everett Research Laboratory in 1955 and developed a missile nose cone capable of resisting the heat of re-entry into the earth's atmosphere. Among other deeds, he joined his brother Adrian in designing an artificial heart valve.

Edwin H. Land, inventor of the Polaroid camera and numerous other optical devices, is probably the nation's most successful scientist-corporate executive. His Cambridge-based Polaroid Corporation is valued at well over $125 million. A strong proponent of a close working relationship between research and industry, Land is a visiting professor at MIT and a member of Harvard's Board of Overseers Visiting Committees for physics and astronomy instruction.

Gerald W. Blakeley Jr., a graduate of Bowdoin College in Brunswick, Maine, stands in Technology Square, an industrial park he built near MIT in Cambridge. The buildings that comprise the square were designed for the scientific research conducted by the industries that occupy them. The location of the square is convenient for MIT and Harvard professors who act as consultants to the businesses.

An abiding commitment to public service

The federal government, no less than private industry, draws on the vast pool of experts in New England colleges and universities to act as consultants or to fill specific full-time posts. Economists, sociologists and linguists are among the academics in constant demand in Washington. The men may be called on to assist in formulating policy toward a particular nation, to advise on government wage scales or to help prepare an agricultural program for a new country. The concept of public service ingrained in New England institutions continues to provide the U.S. with the services of superior men.

In a career of service to the federal government, dating back to 1945, Don K. Price, dean of Harvard's John Fitzgerald Kennedy School of Government, has served Presidents of both parties at such varied tasks as government reorganization, setting federal salary levels and establishing the Atomic Energy Commission. He has also been a trustee of the RAND Corporation, a nonprofit research concern in California.

After serving as the United States Ambassador to Japan from 1961 to 1966, Edwin O. Reischauer returned to Harvard, becoming a University Professor affiliated with the East Asian Research Center. Born in Tokyo, Reischauer is an outstanding authority on Asian history, literature, politics and philosophy. He has been a frequent consultant to the State Department in formulating U.S. policy toward China.

The author of five books and numerous articles on foreign affairs, Henry A. Kissinger, a professor of government at Harvard and director of its International Seminar, is also one of the nation's most valued advisers on foreign policy. He was a special consultant on national security to President Kennedy and has aided both the U.S. Arms Control and Disarmament Agency and the RAND Corporation.

Both the United States and the United Nations have called on the services of economist Max F. Millikan, director of MIT's Center for International Studies. In the 1950s he took a leave of absence from MIT to become Assistant Director of the Central Intelligence Agency. In the following decade he served as a consultant on policy planning in the State Department and as an adviser to the United Nations on international economic programs.

Attacking orthodoxy from the campus

Often the supposed ivory towers of philosophers and educators in New England colleges and universities become intellectual gymnasiums where new and revolutionary ideas are tested before being subjected to the hostile reactions of orthodox critics. For example, an innovator who proposes an entirely new method of teaching science because the established way is dull must have a strong concept that will withstand furious attack. Similarly, a philosopher who explores subjects considered outside his realm must be prepared for intellectual controversy. But upsetting the status quo and questioning deeply held beliefs are old traditions in New England. Fortunately, many men from the region's institutions still refuse to view any intellectual concept as sacred.

With the aid of a blackboard, MIT's physicist Jerrold Zacharias explains a light-velocity experiment. In the late 1950s Zacharias revolutionized the teaching of physics in high schools when he formed a committee to map a wholly new program. It was cautiously adopted by eight schools in 1957; 10 years later it was in use in some 5,000. Zacharias was disenchanted with his own education in science. "Not one course laid a glove on me," he says.

Writer, editor, painter, poet and playwright as well as Sterling Professor of Philosophy at Yale, Paul Weiss is one of the increasingly rare philosophers who can communicate as readily with laymen as with his colleagues. Although a celebrated scholar in his field of metaphysics, Weiss has also brought the discipline of philosophy to sports and other aspects of contemporary life that are seldom, if ever, touched on by more conventional philosophers.

Intellectuals and the nation's social problems

Along with assisting the federal government in solving its manifold problems, adapting the results of scientific research to practical use, acting as consultants to business and providing stimulus in the world of ideas, New England's learned men are deeply involved in America's highly complex social problems. Medical men, urban planners, architects, sociologists and others are engaged in counterattacking the blight that afflicts almost every metropolitan area in the nation. The contribution of the intellectual, it has been said, is to explain what a problem is all about and to offer suggestions about solving it. New England's intellectuals make this contribution in many areas with admirable results.

A crusader for proper medical care for the poor, Dr. H. Jack Geiger, Professor of Preventive Medicine at Tufts University Medical School in Boston, converses in his experimental Columbia Point Health Center. Before the center opened, the nearest hospital to Columbia Point, a low-income housing development, was more than two hours away via bus and subway. Today more than two dozen such centers exist in the U.S., modeled on the Columbia Point project.

The highway complex behind Daniel Patrick Moynihan might well symbolize the multitudinous activities of this outstanding urban expert, writer, public servant (a former Assistant Secretary of Labor) and intellectual gadfly. As director of MIT's and Harvard's Joint Center for Urban Studies, he is concerned with every aspect of municipal life. The center acts as adviser to some 80 cities.

Vincent J. Scully, a professor of art at Yale and an articulate proponent of better urban design, stands behind Aristide Maillol's sculpture *L'Air* in the university art gallery. A popular teacher— a fifth of all Yale students take at least one of his courses—Scully says a building must relate to its setting and to a city's other structures to reveal a pleasing interaction of historical styles.

8

Cradle
of the Future

To the camera-carrying tourist, New England today is America's attic, a pleasant place full of picturesque and stirring reminders of the country's past. A much different view was taken by a French geographer, Jean Gottmann, in a 1961 study of the northeastern seaboard of the United States. That area, which includes a large part of New England, he saw as "the cradle of a new order in the organization of inhabited space . . . the dawn of a new stage of human civilization. . . ."

Gottmann pointed out that the coastal area of the northeast has grown into a "megalopolis": one large supercity created as neighboring urban and suburban areas expanded and overlapped. About one fifth of the total population of the United States lives in this megalopolis—and its boundaries continue to spread. The New England section of the megalopolis is now considered to cover all of Connecticut, Rhode Island and Massachusetts and to extend across southeastern New Hampshire to the Portland area of Maine.

But this does not mean that Vermont and the

mountains and forests of northern New Hampshire and Maine are the only rural-looking places left in New England. A traveler flying over Connecticut and Massachusetts sees, between and beyond the highways and expressways, large areas of pastures, woodlands, tilled farmlands and small villages in a countryside that looks very much the same as it did 50 years ago. But although these country towns in southern and central New England still have their rustic and unspoiled appearance, they have long since lost their rural character.

The economic and social changes that develop when the expansion of urban-centered living turns a rural village into a suburb do not necessarily alter the physical appearance of the place. The townspeople can continue to live in the same houses, enjoy the same view of the green, countryside hills as their grandfathers did and keep their automobiles in the same barns where farm horses were once stabled. The big difference, of course, is simply that most of the wage earners no longer earn their living as their fathers did, either by farming their own land or by serving the needs of the local farmers as tradesmen; now workers commute to jobs outside the town. Many of the smaller farms in the areas of New England's megalopolis are operated by farmers who do not depend entirely on agriculture for their income; they or their wives hold other jobs. "We hurry through the chores and the milking before we rush off to Pratt and Whitney," says one part-time dairy farmer who commutes from his village in western Massachusetts to a jet-engine plant in East Hartford, Connecticut, on a bus chartered by the company.

How drastically urban intrusions have changed the traditional New England village way of life can be seen in the small dairy-farming community of New Braintree, located on the back-country roads of western Massachusetts between the spreading metropolitan areas of Worcester and Springfield. New Braintree still has the appearance of an early-19th Century community. A town of 550 people who live on 20 green and hilly square miles, it is so removed from the main highways that a stranger would have trouble finding it. If he did make his way along the narrow stone-walled roads past a few hilltop farmhouses to the center of the town, he would see the white-steepled Congregational church, a small common with a soldiers-and-sailors monument, and a vacant red-brick building that once housed the general store and post office. Such a visitor might wonder if he had traveled backward in time to a rural village of 100 years ago. There is nothing in the quiet scene around him that could not have been there during the 1860s, except perhaps the monument and a tractor parked in the farmyard near the common. But if the scene of New Braintree has changed little over the past century, the daily lives of its people have changed a great deal.

New Braintree's history is typical of a New England country town. In 1675, during King Philip's War, a company of Puritan militia was attacked by Indians along the foothills bordering its Winnimisset Valley. Later the area was settled by colonists from a small town south of Boston, Braintree, for which the new settlement was named. When the community was incorporated as a colonial town in 1751, it had 45 families and a population of nearly 300 people. During the next century, it was more thickly populated than it is today; in 1850, before many of its farmers began to emigrate westward, there were 852 townspeople, and there had been attempts to bring manufacturing to New Braintree. A water-powered woolen mill, started during the War of 1812, soon failed. A shoemaking business, a carriage- and wagon-building shop, and a cheese factory lasted longer, but in time they too went out of business. Between the Civil War and World War II, New Braintree remained at a standstill, a dairy-farming town of 500 people, changing little from year to year.

As recently as the 1930s, when Franklin D. Roosevelt was President, life in the town was about the same as it had been during the Presidency of Grover Cleveland, except for the automobile, which was used mainly for shopping trips to nearby Worcester and North Brookfield, and the radio, which kept families up later, and the party-line telephone that had to be cranked to signal a neighbor's number. Everybody in New Braintree was a dairy farmer except Bill Loftus and Charlie Daley. Loftus was superintendent of town roads, constable, and manager of the red-brick general store and post office across from the church in the town's center; Daley was the village blacksmith. Until World War II the farm work was done with horses and the cows were milked by hand. Tractors and other modern implements did not quickly win favor with tradition-bound New Englanders working small, hilly farms. "Even during the war, I remember people here arguing that you couldn't farm without horses, and they thought hay balers were crazy," says Donald Adams, a former New Braintree farmer who now does storekeeping and construction work. "Now they all use tractors and hay balers."

Like the hard farm work, the home and social life in New Braintree in the early 1930s had not changed much since the turn of the century. The first electric power lines did not reach the town until 1929 and were not extended throughout the surrounding area until several years later, so most of the farmhouses used kerosene lamps for lights and hand pumps to supply the kitchen sinks. Wood-burning stoves heated the homes, cooked the meals and boiled the laundry water. There were no school buses; children walked to one or the other of the town's three one-room schoolhouses, each of which had one teacher for all eight elementary grades. Older students made their own way, somehow, to high school five miles away in North Brookfield.

Highlights of the town's social calendar were Town Meeting Day in March and the Grange's gala Strawberry Festival Supper in June. Town Meeting began about 8 a.m., after the morning chores, and lasted, with prolonged debates and speeches, until it was time to adjourn for milking in the late afternoon. The ladies provided a town-meeting dinner at noon in the basement of the Town Hall. The Grange, a farmers' association, met once or twice a month to exchange information about prices, crops and livestock. Its annual Strawberry Festival, offering baked ham, home-baked beans, brown bread and strawberry shortcake, was a gala affair.

Less formal social gatherings were held around the potbellied stove in Loftus' general store when the townspeople were picking up their mail and groceries. The store also carried hardware, work clothes and shoes, candy, soda pop, dry goods and, in the summer, ice cream of two flavors, which changed weekly. Behind the store, Loftus sold ice from a sawdust-packed ice house for the convenience of the few families in town who did not cut and store their own ice, as dairy farmers had to do.

In only one respect did the people of New Braintree in 1932 present a different aspect from that of their ancestors in 1882, or even in 1832, and that was a difference the passing visitor would probably have failed to notice. The once solidly Yankee population, including many descendants of original Puritan settlers—the Barrs, Pollards, Tufts, Whipples and Thompsons—had become mixed with a few French-Canadian, Polish and Lithuanian farming families with such names as Benoit, Langevin, Vigneault, Wespalis, Wisnewski and Grigas.

But not even the most casual tourist could miss the changes of recent decades. In the 1960s the Loftus general store stood empty and deserted, replaced by distant yet easily reached suburban-type shopping centers. Life in New Braintree, with electric refrigeration and color television, is not much different today from life in the country sections of New York's Westchester County. A number of the townspeople now commute to jobs in cities and the larger industrial towns, some traveling as far as East Hartford and Windsor Locks in Connecticut. The large, old Vigneault farmhouse is now the handsomely restored and attractively landscaped home of a wealthy industrialist, Frederic W. Howe Jr., president of the Worcester textile-machinery firm of Crompton & Knowles, who would not have been found in the New Braintree of the early 1930s. The annual town meeting is held in the evening because there are not enough taxpayers present during the day. The Grange, which has become almost exclusively a social group rather than an organization of working farmers, still serves its Strawberry Festival Supper—but only to families that have made reservations in advance.

Along with a more spruced-up and prosperous look, one prosaic but significant sign of New Braintree's growing change from a purely rural farming community to a kind of suburb is its recent consideration of establishing a town dump. No farming town needs a dump—farmers dispose of trash by carting it to a distant part of their own land—but New Braintree now has so many homeowners on small tracts that a public dumping place is becoming necessary. Another disturbing portent of the town's increasingly suburban character is its rising

tax rate. In 1930 Charlie Daley paid a tax of $20.90 on his home, blacksmith shop and three quarters of an acre of land. His 1967 tax bill for the same property was $451.

Daley and his smithy, oddly enough, were little affected by either the arrival of the farm tractor or the development of megalopolis. Well past the age of 80 in the mid-1960s, Charlie worked steadily every day because he was one of the few expert horseshoe makers left in New England. However, now his service was urgently demanded not by farmers but by owners of saddle horses and harness-racing stables.

As in suburbia everywhere, more than half of the tax revenue in New Braintree goes to school costs. The three old single-room schoolhouses have been replaced by a central elementary school with three teachers and three classrooms, to which children ride in school buses. Older children travel in buses to junior high and high schools in North Brookfield, their tuition paid by New Braintree, but the town will probably soon bow to the inevitable and join with two nearby towns in forming a regional school, incurring still higher tax rates.

New Braintree's scenic countryside looks much the same as it did before World War II, even though there are only about one third as many farms as there were in those bygone years; larger farms cover almost the same area of land. Albert Lefevre, the town clerk and operator of the school buses, runs a 250-acre dairy farm, twice as large as it was in his father's day, with about three times as many cows, the herd currently numbering about 50 head. His neighborhood on the Gilbertville Road in the southwest area of the town, which had 11 farms before the war, had four by the 1960s. But those four farms were able to produce considerably more milk than the 11 did in the 1930s. Lefevre's own work as a modern dairy farmer is as changed as the character of his neighborhood. Like farmers everywhere, he must manage a bigger farm than his father's to make a profit, with none of the manual help that his father had.

"The big difference is that I'm alone here during the day," Lefevre says. "A farm this large thirty-five or forty years ago would have had a hired man helping the farmer, along with the farmer's wife and a few of his older sons. To make ends meet, Margery, my wife, works as a nurse at a hospital in Ware. My twenty-year-old boy, Dwight, our oldest, is studying civil engineering at Northeastern University in Boston, and my nineteen-year-old son, Ralph, is in the Army in Germany. Farm labor in New England is so scarce that apple growers have to import workers from Canada to pick their crops." With the labor shortage and the larger herds of cows, milking by hand is now impossible. Every dairy farm in New Braintree, like most dairy farms in New England, uses automatic milking machinery.

The increasing land taxes and the constant need for a larger capital investment are making farming in a New England megalopolitan town like New Braintree less attractive every year. Lefevre is looking forward to the day when bigger regional schools may enable him to give up dairy farming and to work full time on his school-bus business. Another farmer says, "Pretty soon they'll be shipping frozen milk from the West, just like everything else. Then there won't be any farms left in New England, and we'll all be better off."

The change in small country towns like New Braintree is a reflection of a new spirit and tempo that has stirred up all of New England in recent years. This renaissance of enterprise shows itself in many forms in many places—in the rise of computerized technology in the new industries outside Boston along Route 128, the suburban belt expressway that has become one of the leading space and missile research-and-development centers in the Western world; in the dramatic revitalization of jaded central city areas in Boston, New Haven and Hartford; in the strong economic comeback of idle mill towns such as Manchester, New Hampshire, and Burlington, Vermont; in the boom of both winter and summer tourist resorts; and in the strengthening of the area's position as the nation's leading center of higher education, not only in the long-established prestige universities of Harvard, Yale and M.I.T., but on the newer campuses of Brandeis University, the University of Connecticut, the University of Massachusetts, Boston College and Boston University.

During most of the 20th Century, the economic growth of New England had lagged far behind that of other sections of the country. The region's troubles stemmed immediately from the loss of its textile industry, the main source of prosperity in the 19th Century, which had moved South to take advantage of a cheaper labor market and a location closer to the sources of raw materials. But historians such as Oscar Handlin have suggested that the decline of New England's economy may have been brought about by the disruption of the Yankees' feeling of security. When the region was swept by the sudden influx of immigration from Europe and Canada in the later years of the last century, Handlin points out, the Yankees who controlled New England's capital wealth found themselves suddenly surrounded by strange newcomers; they became apprehensive in business ventures and took pains to protect their family's holdings by tying up their money in what were called "Boston trusts." These trusts limited the heirs' right to use their inherited fortunes, thus "providing restraints against alien ideas" that might threaten the family's stability. Such restrictive trust funds, which controlled many large estates, discouraged the kinds of business risks that had originally built those estates with fortunes won in the China trade and the Merrimack River textile-mill ventures, and this dried up the New England economy.

The Boston trusts were only one among several handicaps that hindered New England's competition against other areas of the nation during the expansion of mass production in the early years of the 20th Century. Geography was one factor. The region was poorly situated, removed from both the coal and ore regions of the U.S. and the growing markets of the Midwest and Far West and thus ill-favored for the development of heavy industry. But the dominating restraint was the conservative Yankee reluctance to get involved in anything strange or different. "I wish there weren't quite so many new ideas," wrote George Apley, John P. Marquand's fictional prototype of the 1930s Bostonian, in a letter to his son. "Where do they come from? Why is everyone trying to break away from what we all know is sane and good?"

The big change that finally shook up New England and started it on its present road to lively prosperity came from ideas much newer than those that had troubled George Apley. One great regional resource that New England had never tapped for economic advantage until World War II was its universities' brain power, especially the wealth of scientific knowledge concentrated at Harvard and M.I.T. During the war, the academic scientists at Cambridge set aside scholarly studies to develop electronic computers and radar for the government, and after the war they became involved in industrial research in the electronics field. When the Soviet Union exploded a nuclear bomb in 1949 and became a dangerous threat to the U.S. homeland, Cambridge—by then well established as America's leading center of electronic knowledge and experience—was the logical place to be selected for the work of designing the U.S. government's attack-detecting, early-warning systems.

For this big task M.I.T. in 1954 built a special laboratory in the town of Lincoln, near Lexington and Concord, not far from the recently completed

Route 128. While the Lincoln Laboratory was developing the high-speed computers and sensitive radar equipment for the defense systems, its staff of 600 scientists and engineers were also devising new equipment and methods that were applicable to private industry. Attracted by this example and the concentration of scientific knowledge available in the universities of the region, companies from all over the country—RCA, Avco, Minneapolis-Honeywell—as well as many from the Boston area —especially Raytheon and Polaroid—began to establish research-and-development plants in industrial parks along Route 128. A few years later, when the U.S. astronauts were beginning to travel in space, the roadside industrial parks boomed as a world-famous complex of highly sophisticated scientific laboratories. Many of the firms producing equipment for spaceships and satellites have been founded on the basis of ideas from university consultants, and they have been generously financed by eager Wall Street and Boston investors.

The products turned out on Route 128 would certainly bewilder Paul Revere, who rode through the area on his way from Lexington to Concord. A typical shipment from one of the plants, consisting of instruments for a planet-circling satellite, has been said to be worth $3,000 a pound. An RCA factory on the road makes half of all the memory cores used in the entire computer industry. One core, containing many tiny electronic beads, can store as many bits of factual data as a man could memorize in 20 years. By a recent count, Route 128, also known as "The Golden Semicircle" and "Space Highway," had more than 550 companies employing 55,000 people.

Electronics is now one of New England's biggest industries. It overcomes the costly transportation problem that hinders other industries in the region because electronic products are mostly so small, lightweight and expensive that the expense of shipping is inconsequential. Unlike the prodigal textile business, which was not firmly rooted in New England, the electronics industry is an integral part of the region because it grows out of the scientific knowledge and research of experts in the local academic community. Brains are its raw material, and the brains will stay in New England as long as the universities do. "The scientists like the cultural atmosphere here in New England," one electronics man says, "so we've got to keep our company here whether we like it or not, because we must stay close to the scientists."

By now the electronics firms have spread to distant parts of New England, far from the golden parks of Route 128, and with them have come several other new types of industry, also related to space and missile work. Some of the companies have turned up in unexpected places. In an old Civil War-vintage, red-brick factory at the small country town of Fiskdale, Massachusetts, a few miles south of New Braintree, there is, for example, a firm called Tod Industries. It manufactures a number of parts used in the space suits of astronauts. These products are typical of the new New England. Nearly half its manufacturing, it has been estimated, involves things that did not exist in the late 1950s.

New England's northern tier—New Hampshire, Vermont and Maine—have shared the employment upswing of the 1960s with the more traditional industrial centers of Rhode Island, Connecticut and Massachusetts. New Hampshire, economically the fastest-growing state in New England, has the lowest unemployment rate in the region. The mill town of Nashua, for example, has made a striking recovery from the economic blow suffered in 1948 when the community's leading employer, a textile factory, moved away. A group of local citizens formed a nonprofit foundation, bought the mill's property and offered to divide it for sale or lease to any firms that would take any part of it. Now, in the buildings that previously housed one company and 3,500 workers, there are 24 firms employing more than 6,000 workers. The nearby town of Manchester, once hard-hit, has also diversified its industry and is enjoying full employment. When a woolen mill closed down on the outskirts of Burlington, Vermont, creating widespread unemployment, local citizens built an entirely new industrial plant on speculation and landed International Business Machines as a tenant. IBM has 3,000 people on the payroll.

Even in Vermont, cherished by visitors and Vermonters alike as New England's most rural state, industry has passed farming as Vermont's chief source of income. Among other Vermont products, 10 per cent of all the machine tools made in the United States are manufactured there. The precision machines that come from the Fellows Gear Shaper Company of Springfield produce about 90 per cent of all the gears in American automobiles.

Traditional machine-oriented business also continues to thrive in Connecticut, long the most heavily industrialized of the New England States. One big factor in this prosperity is United Aircraft, the largest private employer in the entire region, keeping some 70,000 people busy in its jet-engine and helicopter plants and research-and-development laboratories. The dramatic change in Connecticut —one of the most remarkable civic achievements in modern New England—is the refurbishing and rebuilding of downtown New Haven, under the leadership of Mayor Richard Lee. Experts on the subject have hailed the project as the most successful example of urban renewal in the United States. With the aid of Edward Logue, the gifted city renovator who later moved on to a bigger task in Boston, Lee in 1955 started his major drive against the economic decline of decaying New Haven. It desperately needed rebuilding. No new privately owned office or hotel building, and except for two schools, not a single public building, had been built in New Haven during the previous 30 years. Near the downtown business area, the Oak Street slum district, with 42 acres of rat-infested, overcrowded and run-down houses, was costing the city more in police and fire protection than the area was paying in taxes. Retail business was fading and several large employers were about to move away.

Lee began his campaign by persuading reluctant state officials to build the Oak Street Connector, a $15 million link between New Haven and the Connecticut Turnpike then being constructed along the shorefront of Long Island Sound. With a combination of federal, state and city funds and the support of private capital, the Mayor proceeded to demolish the Oak Street slum area. Its 900 families were moved to respectable low-cost housing and the tenements were replaced with new office buildings, a retail shopping plaza, high-rise apartment buildings, garages and an industrial park. In another downtown section, Lee launched the Church Street redevelopment project, which revitalized a 96-acre tract with a huge new department store and a municipal parking garage, a 350-room hotel, an office building and retail stores, more apartments, a bank building, a medical office building and a junior high school, among many other structures. The Mayor made 30 trips to New York to persuade Macy's to take over the department store in the Church Street center. He was able to stop a hardware concern, an important local employer, from leaving the city by buying its outmoded old factories and giving the company land for a new plant on a site near New Haven's harbor.

Providence is another New England city that has taken a new lease on life. Long listed by the Department of Labor as a depressed area, the Rhode Island capital's unemployment rate dropped in 1966 to only 4.2 per cent, its lowest in 15 years. National Interstate Highway 95, the coastal expressway from Boston to New York, now passes through the heart of Providence, opening up excellent industrial sites in Rhode Island.

The revenue brought to New England by its rejuvenated industry is supplemented by the income from its increasing tourist trade. For example, tourists spend well over $300 million a year in Maine and about $165 million a year in Vermont. In one area of Vermont where land was selling in 1960 for five dollars an acre—less than its value in 1760— the opening of a big new ski resort quickly pushed up the price of real estate to more than $200 an acre.

To bring the economic value of the tourist trade in a small country town into focus, one can cite the example of Sturbridge, Massachusetts, which was an obscure crossroads village until 1946. Then Albert and Joel Cheney Wells, two brothers from the local family who owned the prosperous American Optical Company, decided to re-create an early 19th Century New England rural town there. The resulting regional museum—a fascinating exhibit called Old Sturbridge Village and consisting of 18th and 19th Century Yankee homes, craft shops, a gristmill, a wool-carding mill, a meeting-house and various other old buildings and artifacts —has become one of New England's best-known tourist attractions. In 1946, the year the exhibit was opened, it drew some 5,000 people. At the time, the town of Sturbridge had one old inn, three guest homes offering rooms for visitors, and 12 old-style tourist cabins; the taxes on all of them amounted to $467 a year. In 1966 Old Sturbridge Village welcomed 550,000 visitors from every state in the Union and from many foreign countries. By then the town had done considerable building; there were now overnight accommodations for more than 700 transient guests, and those new facilities were the source of more than $50,000 in tax revenue.

Increasing tourism, though handsomely profitable, is only a comparatively minor part of the vast rebuilding job that is being done on New England's economic structure. As the modern world becomes more and more oriented to technology and computers, the region, as probably the nation's greatest center of scientific knowledge, seems certain to continue to grow in importance as a wellspring of research, technical guidance and the production of the sophisticated equipment of this age. Many knowledgeable observers feel that New England today is in a position comparable to the one it held in the late 18th and the 19th Centuries, when it had exactly the right assets and background to take advantage of the coming of the machine age and the vast expansion of world trade.

Built between 1882 and 1911 as a textile mill, and now providing quarters for a number of small firms representing several industries, a grim building in Lawrence, Massachusetts, stands as a symbol of New England's decline and recent rebirth.

From bust to boom: a Yankee saga

Served by an antiquated transport system and largely dependent on an ailing textile industry, much of New England only a few years ago seemed on the road to ruin. As textile plant after textile plant closed down, a pall of economic doom settled over the region. Today, however, the picture is far different. A great network of superhighways now connects New England with the rest of the country. New space-age industries, drawing on one of the region's most valuable—but long-neglected—economic resources, the brilliance of its scholars and scientists, have generated a boom that is turning staid old cities into soaring metropolises and renewing old Yankee traditions of ingenuity, audacity and imagination. What was—and still is—America's curator of yesterday is quickly becoming a resolute pathfinder into tomorrow.

167

Hartford insures
its own future

A tangle of narrow streets and decaying buildings choked the core of Hartford, Connecticut, before the start of major renovation of the area in 1960. State Street, across the foreground of the picture, is the only avenue that survived the renewal project intact.

Rising in a series of gleaming structures beside the Connecticut River, Hartford's Constitution Plaza *(right)* exemplifies the spirit of renascent New England. The plaza, built at a cost of $40 million, most of which was supplied by private capital, comprises six large commercial buildings—a hotel, a television-and-radio broadcasting center and four office buildings. The plaza also has landscaped pedestrian malls and contains parking facilities for 1,800 cars. Dominating the plaza is the Phoenix Mutual Life Insurance Building *(far right),* popularly called "The Boat," rising near the now refurbished State Street, which leads to a new bridge across the river. Aside from attracting business to Hartford and giving its core a new look, the plaza has been a financial boon for the city. It is expected to return about $1.3 million each year in taxes compared with the $90,000 that the district formerly contributed annually.

168

The highway of science around Boston

A great concrete swath cuts through the suburb of Waltham, Massachusetts, in 1952, marking the site of the new Route 128. Critics at the time denounced the route as needlessly extravagant.

Route 128 today is the spine of a successful industrial complex that is helping to spark the economic rebirth of the region. Most of the firms along the route are concerned with such fields as electronics and precision manufacturing, and often call upon the services of scientists at Harvard and the Massachusetts Institute of Technology. Of some 30 industrial parks along Route 128, three are located at Waltham *(left)*, not far from Cambridge. Some concept of the diversity of factories, research laboratories and service organizations in this one square mile can be gleaned from the keyed photograph: (1) Polaroid (cameras and film); (2) Geodyne (ocean- and weather-study instruments); (3) Actronics (aircraft control instruments); (4) Invac (computer equipment); (5) Spectrum Systems (lens coatings); (6) Tyco (electronics research); (7) Adams-Russell (radio components); (8) Litton (communications research); (9) Adcole (electronic devices); (10) Sanborn (medical and electronic devices); (11) Tektronix (electronics); (12) Xerox (copying machines); (13) Little, Brown (publishers); (14) Raytheon (electronic research); (15) Wintex (vinyl textiles); (16) Sylvania (electronic research); (17) Baird Atomic (electronic instruments); (18) Thermo Electron (energy-conversion research); (19) Pickard & Burns (electronics); (20) Scientific Engineering (professional employment agency); (21) Chicago Pneumatic Tool (industrial and building tools); (22) Arthur A. Crafts (diamond and tungsten carbide tools and gauges); (23) A. B. Dick (office copying equipment); (24) Infrared Industries (electrical and electronic equipment); (25) Baldwin-Lima-Hamilton (electronic instruments); (26) John Hancock Life Insurance Company; (27) Air General (heliport). In addition to the quarters of these organizations, other buildings in the picture house firms that make or distribute such products as dispensers, safes, soft drinks, plastics and aluminum. The area also includes several office buildings, two motels and a car-rental agency.

171

Old and new juxtaposed in Boston

Changes in downtown Boston are indicated by this picture of the West End, whose early-19th Century West Church *(center of picture)* stands proud near the rising towers of the new Government Center. As Boston continues its urban-renewal activities—some city planners estimate that in 15 years between 1961 and 1975 a total of two billion dollars will have been spent on construction—the city will be increasingly hard-pressed to balance the claims of historic buildings against the need to make economic use of valuable land. So far, a balance has been maintained, and the parts of a city grown dowdy and decayed have been at least partially modernized while losing little of their centuries-old charm. Central to Boston's plans for the future is the Government Center, shown here as it neared completion. Among its structures are the twin-towered, 26-story John F. Kennedy Federal Building *(extreme right)*, the lofty State Office Building *(extreme left)* and the crescent-shaped commercial structure One Center Plaza *(lower left)*. Nearby, but not shown in the picture, are a big apartment-house complex along the banks of the Charles River, and across the Charles, the National Aeronautics and Space Administration's $60 million electronic-research center. In 1911 the British author Arnold Bennett wrote: "What primarily differentiates Boston from all other American cities is this: It is . . . complete." Obviously Bennett was a better writer than prophet.

J.W. BATESON COMPANY INC.

Suggested tours

On the following pages seven maps show sections of New England that are of particular interest to the tourist. No attempt has been made to show every road and town. Instead, scenic routes, parks, historic sites and other special features are emphasized. The text accompanying each map gives a description of the area. Opening dates and hours, especially for tours of business enterprises, should be confirmed locally, since they may vary with the season of the year. The seven areas covered are numbered on the small map below to correspond with the descriptive text.

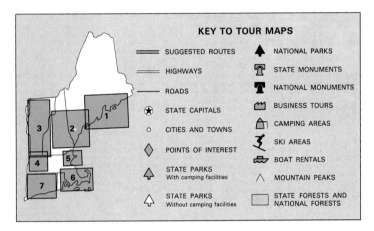

KEY TO TOUR MAPS

▬▬ SUGGESTED ROUTES	▲ NATIONAL PARKS
═══ HIGHWAYS	⚱ STATE MONUMENTS
── ROADS	⚱ NATIONAL MONUMENTS
★ STATE CAPITALS	⌂ BUSINESS TOURS
○ CITIES AND TOWNS	⛺ CAMPING AREAS
◆ POINTS OF INTEREST	⚡ SKI AREAS
▲ STATE PARKS With camping facilities	⛵ BOAT RENTALS
△ STATE PARKS Without camping facilities	∧ MOUNTAIN PEAKS
	▢ STATE FORESTS AND NATIONAL FORESTS

1. The upper coast of Maine

The ruggedly scenic coastline of Maine, from Casco Bay in the southwest all the way to Bar Harbor on Mount Desert Island near the northeast corner of the coast, would be, by itself, enough to make this part of the state one of the most beautiful sections of New England. Bath, Damariscotta, Wiscasset, Rockland and Camden are handsome seacoast towns filled with graceful old houses. But the area includes a geographic bonus—many of the state's numerous and lovely lakes. Maine is also a heavily forested state, and the woods make it one of the country's most attractive vacation spots. There are hundreds of campsites and picnic areas and many canoe routes. Good sites for vacation homes abound, especially around Camden and the Camden Hills State Park, and around Bar Harbor and Acadia National Park on the ocean.

Maine is noted for its lobsters, and particularly in the Damariscotta area east of Brunswick, visitors will see lobster boats, traps and the men who operate them. Also in the Damariscotta area are several fascinating forts that were built to protect Maine's coast at various times in the state's history: Fort Popham, a semicircular Civil War fort near the spot where the English first attempted to colonize Maine in 1607; Fort William Henry, a replica of a fort destroyed in 1696 by Indians; and Fort Edgecomb, an old (1808-1809) blockhouse. Northeast of this concentration of forts is Bangor, the largest city in this region and site of an interesting historical museum.

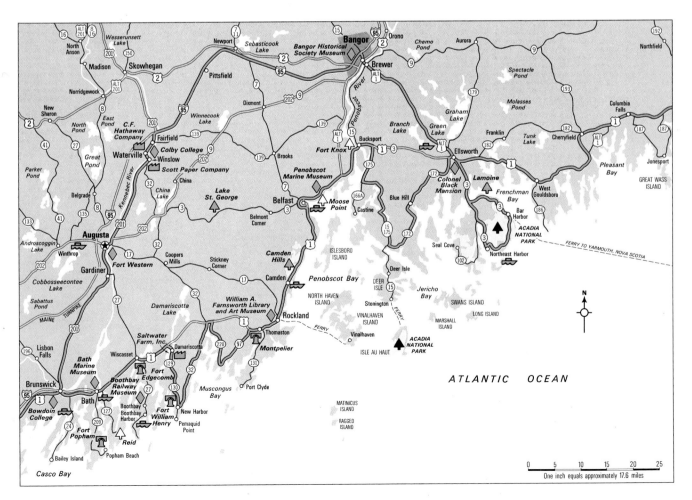

0   5   10   15   20   25
One inch equals approximately 17.6 miles

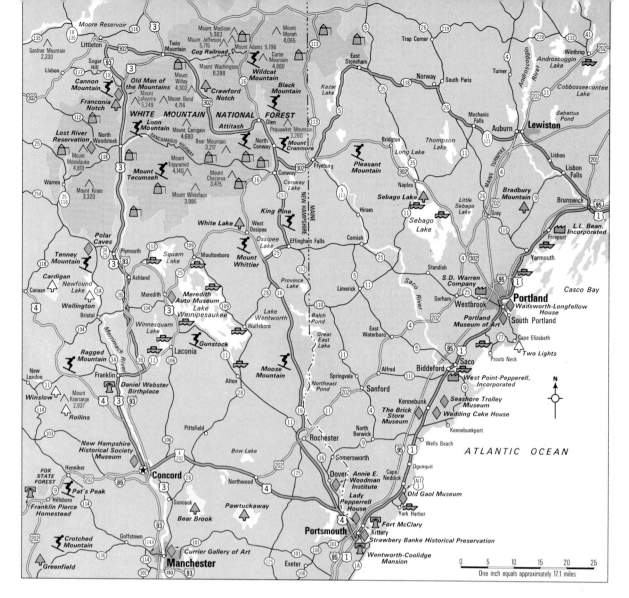

2. New Hampshire and southern Maine

Few areas of New England can boast such scenery as southern Maine and south and central New Hampshire, shown above. Here, within a day's drive of one another, are lakes, mountains, sandy beaches and rock-bound coasts. There are many sites of historical interest, and some of the country's best skiing, fishing and hunting.

Travelers often approach this portion of New England from the south, via Route 1 and New Hampshire's short (18 miles) coastline. Here are found excellent sand beaches and the town of Portsmouth. In Portsmouth is a section called Strawbery Banke, so named for the wild strawberries that grew there and that enticed European settlers, in 1630, to establish the first village in the state there. A number of 17th, 18th and 19th Century buildings on this 10-acre expanse are open to the public.

Route 1 continues northward into Maine and passes through or near such picturesque coastal communities as Kittery, York Harbor, Ogunquit and Kennebunkport. These towns, all famous for swimming, fishing and boating, contain many 18th and 19th Century buildings. Of particular interest is Kittery, with its 18th Century Lady Pepperrell House, a small museum that contains many

fine examples of period furniture and Waterford glass.

Farther along Route 1 is Portland, Maine's largest city and site of the Wadsworth-Longfellow House, now kept as a shrine to the poet. Swinging inland from Brunswick, the road passes close to the Sebago Lake region, noted for its camping facilities and fine fishing. Then, turning southwest along Routes 5 and 302, the New Hampshire border is crossed and the landscape becomes more mountainous. These are the White Mountains and here the federal government maintains a nearly 800,000-acre national forest. Tallest of the peaks is Mount Washington, rising to 6,288 feet above sea level. The top can be reached by car, but many sightseers prefer to take the 1869 cogwheel railroad. This area is a mecca for skiers and hikers. One of the most popular attractions is the Old Man of the Mountains, a startlingly realistic face formed by a series of cliffside ledges in Franconia Notch on Route 3. An alternate route is the spectacularly scenic Kancamagus Highway, between Conway and Lincoln (near North Woodstock). Route 3 continues its southern course winding through or near several charming towns, including Franklin, birthplace of Daniel Webster.

175

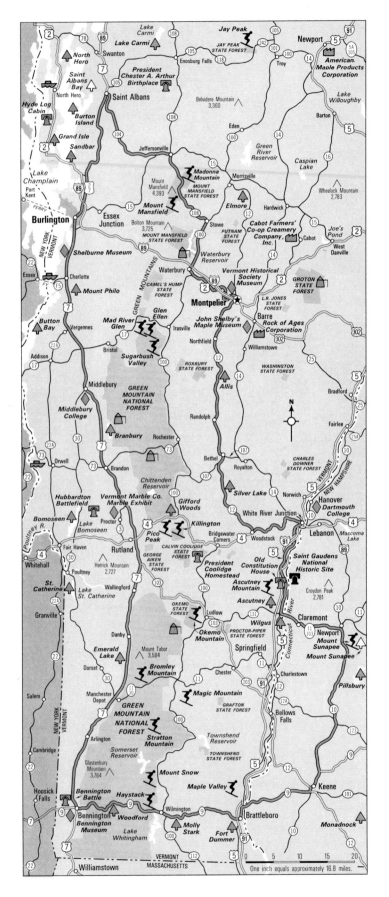

3. The Green Mountain State

Vermont—most of which is shown on the map at left along with a small portion of New Hampshire—could be called the "four seasons' state." Whatever the time of year, the visitor, especially if he is a sportsman, can find much to enthrall him. In winter there is skiing on the Green Mountain slopes; in spring there is fishing in the state's many mountain streams; in summer, swimming and hiking; in autumn, hunting for deer, rabbit, game birds and even bear. For the less athletic visitor, Vermont, with its many museums, historical restorations and quiet country towns, offers the lover of Americana a glimpse into the nation's rural past. In the autumn, especially between September 25 and October 15, the changing foliage everywhere makes a brilliant display.

Bennington, in the southwest corner of Vermont, is a good starting point for a tour by car. Its museum includes numerous memorabilia of the Revolutionary and Civil Wars, including the oldest Stars and Stripes in existence—a flag made before the Battle of Bennington (1777). To the east of Bennington, along Route 9, lies the town of Brattleboro. Among Brattleboro's sights are two houses dating back to about 1850, each built in the shape of an octagon, a Victorian design.

To the northeast and across the state line in New Hampshire is Mount Sunapee State Park, where a four-passenger gondola whisks visitors from the mountain's base to its summit, 2,700 feet above sea level, for a panoramic view of Lake Sunapee and the surrounding mountainous countryside. North of Sunapee is Hanover, New Hampshire, the site of Dartmouth College—one of the most beautiful campuses in the nation. Returning to Vermont, along Route 12, the traveler comes to Montpelier, the state capital. Here a historical museum displays Vermont's first printing press, dioramas depicting scenes in the life of Admiral George Dewey and natural-history exhibits. From Montpelier it is only a short jaunt to the town of Barre, where John Shelby's Maple Museum contains a fascinating display of antique and modern sugaring equipment. Also the world's largest granite quarry is near there and is open for tours.

Turning northwest, the visitor reaches, via a bridge, Hyde Log Cabin, on an island in Lake Champlain, the oldest structure of its type still standing. To the south, beyond Burlington (Vermont's largest city), is the Shelburne Museum—a large group of restored buildings that display a variety of architectural and furnishing styles ranging from the colonial period to late-19th Century Victorian. Among its attractions are a side-wheel riverboat, now landbound, and an 18th Century inn.

Continuing south along Route 7, the visitor passes near a number of state forests and parks where he can camp as well as fish and swim in mountain lakes. At Proctor the Vermont Marble Company, which supplied the stone for many noted U.S. public buildings, offers an interesting exhibit. Nearby are several famous ski areas and the Green Mountain National Forest, containing almost a quarter million acres of lakes, mountains and woodlands.

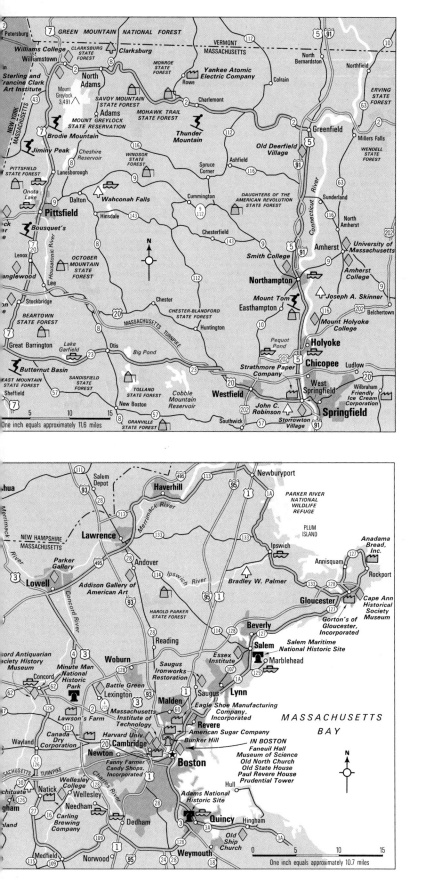

4. Western Massachusetts

Western Massachusetts, adorned by the lovely wooded Berkshire Hills in the west and the richly fertile Connecticut Valley in the east, is one of New England's most beautiful areas. In addition to scenic beauty, the area offers a variety of other attractions such as winter skiing, a summer music festival, historic villages, outstanding art museums and handsome campuses, including those of Amherst, Mount Holyoke, Smith and Williams.

On the grounds of Springfield's Eastern State Exposition is Storrowton Village, a collection of restored buildings that date back to colonial times. North of Springfield, on Route 5, is another group of 17th and 18th Century structures in Old Deerfield Village, a town that endured several Indian attacks. Just north of Deerfield is Route 2, called the Mohawk Trail, which follows a track originally blazed by Indians. Route 2 westward passes through the Mohawk Trail State Forest and on to Williamstown. There, in the Sterling and Francine Clark Art Institute, is a fine collection of European and American painting; Renoir is especially well represented. To the south, on Route 20 west of Pittsfield, is the restored Hancock Shaker Village, a settlement founded by the Shaker religious sect in about 1780. Near Lenox lies Tanglewood, site of the famous Berkshire Festival, where, during July and August, audiences of 6,000 can listen to the Boston Symphony and guest artists. A former home of Nathaniel Hawthorne, the author of *The Scarlet Letter*, is also at Tanglewood and is open to the public before concerts.

5. Boston and its vicinity

Boston is a treasure trove of early American landmarks, particularly along its Freedom Trail (*page 121*), and of fine museums and other public buildings, such as the Museum of Science and the new Prudential Tower. It is also the focus of a great educational complex, with Harvard and the Massachusetts Institute of Technology just across the Charles River in Cambridge and Wellesley in the town of Wellesley. Nearby are sites famous in American history: west of Boston lie Concord and Lexington, where Minutemen fought the first skirmishes of the Revolution; Quincy has the handsome homes of Presidents John Adams and John Quincy Adams; and Charlestown offers the Bunker Hill Monument.

Heading north of Boston, one comes to a string of old, handsome port towns—Marblehead, Salem, Gloucester, Rockport and Newburyport—that provided much of the area's early maritime wealth. Salem is especially notable for its streets lined with magnificent 18th Century mansions, many built by rich sea captains. Inland from Newburyport lie the old textile towns of Haverhill, Lawrence and Lowell, now flourishing again with science-oriented industries. Andover, just south of Lawrence, is the site of the famous preparatory school, which owns the excellent Addison Gallery of American Art. South from Lowell, the tour passes Concord, with its Revolutionary battle site as well as its Antiquarian Society History Museum, exhibiting memorabilia of many 19th Century writers.

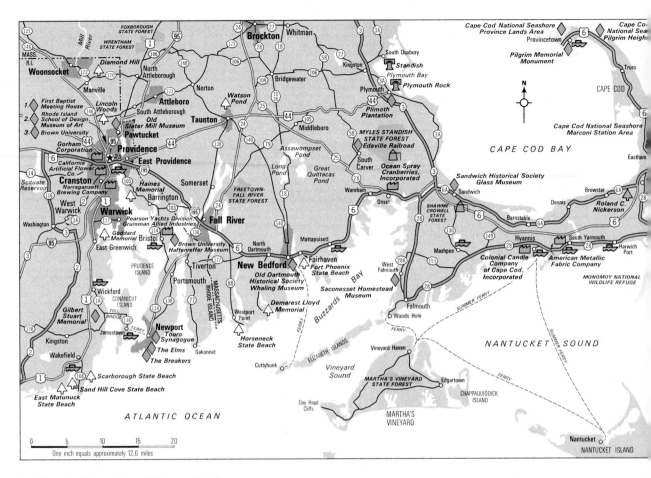

6. Rhode Island and Cape Cod

The jagged coastline of this part of New England is dotted with a number of historic ports and many well-known summer resorts with fine beaches. The area also boasts the busy and interesting city of Providence, which has many historical and cultural attractions, including the Rhode Island School of Design Museum of Art, Brown University and the First Baptist Meeting House.

The area may be reached from the west via Interstate 95 East, but a more scenic road is Route 2. The visitor may, if he wishes, leave Route 2 near Kingston and drive to Jamestown, taking the car ferry there to Newport, which has a matchless combination of fine colonial buildings and astonishingly lavish vacation "cottages" built by the very rich of the late 19th Century.

Proceeding eastward either from Newport or Providence, the visitor will find himself on Route 6, which leads to New Bedford, once a great center of whaling and still an active fishing port. The city's Old Dartmouth Historical Society Whaling Museum is filled with relics of whaling days. Across the street is the Seaman's Bethel, looking exactly as it is described in a memorable scene in Herman Melville's novel *Moby Dick*. A chapel much frequented by the crews of 19th Century whaling vessels, it has plaques on the walls commemorating men lost at sea and a pulpit shaped like a whaling boat's prow.

East of New Bedford, Route 6 skirts the shoreline of

Buzzards Bay and crosses on to Cape Cod via either of two bridges over the canal that separates the cape from the mainland. On the cape, Routes 6A and 28 are the most scenic, going through such fine old New England villages as Barnstable and Brewster on the northern shore, South Yarmouth and Chatham on the ocean side. At Orleans both roads rejoin Route 6, which heads north toward Provincetown through the Cape Cod National Seashore. The seashore includes the Great Beach (so named by an early visitor, Henry David Thoreau), a magnificent 30-mile stretch of dune and sand facing the Atlantic. Provincetown itself, while still an active fishing port, has scores of inns for visitors, a selection of good restaurants and continues to play host in the summer to many artists. The atmosphere is bohemian without being raucous and the local beaches are excellent.

Two islands off the cape—Martha's Vineyard and Nantucket—are also popular resorts and may be reached by ferry from either Woods Hole or Hyannis. Both islands have good beaches but perhaps the one with the most spectacular setting is Gay Head on the Vineyard. Here multicolored clay cliffs swoop down almost to the edge of the breaking surf.

After a sojourn on the cape it is only a short trip from the canal to Plymouth, site of the Pilgrims' first settlement. Here a replica of the *Mayflower* is open to visitors.

7. Connecticut

Though Connecticut's area (5,009 square miles) is small enough for a convenient tour during a long weekend, the state offers a host of cultural, historical and scenic attractions as well as many opportunities for recreation. Many of its 245 miles of shoreline are easily reached from New York City via the Connecticut Turnpike (Route 95). Also near the turnpike and little more than an hour's drive from New York is the American Shakespeare Festival Theatre in Stratford, where the bard's works are performed during the summer in a theater resembling the original Globe. Farther up the turnpike is New Haven, site of Yale University, to whose traditional Gothic architecture a number of fine modern structures have been added, among them the University Art Gallery and the Beinecke Rare Book and Manuscript Library.

Just off Route 95, beyond New Haven, is the Henry Whitfield State Historical Museum; built in 1639, it is the oldest stone structure in New England, and its 17th Century antiques offer a glimpse into life during colonial times. East of New Haven along Route 95 is New London, where visitors can tour the U.S. Coast Guard Academy and watch the midshipmen on parade. From New London it is but a short distance to Mystic Seaport, a re-creation

of a mid-19th Century port. Several old high-masted sailing ships there are open for inspection.

After heading north on Routes 12 and 169 and west on 44, tourists may make an interesting side trip to South Coventry, with its Nathan Hale Homestead, the restored residence of the Revolutionary War hero. From there it is a short hop to Hartford, capital of Connecticut and center of much of the nation's insurance industry. Hartford's Wadsworth Atheneum—with its collection of paintings, antique furniture and period costumes—is one of the nation's major museums. Citizens of Hartford are also justly proud of their downtown area, which has been widely acclaimed as an outstandingly successful urban-renewal project. In Bloomfield, just outside Hartford, there are tours of the Connecticut General Life Insurance Building, listed by the American Institute of Architects as one of "ten buildings in America's future."

Beyond Hartford, along Route 44 to the northwest, the countryside becomes rural and forested, a splendid area of hills, lakes and streams where campers may pitch their tents and enjoy nature. South on Route 63 is the beautiful town of Litchfield. There, on elm-lined streets, stand a number of colonial homes that are still in use.

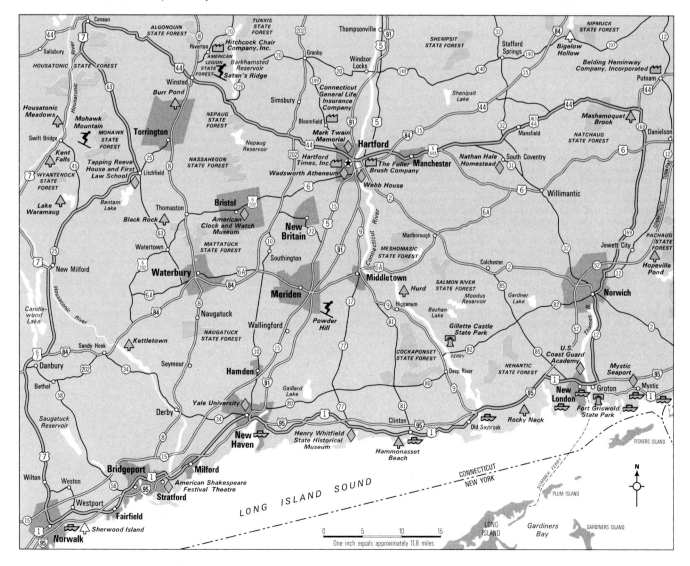

Museums and galleries

Connecticut

Bristol
American Clock and Watch Museum, 100 Maple St. Exhibits on history of clock industry. Apr—Oct: Tues-Sun 1-5.

Farmington
Hill-Stead Museum, Farmington Ave. Country home with its original 18th and 19th Century furnishings. Wed, Thurs, Sat, Sun 2-5.

Groton
The Submarine Library and Museum, U.S. Naval Submarine Base. Submarine memorabilia and models. Mon-Fri 9-4; Sat, Sun 10-4.

Hartford
Connecticut State Library Museum, 231 Capitol Ave. The Colt collection of firearms; state history and archeology. Mon-Fri 8:30-5; Sat 9-1.

Mark Twain Memorial, 351 Farmington Ave. Remarkable house partly designed by Twain. Tues-Sat 10-5; Sun 2-5.

Wadsworth Atheneum, 25 Atheneum Sq. N. Superior art collection. Tues-Sat 10-5; Sun 1-6.

Mystic
Mystic Seaport Marine Historical Association, Inc., Greenmanville Ave. Replica of a mid-19th Century port community; maritime relics and antique sailing ships. Daily 9-5.

New Britain
New Britain Museum of American Art, 56 Lexington St. American art of 18th through 20th Centuries. Tues-Sun 2-5:30.

New Haven
Peabody Museum of Natural History, Yale University, Whitney Ave. Geology, anthropology and oceanography. Mon-Sat 9-5; Sun 1-5.

Yale University Art Gallery, 1111 Chapel St. Fine general collection. Tues-Sat 10-5; Sun 2-5.

New London
Lyman Allyn Museum, 100 Mohegan Ave. American, European and Oriental art; Federal furnishings. Tues-Sat 1-5; Sun 2-5.

Stamford
The Stamford Museum and Nature Center, 39 Scofieldtown Rd. Natural history museum, art gallery, planetarium and dairy farm. Mon-Sat 9-5; Sun 2-5.

Maine

Andover
Telstar, Andover Satellite Station, near Route 120. Complete display of history of communications satellites. Daily 9-5.

Brunswick
Bowdoin College Museum of Art, Walker Art Building. Good small collection of fine arts; memorabilia of Winslow Homer. During school year: Mon-Fri 10-4; Sat 10-5; Sun, hols 2-5; July—Labor Day: Mon-Sat 10-5, 7:30-8:30; Sun 2-5.

Kennebunk
The Brick Store Museum, 117 Main St. Exhibits on local history, painting and marine life in 1825 building. Apr 1—Oct 15: Tues-Sat 10-4:30.

Portland
Portland Museum of Art, 111 High St. Works by Maine artists. Tues-Sat 10-5; Sun 2-5.

Portland Society of Natural History, 22 Elm St. Maine natural history. Mon-Sat 9-5.

Rockland
William A. Farnsworth Library and Art Museum, 19 Elm St. Eighteenth and 19th Century American and European art; Wyeth collection. Tues-Sat 10-5; Sun 1-5; June—Labor Day: also Mon 10-5.

Searsport
Penobscot Marine Museum, Church St. Ship models, paintings, prints and charts. May 30—Sept 10: Mon-Sat 9-5; Sun 1-5.

Waterville
Jette Art Museum, Colby College. American painting, sculpture. Mon-Sat 10-12, 1-5; Sun 2-5.

Massachusetts

Andover
Addison Gallery of American Art, Phillips Academy. Fine collection of American art, furniture. Mon-Sat 9-5; Sun 2:30-5.

Boston
Institute of Contemporary Art, 100 Newbury St. Major exhibitions of modern art. Tues-Sun 11-6; Wed eves to 9. Closed Aug.

Isabella Stewart Gardner Museum, 280 The Fenway. Distinguished collection of European, American and Far Eastern art exhibited in a Venetian palace. Tues, Thurs, Sat 10-4; Sun 2-5; first Thurs of month 10-10. Closed Aug.

Museum of Fine Arts, 469 Huntington Ave. Superb general collection. Tues-Sat 10-5; Sun 1:30-5:30; Oct—May: also Tues eves until 10.

Museum of Science, Science Park. Unusual industrial and scientific exhibitions; planetarium. Tues-Sat 10-5; Sun 1-5.

Cambridge
Fogg Art Museum, Harvard University, Quincy St. Fine collection of Eastern and Western art. Mon-Sat 9-5; Sun 2-5. Closed Sat, July—Labor Day; Sun, mid-June—Oct.

Francis Russell Hart Nautical Museum, Massachusetts Institute of Technology, 55 Massachusetts Ave. Large collection of ship models; maritime memorabilia. Daily 8-10.

Harvard University Museums: Harvard possesses a wide range of museums in addition to the Fogg. They span many of the natural sciences, such as zoology and botany, and include other special collections, such as the one housed in the Semitic Museum. Most of them are located near the Harvard Yard. Information about hours and about unusual exhibits may be obtained from the university.

Dalton
Crane Museum, South St. Exhibits showing history and techniques of papermaking. June—Sept: Mon-Fri 2-5.

New Bedford
Old Dartmouth Historical Society Whaling Museum, 18 Johnny Cake Hill. Marine items; half-size replica of a whaling ship. Winter: Tues-Sat 10-5; Sun, hols 1-5; summer: Mon-Sat 9-5; Sun, hols 12-5.

North Andover
Merrimack Valley Textile Museum, Massachusetts Ave. Exhibits illustrating the role of wool manufacturing in U.S. history. Tues-Sat 10-4; Sun 1-5.

Pittsfield
Hancock Shaker Village, off Route 20. Restoration of colonial Shaker community. July 1—Oct 15: daily 9:30-5.

Plymouth
Plimoth Plantation, Inc., Warren Ave. Re-creation of original Plymouth colony of 1627; *Mayflower II*. Summer: daily 9-7; spring and fall: daily 9-5.

Salem
House of Seven Gables, Turner St. House made famous by Hawthorne's story; contains memorabilia of the author. July—Aug: daily 9:30-7:30; Sept—June: daily 10-5.

Sturbridge
Old Sturbridge Village. Re-created New England village of 1790-1840 era; crafts and decorative arts collection. Apr-Nov: daily 9:30-4:30; winter weekends: 9:30-4.

Williamstown
Sterling and Francine Clark Art Institute, South St. Fine collection of art and silverware, specializing in 19th Century American and French painting. Tues-Sun 10-5. Closed Feb.

Williams College Museum of Art, Main St. American sculpture, painting and furniture. Mon-Sat 10-12, 2-4; Sun 2-5.

Worcester
Worcester Art Museum, 55 Salisbury St. Excellent collection of American, European and Oriental art. Mon-Sat 10-5; Sun 2-5; Oct—Apr: also Tues 10-10.

New Hampshire

Cornish
Saint-Gaudens Museum, near Route 12A. Works by sculptor Augustus Saint-Gaudens exhibited in his studio. Late May—mid-Oct: daily 10-5.

Hanover
The Hopkins Center Art Galleries, Dartmouth College, E. Wheelock St. American, European and Chinese art. Mon-Sat 12-5; Sun, hols 2-5.

Manchester
The Currier Gallery of Art, 192 Orange St. European and American art. Mon-Sat 10-5; Sun 2-5.

Portsmouth
Strawbery Banke. Remarkable restoration of old section of Portsmouth originally settled in 1630. Mon-Sat 10-5; Sun 12-5.

Rhode Island

Bristol
Heffenreffer Museum, Brown

University, Mount Hope Grant. Indian, Eskimo and African collections. Sept—May: Sat 10-4; Sun 1-4; June—Aug: Tues-Sun 1-4.

Newport
The Breakers, Ochre Point Ave. Famous residence of Cornelius Vanderbilt modeled after 16th Century Italian palace. Late May—Nov: daily 10-5 (Sun 10-9 during July—Aug).

Touro Synagogue, 85 Touro St. Oldest U.S. synagogue building. July—Sept 5: Sun-Fri 10-5.

Providence
Museum of Art, Rhode Island School of Design, 224 Benefit St. Good general collection. Tues-Sat 11-5; Sun, hols 2-5. Closed Aug.

The Rhode Island Historical Society, 52 Power St. State historical items. Mon-Fri 9-5; Sept—June: also Sun 3-5.

Vermont

Bellows Falls
Steamtown, U.S.A. Railroad and fire-engine memorabilia exhibited in old roundhouse. Visitors may take a 26-mile excursion on a train pulled by a steam locomotive. Times of these excursions should be checked by mail (Box 71, Bellows Falls) or telephone (603-445-5408).

Bennington
The Bennington Museum, W. Main St. Exhibits on American crafts and folk art. Winter: daily 9:30-4:30; summer: daily 9-6. Closed Sun Dec—Feb.

Burlington
Robert Hull Fleming Museum, University of Vermont, 61 Colchester Ave. Primitive and ancient art; art of America, Europe and Orient. Mon-Fri 9-4:30; Sun 2-5; summer: also Sat 9-4:30.

Middlebury
Sheldon Museum, 1 Park St. Excellent small collection of early Americana. June—Oct 15: Mon-Sat 10-5; Oct 16—May: Tues, Thurs 1-5.

Montpelier
Vermont Historical Society Museum, State Administration Building, State St. Exhibits on state history and science. Winter: Mon-Fri 8-4:30; summer: daily 8-4:30.

St. Johnsbury
Fairbanks Museum of Natural Science, 83 Main St. Science exhibits, botanical garden, planetarium. Mon-Sat, hols 9-5; Sun 2:30-4:30; July 1—Sept 1: also Mon, Tues eves 8-9:30.

Shelburne
Shelburne Museum, Inc., Shelburne Rd. Early American preservation project; arts, crafts. May 25—Oct 20: daily 9-5.

Local festivals and events

Connecticut
American Shakespeare Festival Theatre, Stratford. Performances of Shakespeare's plays with top-flight actors. June—mid-Sept.

Yale-Harvard Crew Races, New London. Fri of commencement week, June.

Barnum Festival, Bridgeport. Parades, concerts and art shows dedicated to P. T. Barnum. Late June—early July.

Rose Garden Display, Hartford. One of the nation's best flower shows. Late June—early July.

Tour of Old Homes, Litchfield. The town's dignified colonial homes are opened to public. Early July.

American Dance Festival, Connecticut College, New London. Mid-Aug.

Danbury Fair, Danbury. Famous country fair. Late Sept—early Oct.

Maine
St. John's Day Parade. A very colorful parade held in various Maine cities by Knights Templar Masons. Late June.

Maine Rose Show, Portland. Most popular flower show in state. Late June—early July.

Colonial Days, Kennebunkport. Antique and flower shows, sporting events and entertainment. Early July.

Windjammer Days, Boothbay Harbor. Old schooners sail en masse into harbor. Second week in July.

Maine Potato Blossom Festival, Fort Fairfield. Parade, displays, sports events, concerts. Late July.

Bangor Fair, Bangor. One of country's oldest fairs: horse racing, exhibits, stage shows. First week in Aug.

Seafoods Festival, Rockland. Parade, bands, entertainment, Lobster Queen contest. First weekend in Aug.

Skowhegan State Fair, Skowhegan. Another long-held country fair, this one dating back to 1818. Mid-Aug.

Retired Skippers Race, Castine. Sailboat race contested by salts 65 years old or older. Third Sun in Aug.

Fryeburg Fair, Fryeburg. Unspoiled country fair with such events as oxen pulling contests. Early Oct.

Massachusetts
Patriot's Day, Lexington. Parade and exercises at Old North Bridge in commemoration of skirmish between Minutemen and British on Apr 19, 1775. Apr 19.

Militia Day, Old Sturbridge Village. "Ancient and honorable" military units parade in historic uniforms. Mid-June.

St. Peter's Fiesta, Gloucester. Sports events, fireworks, procession, blessing of the fishing fleet. Late June.

Berkshire Music Festival, Tanglewood (near Lenox). Boston Symphony Orchestra and distinguished guest performers. July—Aug.

Grand Illumination, Martha's Vineyard. Combination community sing and band concert held under glowing lanterns. Third Wed eve in Aug.

Eastern States Exposition, Springfield. Biggest agricultural fair in the East. Sept.

New Hampshire
Laconia Winter Carnival, Laconia. World championship dog-sled derby. Last weekend in Feb.

U.S. Alpine Ski Championships, Mt. Cranmore, Wildcat Mt., Cannon Mt. or Franconia Notch. Mar.

New Hampshire Art Association Traveling Exhibition. Art show held in Exeter, Sharon and Mt. Sunapee State Park. Apr—Aug.

Lobster Festival, East Kingston. Fair with rides, exhibits. Aug.

Fifty-Mile Water-Ski Marathon, Laconia. Starts from Weirs Beach on Lake Winnipesaukee. Late Aug.

Lancaster Fair, Lancaster. Agricultural exhibit, horse show and entertainment. Sept.

Foliage Spectacular. Festival held all over state, featuring tours, county fairs and harvest suppers. Late Sept—early Oct.

Sandwich Fair, Sandwich. Agricultural fair. Oct 12.

Rhode Island
Bermuda Race, Newport. Yachts start 635-mile race. Mid-June in even-numbered years.

Jazz Festival, Newport. Top performers in a series of concerts. Weekend closest to July 4.

Block Island Week Sailing Regatta. Mid-July in odd-numbered years.

Rocky Hill State Fair, East Greenwich. One of best of the many country fairs. Late Aug.

Annual U.S. Atlantic Tuna Tournament, Galilee. Early Sept.

Vermont
Winter Carnival, Brattleboro. Includes ski jump and races, parade, ice show and ball. Feb.

Maple Syrup Festival, St. Albans. Producers welcome visitors who join sugarhouse parties for sugar-on-snow, sour pickles and raised doughnuts. Early spring.

Champlain Shakespeare Festival, Burlington. Professional actors. Late July—Sept.

Bennington Battle Day, Bennington. Commemorating the 1777 Battle of Bennington. Aug 16 or nearest weekend.

Fall Foliage Festival, Northeast Kingdom (involves Walden, Cabot, Marshfield, Peacham, Barnet Center and Groton). Sept—Oct.

Green Mountain Horse Association 100-Mile Trail Ride. Starts at South Woodstock. First week in Sept.

Forest Festival Week. Dramatizes the need for conservation of Vermont's beautiful, green woodlands. Late Sept.

Folk Festival, Stowe. Folk singing and other events. Last week in Sept.

Wildlife of New England

A sampling of the natural life frequently found in New England is given on this and the following pages. In each case both the common name and scientific name of the plant or animal are given. The information supplied is not intended to be comprehensive; for additional material on the fauna and flora of the region the reader should refer to specialized books on wildlife. A number of useful reference works that contain such information are listed on page 188.

Mammals

New England cottontail

This small creature *(Sylvilagus transitionalis)* prefers to live in open woods or shrubby areas and is especially active in the hours immediately after sunset.

Woodchuck

Despite its name, the woodchuck *(Marmota monax)* subsists mainly on grasses. Also called the ground hog, it piles up mounds of earth at the entrance to its burrow.

Gray squirrel

A familiar sight throughout New England, *Sciurus carolinensis* spends much of its time either seeking food or storing it away in holes it digs in the ground.

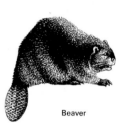

Beaver

Castor canadensis is the craftsman among New England animals: its sturdy dams, incorporating lodges with underwater entrances, average 75 feet in length.

Red fox

Long hunted by sportsmen, *Vulpes fulva* is almost as prized as the mink for its beautiful, silky fur, which varies in color between bright reddish and pale tawny.

Black bear

The heavy, lumbering black bear *(Ursus americanus)* is found in northern New England. It is equipped with fierce claws, but subsists largely on berries and nuts.

Raccoon

Clever, agile and appealing, the black-masked raccoon *(Procyon lotor)* prefers wooded or swampy areas. A good swimmer and climber, it is mainly nocturnal.

White-tailed deer

The ranks of the white-tailed deer *(Odocoileus virginianus)* seem to be growing despite hunters. It has keen senses of smell and hearing and can run 40 miles per hour.

Fish and reptiles

Atlantic mackerel

One of the fish most sought by commercial fishermen along the New England coast, *Scomber scombrus* often swims in huge schools as much as 20 miles long.

Bluefish

Pomatomus saltatrix is a superb game fish. It ranges in predatory schools from Maine to the northern coast of South America, eating mackerel and other fish.

Cod

A favorite food fish in New England —particularly in Boston—*Gadus callarias* is extremely prolific: a female may produce as many as four million eggs in a year.

Pollock

Found in great quantities off the New England coast, *Pollachius virens* is a major food fish that voraciously devours the young of other species, especially cod.

Haddock

Melanogrammus aeglefinus is unusually tasty and is much sought after by commercial fishermen; the annual catch in recent years has averaged 118 million pounds.

Winter flounder

Pseudopleuronectes americanus swims with its left side facing down. Its left eye, normally placed at birth, gradually migrates to the top side of the adult fish.

Sebago salmon

A victim of pollution and of the erection of dams that prevent it from reaching spawning grounds, lake-dwelling *Salmo salar sebago* is becoming extinct.

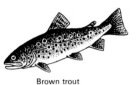

Brown trout

The brown trout *(Salmo trutta)* was originally a native of Europe. Introduced into the U.S. in the 1880s, it is replacing native trout in many streams.

Yellow perch

An inhabitant of lakes, ponds and slow-moving streams, *Perca flavescens* is a small game fish. It cruises in schools of 50 to 200 and is marked by dark bands.

Wood turtle

Clemmys insculpta has a rough shell that looks deeply chiseled. An active swimmer and an astonishingly good climber, it is often found near bodies of water.

Northern red-bellied snake

A secretive but harmless creature, the northern red-bellied snake *(Storeria occipitomaculata occipitomaculata)* seldom grows to more than a foot in length.

Eastern smooth green snake

Inconspicuous *Opheodrys vernalis vernalis* is uniformly green on top and is thus difficult to see in grassy areas, where it hunts soft-bodied insects and larvae.

Birds

Wood duck

The most brilliantly colored American duck, the male wood duck *(Aix sponsa)* is decorated on head and back with green, bronze and purple markings.

Mourning dove

Known for its mournful, cooing call, *Zenaidura macroura* ranges throughout New England. The bird is prolific; a pair may raise four broods in a single season.

Chimney swift

Fond of nesting against the sides of vertical surfaces like the inner walls of chimneys, the chimney swift *(Chaetura pelagica)* is possibly the world's fastest flyer.

Yellow-shafted flicker

The yellow-shafted flicker *(Colaptes auratus),* a diligent woodpecker, is a voracious eater: 5,000 ants have been found in the stomach of a single bird.

Tree swallow

A tree dweller often seen perched in groups on telephone wires, *Iridoprocne bicolor* is the only American swallow with pure-white underparts.

Blue jay

A noisy bird that imitates other birds by screaming, whistling or singing, *Cyanocitta cristata* can be recognized by its crested head and vivid blue markings.

Black-capped chickadee

A little bird, the black-capped chickadee *(Parus atricapillus)* is attracted by suet at home feeders. "Chic-a-dee" is the most famous of its several tuneful calls.

White-breasted nuthatch

The white-breasted nuthatch *(Sitta carolinensis)* often creeps headfirst down tree trunks, usually looking for insects and their eggs.

Eastern hermit thrush

A melodious bird, *Hylocichla guttata faxoni* has a distinctive habit of raising and lowering its tail when disturbed or when it focuses attention on some object.

Eastern meadowlark

Fond of fields and meadows, the Eastern meadowlark *(Sturnella magna)* nests in dense, tall grass but usually perches to sing on trees or fences.

Red-winged blackbird

A courageous fighter, a male red-winged blackbird *(Agelaius phoeniceus)* will attack even a hawk to defend its young. These birds eat insect pests on farms.

Common grackle

A long-tailed bird, *Quiscalus quiscula* is frequently seen near shade trees in the parks of New England cities, usually in large, raucously screeching flocks.

Eastern evening grosbeak

Unlike female Eastern evening grosbeaks, *Hesperiphona vespertina vespertina* males are very colorful, bearing yellow and black markings on a brown body.

Eastern purple finch

In the courtship of Eastern purple finches *(Carpodacus purpureus purpureus)*, the male, which is not purple but reddish in color, does an elaborate airborne dance.

Slate-colored junco

Junco hyemalis is most often seen in New England in the winter, feeding in large or small flocks in forested areas where weeds survive the cold.

Song sparrow

One of the most widely known birds of New England, *Melospiza melodia* is inquisitive and busy, and is found wherever there is bushy cover near water.

Flowers and trees

Painted trillium

Often found in valley woodlands, *Trillium undulatum* has three leaves surrounding a single flower, its white petals marked by a pink or crimson V at their base.

Pink lady's slipper

The pink lady's slipper *(Cypripedium acaule)* is shaped somewhat like a shoe. Also called the moccasin flower, it blooms in spring in New England forests.

Bloodroot

The bloodroot *(Sanguinaria canadensis)* has a reddish sap in both stem and roots. Its petals are so fragile that they fall at the slightest touch.

Northern white violet

Hardy *Viola pallens* is the only white-flowered violet likely to be found on New England mountain slopes. Its lower petals are marked by purple veins.

184

Fireweed

The fireweed *(Epilobium angustifolium)* is often found growing in burned-out forest areas. Its magenta blossoms form a cluster that may be a foot long.

Labrador tea

The base for a substitute for tea used during the Revolutionary War, Labrador tea *(Ledum groenlandicum)* is an evergreen shrub often found in bogs.

Eastern white pine

A highly valued commercial tree, *Pinus strobus* no longer exists in extensive tracts. It is the state tree of Maine, and its cone and tassel are the state flower.

Tamarack

The durable and coarse-grained wood of the tamarack *(Larix laricina),* also known as the American larch, is often used for telephone poles and railroad ties.

Red spruce

Growing in low country and on mountaintops, *Picea rubens* is one of the most abundant of New England trees. Its light wood is used to make pulp.

Eastern hemlock

Frequently planted by landscapers, *Tsuga canadensis* has slender branches with feathery foliage. Its coarse wood is used for construction purposes.

Butternut

Common throughout the region, *Juglans cinerea* is sometimes tapped for its sweet sap to make syrup. Pioneers used the husks of its fruit to make a yellow dye.

Paper birch

Indians found a host of uses for *Betula papyrifera*. Its bark was used to make the skin of canoes; paddles and snowshoes were produced from its wood.

White oak

This short-trunked tree *(Quercus alba)* is valuable commercially. Common in the Eastern United States, it is the state tree of Connecticut.

American elm

One of the noblest American trees, and a favorite ornamental species, the American elm *(Ulmus americana)* is seriously threatened by Dutch elm disease.

American mountain ash

Sorbus americana is widely planted as an ornamental tree because of the beauty of its red or scarlet fruit and the brilliance of its yellow autumn foliage.

Sugar maple

The source of sap from which maple sugar and syrup are made, *Acer saccharum* is also known for its lovely fall coloring. It is the state tree of Vermont.

Statistical information

State name and its source, state nickname, date of admission, capital

Connecticut: Name is an adaptation of an Indian word meaning "long river place"; nicknamed Nutmeg State because its Yankee traders are reputed to have peddled wooden nutmegs; admitted 1788 (the 5th state); Hartford.

Maine: Probably named by French trappers for a onetime province of France; called the Pine Tree State for its extensive forests; admitted 1820 (the 23rd state); Augusta.

Massachusetts: Named by Puritan settlers for native Indian tribe; called the Bay State after its large Cape Cod Bay; admitted 1788 (the 6th state); Boston.

New Hampshire: Named after the English county of Hampshire; called the Granite State because of its extensive quarries; admitted 1788 (the 9th state); Concord.

Rhode Island: Name is an adaptation of "Roodt Eylandt" (red island), a descriptive phrase used by an early Dutch navigator; called Little Rhody because of its small size; admitted 1790 (the 13th state); Providence.

Vermont: Name is an anglicization of a phrase Champlain inscribed on his map of the area, "verd mont," meaning "green mountain"; called the Green Mountain State for its principal range; admitted 1791 (the 14th state); Montpelier.

Population

By state (U.S. Census, 1965 estimate):
Massachusetts: 5,349,000.
Connecticut: 2,833,000.
Maine: 993,000.
Rhode Island: 891,000.
New Hampshire: 669,000.
Vermont: 397,000.

By city (region's eight largest cities are listed below, followed by their population and rank in the U.S. according to the estimate of the *1967 Editor and Publisher Market Guide*):

City	Population	Rank
Boston, Mass.	681,859	16
Springfield, Mass.	183,710	75
Providence, R.I.	178,863	77
Worcester, Mass.	177,817	79
Hartford, Conn.	163,475	87
Bridgeport, Conn.	157,062	93
New Haven, Conn.	153,873	95
Waterbury, Conn.	120,843	125

Land areas

Maine: 33,215 square miles.
Vermont: 9,609 square miles.
New Hampshire: 9,304 square miles.
Massachusetts: 8,257 square miles.
Connecticut: 5,009 square miles.
Rhode Island: 1,214 square miles.

Principal lakes and other bodies of water

Long Island Sound (between Connecticut and New York's Long Island): Approximately 1,000 square miles; maximum depth, some 150 feet.

Cape Cod Bay (Massachusetts): Approximately 520 square miles; maximum depth, some 110 feet.

Moosehead Lake (Maine): 117 square miles; maximum depth, 246 feet.

Lake Winnipesaukee (New Hampshire): 71.5 square miles; maximum depth, 120 feet.

Lake Sebago (Maine): 45.5 square miles; maximum depth, 316 feet.

Chesuncook Lake (Maine): 43 square miles; maximum depth, 150 feet.

Principal rivers (lengths in miles)

Connecticut (New Hampshire, Vermont, Massachusetts and Connecticut): 407.

Androscoggin (New Hampshire and Maine): 175.

Kennebec (Maine): 164.

Housatonic (Massachusetts and Connecticut): 148.

West Branch Penobscot (Maine): 112.

Merrimack (New Hampshire and Massachusetts): 110.

Penobscot (Maine): 101.

Major ranges and mountain peaks

White Mountains: Region's principal mountain system, containing many peaks of more than 5,000 feet, that stretches from southwest Maine through New Hampshire. It includes New Hampshire's Presidential Range, whose highest peaks are Mount Washington (6,288 feet), Mount Adams (5,798) and Mount Jefferson (5,725).

Green Mountains: This range dominates Vermont's topography and, in a southern extension called the Berkshire Hills, western Massachusetts'. The highest peak in Vermont is on Mount Mansfield (4,393 feet). Highest point in Massachusetts is Mount Greylock (3,491 feet).

Mount Katahdin: The highest point in Maine (5,268 feet) and the northern terminus of the Appalachian Trail.

Outstanding New England inventors and their most famous inventions

Eli Whitney	Cotton gin (1794)
Samuel Colt	Revolver (1836)
Samuel F. B. Morse	Electric telegraph (1844)
Charles Goodyear	Vulcanized rubber (1844)
Elias Howe	Sewing machine (1846)

Some U.S. superlatives

Smallest state in the Union: Rhode Island.

Oldest university in the U.S.: Harvard; founded 1636.

First free public library in U.S.: Dublin, New Hampshire; established 1822.

Oldest synagogue in the U.S.: Newport, R.I.; founded 1763.

Largest wool market in the U.S.: Boston.

Agricultural statistics (1965)

State	Total income from agriculture	Some leading agricultural products
Maine	$124 million	Potatoes, broilers, eggs, dairy products, cattle.
Massachusetts	$70 million	Dairy products, horticultural specialties, eggs, cranberries, tobacco.
Connecticut	$67 million	Dairy products, eggs, tobacco, cattle.
Vermont	$39 million	Dairy products, cattle, eggs, forest products, hay.
New Hampshire	$13 million	Dairy products, eggs, cattle, apples, greenhouse and nursery products.
Rhode Island	$6 million	Dairy products, horticultural specialties, potatoes, eggs, cattle.

Pronunciation glossary

Amherst (AMM urst). Towns in Massachusetts and New Hampshire.
Arlington (ARE ling ton, but pronounced AAH ling tun by natives). A Boston suburb.
Bar Harbor (BAR HAR bor, but pronounced BAH HAH buh by natives and most summer residents). A Maine resort.
Barnstable (BARN stuh bul). Town on Cape Cod.
Barre (BAA ree). Towns in Vermont and Massachusetts.
Berlin (BURR lin). Towns in New Hampshire and Connecticut.
Billerica (BILL ri kuh). Town in Massachusetts.

Calais (CAL is) Town in Maine.
Castine (cas TEEN). Town in Maine.
Chatham (CHAT um). Towns in Massachusetts and New Hampshire.
Faneuil Hall (FAN ul or FAN yul). Historic building in Boston.
Gloucester (GLOSS ter). Town in Massachusetts.
Greenwich (GREEN witch, but more commonly GREN itch or GRIN itch). Town in Connecticut.
Harwich (HAR witch or, more colloquially, HAR itch). Town on Cape Cod.
Haverhill (HAY vril or HAY ver ill). Towns in Massachusetts and New Hampshire.

Kancamagus (kan cah MAWG us). Highway in White Mountains.
Leominster (LEM in ster). Town in Massachusetts.
Milan (MY lan). Town in New Hampshire.
Montpelier (mont PEEL yur). Capital of Vermont.
Mount Desert (di ZERT). Island off Maine coast.
Mount Katahdin (kuh TAH dun). Peak in Maine.
Nahant (na HAHNT). Resort village in Massachusetts.
Orleans (orr LEENS). Towns in Vermont and on Cape Cod.
Padanaram (PAD uh neer um). Town in Massachusetts.
Peacham (PEE chum). Town in Vermont.

Portsmouth (PORTS muth). City in New Hampshire and town in Rhode Island.
Quincy (QUIN zee). City in Massachusetts.
Saco (SAH co or SACK oh). Town and river in Maine.
Scituate (SIT u ate or SIT u et). Towns in Massachusetts and Rhode Island.
Sebago (seh BAY go). Village and lake in Maine.
Thames (pronounced locally as written, with the "th" and a broad "a"). River in Connecticut.
Warwick (WAH rick). Town in Rhode Island.
Wianno (we ON o). Village on Cape Cod.
Worcester (WUSS ter). City in Massachusetts.

Credits and acknowledgments

Maps for front and back end papers by Jeppesen & Company, Denver, Colorado.
Maps on pages 174 through 179 © The H. M. Gousha Company, San Jose, California.
Maps on pages 10, 14, 15, 118 and 119 by Lothar Roth.

The sources for the illustrations that appear in this book are shown below. Credits for the pictures from left to right are separated by commas, from top to bottom by dashes.
Cover—Dennis Hallinan from Freelance Photographers Guild. Front end papers—Drawings by Richard Boland.
Chapter 1: 8, 9—John Lewis Stage. 12—Drawings by Rudolf Freund. 16—Drawing by Donald Spaulding. 17—Drawing by Rudolf Freund. 19—Kosti Ruohomaa from Black Star. 20 through 28—Drawings by Gaetano di Palma. 20, 21—Dmitri Kessel. 22 through 25—Richard Meek. 26, 27—Left Jay Maisel, Lee Freidlander (2). 28—Richard Meek. 29—Robert Perron.
Chapter 2: 30—United Press International. 32—Courtesy Yankee, Inc., Dublin, New Hampshire. 34, 35—Drawings by Donald Spaulding. 36—Courtesy the American Antiquarian Society. 37—Drawings by Donald Spaulding. 38—Adapted from *A Word Geography of the Eastern United States* by Hans Kurath courtesy the University of Michigan Press. 39—Courtesy the Secretary of the Commonwealth of Massachusetts. 41 through 53—Clemens Kalischer.
Chapter 3: 54—Fernand Bourges. 56—The New York Public Library. 57—Brown Brothers. 60—Adapted from *River Towns of Connecticut* by Charles M. Andrews, Johns Hopkins University Press, Baltimore, 1889. 63—Drawings by Donald Spaulding. 65 through 79—Richard Meek, drawings by Leo and Diane Dillon. 70, 71—Courtesy The Lexington Historical Society.
Chapter 4: 80, 81—The I. N. Phelps Stokes Collection of American Historical Prints, Prints Division, The New York Public Library. 83—Courtesy The Brimfield Public Library. 84—Reprinted with the permission of The Macmillan Company from *The World of Eli Whitney* by Jeannette Mirsky and Allan Nevins, copyright 1952 by the authors. 86—Bill Finney courtesy The New Hampshire Historical Society. 88—Prints Division, The New York Public Library. 89—Courtesy the Weld Family, Indian Neck, Wareham, Massachusetts. 91, 92, 93—Courtesy The Peabody Museum of Salem. 94, 95 —Courtesy The Merrimack Valley Textile Museum. 96, 97 —Department of the U.S. Army, U.S. Army Weapons Command Springfield Armory, Courtesy the Stetson Shoe Co.—Courtesy the American Clock and Watch Museum. 98, 99—Courtesy The John Hancock Mutual Life Insurance Co., Courtesy The First National Bank of Boston.
Chapter 5: 100—Ted Polumbaum. 105—Courtesy *The Boston Globe.* 107, 108, 109 —Courtesy the Fulham Family. 110, 111—Courtesy Henri A. Benoit. 112, 113—Courtesy Judge Raymond Pettine. 114, 115—Courtesy Frank L. Nunes.
Chapter 6: 116—Richard Meek. 121—Map by Joseph Bertelli. 122—The Bettmann Archive, The New York Public Library. 123— The Bettmann Archive. 124 —Courtesy The Harvard University Archives. 125—James F. Coyne, Robert Crandall courtesy The Isabella Stewart Gardner Museum. 127—Ted Polumbaum. 128 through 137—Richard Meek.
Chapter 7: 138—Alfred Eisenstaedt. 142—The Bettmann Archive, Culver Pictures Inc. —Courtesy The Museum of Modern Art, New York, Gift of A. Conger Goodyear, Culver Pictures Inc. 144—Culver Pictures Inc. except bottom center Brown Brothers. 145 —Bottom right Culver Pictures Inc. 149 through 159— Alfred Eisenstaedt.
Chapter 8: 160—Ted Polumbaum. 167—Marvin Newman. 168, 169—The Hartford Redevelopment Agency, Richard Meek. 170, 171—Robert Perron, New England Survey Service Inc., Boston. 172, 173 —Richard Meek. 182 through 185—Drawings by Rudolf Freund.
Back end papers—Drawings by Richard Boland.

The editors of this book wish to thank the following persons and institutions for their assistance: Roland Chauvin, Bristol, Rhode Island; John T. Galvin, Director of Public Relations, Tufts-New England Medical Center, Boston; Sidney S. Horenstein, Department of Fossil Invertebrates, The American Museum of Natural History, New York; James Keeney, Old Sturbridge Village, Sturbridge, Massachusetts; Richard M. Klein, Curator of Plant Physiology, The New York Botanical Garden; Louis A. Lamoureux, Peacham, Vermont; Eugene Moriarty, Boston *Herald-Traveler;* Admiral Samuel Eliot Morison, Jonathan Trumbull Professor of American History, Emeritus, Harvard University; Robert Mount, Assistant Professor, Department of Speech, The City College of New York; Dean M. Schmitter, Associate Professor, Department of English, Columbia University; Walter Muir Whitehill, Director, Boston Athenaeum.

Bibliography

*Available also in paperback.
†Available only in paperback.

General and historical reading
Andrews, Charles M., *The Colonial Period of American History,* Vol. 1.* Yale University Press, 1934.
Callahan, North, *Henry Knox, George Washington's General.* Rinehart, 1958.
Faulkner, Harold U., *American Political and Social History.* Appleton-Century-Crofts, 1957.
Faulkner, Harold U., and Tyler Kepner, *America: Its History and People.* Harper, 1934.
Fite, Emerson D., and Archibald Freeman, eds., *A Book of Old Maps.†* Dover, 1966.
Forbes, Esther, *Paul Revere.* * Houghton Mifflin, 1962.
Fuess, Claude M., *Calvin Coolidge.* Little, Brown, 1940.
Greenslet, Ferris, *The Lowells and Their Seven Worlds.* Houghton Mifflin, 1946.
Gunther, John, *Inside U.S.A.* Harper, 1951.
Hale, Nancy, ed., *New England Discovery.* Coward-McCann, 1963.
Howe, Helen, *The Gentle Americans.* Harper & Row, 1965.
Marquand, John P., *Timothy Dexter Revisited.* Little, Brown, 1960.
Matthiessen, Francis O., *The James Family.* Knopf, 1947.
Miller, John C.:
The Federalist Era. * Harper, 1960.
Sam Adams. * Little, Brown, 1936.
Morison, Samuel Eliot:
The Maritime History of Massachusetts, 1783-1860. * Houghton Mifflin, 1961.
The Oxford History of the American People. Oxford University Press, 1965.
Morris, Richard B., and the Editors of LIFE, *The LIFE History of the United States,* Vols. 1 and 2. Time Inc., 1963.
Nettels, Curtis P., *The Roots of American Civilization.* Appleton-Century-Crofts, 1963.
Phillips, James D., *Salem and the Indies.* Houghton Mifflin, 1947.
Scheer, George F., and Hugh F. Rankin, *Rebels and Redcoats.†* New American Library, 1963.
Shannon, W. V., *The American Irish.* Macmillan, 1966.
Stephenson, George M., *A History of American Immigration, 1820-1924.* Russell, 1964.

Van Dusen, Albert E., *Connecticut.* Random House, 1961.
Weeden, William B., *Economic and Social History of New England, 1620-1789.* 2 vols. Hillary House, 1963.
White, William Allen, *A Puritan in Babylon.* * Macmillan, 1938.
Willison, George F., *Saints and Strangers.†* Ballantine, 1965.

Literary and intellectual
Bode, Carl, ed., *The Portable Thoreau.* * Viking, 1947.
Brooks, Van Wyck:
The Flowering of New England. * Dutton, 1952.
New England: Indian Summer, 1865-1915. * Dutton, 1940.
Hofstadter, Richard, *Anti-Intellectualism in American Life.* * Knopf, 1963.
Morison, Samuel E., *The Intellectual Life of Colonial New England.†* Cornell University Press, 1960.
Spiller, Robert E., and others, *Literary History of the United States.* Macmillan, 1963.

Boston
Amory, Cleveland, *The Proper Bostonians.* * Dutton, 1947.
Cutler, John H., *Honey Fitz.* Bobbs-Merrill, 1962.
Handlin, Oscar, *Boston's Immigrants.* Harvard University Press, 1959.
Jennings, John, *Boston: Cradle of Liberty, 1630-1776.* Doubleday, 1947.
Kirker, Harold and James, *Bulfinch's Boston, 1787-1817.* Oxford University Press, 1964.
Peabody, M. L., *To Be Young Was Very Heaven.* Houghton Mifflin, 1967.
Ross, Marjorie D., *The Book of Boston.* * 3 vols. Hastings House, 1960-1964.
Tharp, Louise Hall, *Mrs. Jack.* Little, Brown, 1965.
Weeks, Edward, *The Lowells and Their Institute.* Little, Brown, 1966.
Weston, George F., Jr., *Boston Ways: High, By and Folk.* Beacon Press, 1961.
Whitehill, Walter Muir:
Boston: A Topographical History. Harvard University Press, 1963.
Boston in the Age of John Fitzgerald Kennedy. University of Oklahoma Press, 1966.

Special topics
Chamberlain, John, *The*

Enterprising Americans. * Harper & Row, 1963.
Cutler, Carl C., *Greyhounds of the Sea.* U.S. Naval Institute, 1961.
Eisenmenger, Robert W., *The Dynamics of Growth in New England's Economy, 1870-1964.* Wesleyan University Press, 1966.
Fitch, James Marston, *American Building: The Historical Forces That Shaped It.* Houghton Mifflin, 1966.
Gottmann, Jean, *Megalopolis.* * Twentieth Century Fund, 1961.
Kurath, Hans, *Handbook of the Linguistic Geography of New England.* Brown University Press, 1939.
Kurath, Hans, and Raven I. McDavid, Jr., *The Pronunciation of English in the Atlantic States.* University of Michigan Press, 1961.
McCarthy, Joseph P., *The Remarkable Kennedys.* * Dial Press, 1960.
Morrison, Hugh, *Early American Architecture.* Oxford University Press, 1952.
Paine, Ralph D., *The Old Merchant Marine.* Yale University Press, 1919.
Rand, Christopher, *Cambridge, U.S.A.* Oxford University Press, 1964.
Sloane, Eric, *American Barns and Covered Bridges.* Wilfred Funk, 1954.
Struik, Dirk J., *Yankee Science in the Making.†* Collier, 1962.

Natural setting and wildlife
Burt, F. Allen, *The Story of Mount Washington.* Dartmouth Publications, 1960.
Chamberlain, Barbara Blau, *These Fragile Outposts.* Doubleday, 1964.
Conant, Roger, *A Field Guide to Reptiles and Amphibians of Eastern North America.* Houghton Mifflin, 1958.
Fenneman, Nevin M., *Physiography of Eastern United States.* McGraw-Hill, 1948.
Hay, John, and Peter Farb, *The Atlantic Shore.* Harper & Row, 1966.
La Gorce, John Oliver, ed., *The Book of Fishes.* National Geographic Society, 1952.
Matthews, F. Schuyler, and Norman Taylor, *Field Book of American Wild Flowers.* Putnam's, 1955.
Migdalski, Edward C., *Salt Water Game Fishes.* Ronald, 1958.
Morison, Samuel E., *The Story of*

Mount Desert Island. Little, Brown, 1960.
Ogburn, Charlton, Jr., *The Winter Beach.* Morrow, 1966.
Palmer, Ralph S., *The Mammal Guide.* Doubleday, 1954.
Peattie, Roderick, ed., *The Friendly Mountains.* Vanguard, 1942.
Peterson, Roger Tory, *A Field Guide to the Birds (East of the Rockies).* Houghton Mifflin, 1947.
Sargent, Charles S., *Manual of the Trees of North America.* 2 vols. Dover, 1949.
Strahler, Arthur N., *A Geologist's View of Cape Cod.* * Natural History Press, 1966.
Thomson, Betty Flanders, *The Changing Face of New England.* Macmillan, 1959.
Underhill, M., ed., *Mountain Flowers of New England.* Appalachian Mountain Club, 1964.
Wetmore, Alexander, *Water, Prey and Game Birds of North America.* National Geographic Society, 1965.

Guidebooks
Chase, Mary Ellen, and the Editors of *Look, Look at America: New England.* Houghton Mifflin, 1947.
Federal Writers' Project:
Connecticut. Houghton Mifflin, 1938.
Maine. Houghton Mifflin, 1937.
Massachusetts. Houghton Mifflin, 1937.
New Hampshire. Houghton Mifflin, 1938.
Rhode Island. Houghton Mifflin, 1937.
Vermont, 2nd ed. Houghton Mifflin, 1966.
Fodor, Eugene, Robert C. Fisher and Barnett D. Laschever, eds., *Fodor Shell Travel Guides U.S.A.; New England.* David McKay, 1966.
Hepburn, Andrew, *Complete Guide to New England.* * Doubleday, 1962.
Holiday Editors, *American Panorama: East of the Mississippi.* Doubleday, 1960.
Mobil Travel Guide, *Northeastern States.* Simon & Schuster, 1966.
Sloane, Howard N. and Lucille L., *The Goodyear Guide to State Parks: Region 1—New England and New York.* Crown, 1967.
White Mountain Guide Committee, eds., *The A.M.C. White Mountain Guide.* Appalachian Mountain Club, 1966.

Index

189

X

PRODUCTION STAFF FOR TIME INCORPORATED
John L. Hallenbeck (Vice President and Director of Production),
Robert E. Foy, Caroline Ferri and Don Sheldon
Text photocomposed under the direction of Albert J. Dunn and Arthur J. Dunn